The Illustrated Dust Jacket

1920—1970

JAMS

BY MRS C.F. LEYEL

KHALE

The
Complete
Jam
Cupboard

By
Mrs. C. F.
LEYEL

The
ture of
ookery

1/6
Net

ROUTLEDGE

THE
ILLUSTRATED
DUST JACKET
1920–1970

MARTIN SALISBURY

371 illustrations

Thames & Hudson

Frontispiece –
Jams
Mrs C. F. Leyel
George Routledge
and Sons · *c.* 1925
190 × 125 mm · 7½ × 5 in.

Before creating her hugely
successful *Orlando the Marmalade
Cat* series of picture books, Kathleen
Hale (UK, 1898–2000) spent some
time in the 1920s painting and
accepting illustration commissions,
such as this exquisite three-colour
design.

Contents

INTRODUCTION

In 1949, the then editor of *Graphis*, Charles Rosner, curated the first international exhibition of book-jacket design at the Victoria and Albert Museum in London. Of around 8,000 jackets in the museum's collection, 460 were selected that were 'deemed to be worthy of hanging on the walls of a national museum'.[1] Presumably, such a statement addressed the possibility of the illustrated dust jacket's aspirations to the status of art. The jacketed books in question were selected for the outstanding quality of the artwork that adorned them and the extent to which each one fulfilled its function in exciting interest in the book itself. The word 'illustrated' of course embraces the use of a variety of forms of imagery, including photographic, hand drawn or painted. This book is particularly concerned with the last of these – the work of artists whose hand-rendered pictorial illustrations were reproduced on book jackets over a period of fifty years, from a time when publishers were beginning to see the possibilities of high-quality artwork in this context around 1920, to one when photography increasingly began to usurp the traditional artist's skills at the end of the 1960s. The purely typographic tradition, exemplified by the work of Berthold Wolpe at Faber and Faber in these years, is also outside this book's remit.

In Rosner's later publication, *The Growth of the Book Jacket* (1949),[2] he quotes from a deliciously pompous comment on the exhibition in the *Observer* newspaper by the essayist, caricaturist and general wit Sir Max Beerbohm. Writing from his home in Italy Beerbohm pronounces:

> I gather that to many other arts has now been added the art of the book-jacket, and that there is an exhibition of it in the Victoria and Albert Museum. I doubt whether, if I were in England, I would visit this, for I have in recent years seen many such exhibitions. To stand by any book-stall or to enter any book-shop is to witness a terrific sense of internecine warfare between the innumerable latest volumes, almost all of them violently vying with one another for one's attention, fiercely striving to outdo the rest in crudity of design and colour. It is rather like visiting the parrot-house in the Zoological Gardens, save that there one can at least stop one's ears with one's fingers, whereas here one merely wants to shut one's eyes.[3]

Beerbohm, by then in his late seventies, was of a generation that had seen the book jacket grow from its humble origins as a purely functional plain protective bookseller's wrapping in the nineteenth century, to something closer to the illustrated jacket with which we are familiar today. Beerbohm was not alone in being somewhat underwhelmed by the virtues of this emerging area of the graphic arts. In his Dent Memorial Lecture in 1936, Richard de la Mare, a member of the board of Faber and Faber, commented that:

> The history of the book jacket is a strange one. The wretched thing started as a piece of plain paper, wrapped round the book to protect it during its sojourn in the bookseller's shop; but it has become this important, elaborate, not to say costly and embarrassing affair, that we know today, and of which we sometimes deplore the very existence. How much better might this mint of money, that is emptied on these ephemeral wrappers – little works of art though some of them may be – be spent upon improving the quality of the materials that are used in the making of the book itself![4]

Roads to Glory
Richard Aldington
Chatto & Windus · 1930
188 × 125 mm · 7⅜ × 5 in.

The painter and war artist Paul Nash (UK, 1889–1946) produced a small amount of commercial illustration and design work, including this striking dust jacket for Aldington's thirteen stories about the First World War.

London Fabric
James Pope-Hennessy
B. T. Batsford · 1939
225 × 146 mm · 8⅞ × 5¾ in.

There has been a surge of interest in recent years in the strangely luminous artworks of Eric Ravilious (UK, 1903–1942). During his short working life he produced a substantial volume of painting, printmaking, ceramic design and illustration. An official war artist, he was lost, presumed dead, in 1942 when the flight that he was on failed to return to Iceland. He was 39. The poor quality paper used for this dust jacket means that few have survived in good condition.

The Art of the Book Jacket
Victoria and Albert Museum · 1949
220 × 140 mm · 8⅝ × 5½ in.

The distinctive hand-rendered typography of Hans Tisdall created a dynamic design for the cover of the booklet accompanying Charles Rosner's exhibition at the Victoria and Albert Museum in London.

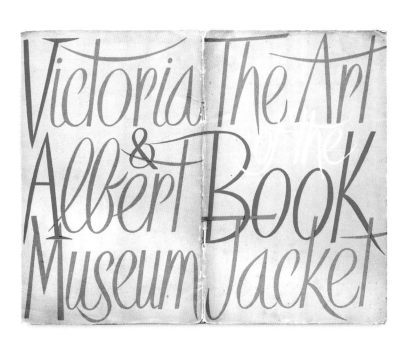

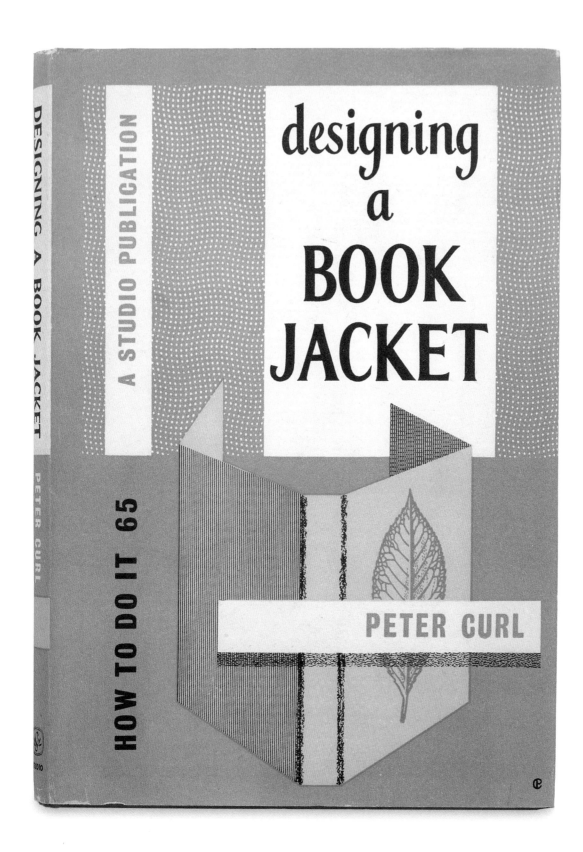

Designing a Book Jacket
Peter Curl
The Studio Publications · 1956
210 × 135 · 8¼ × 5⅜ in.

Peter Curl designed many dust
jackets as well as this one for his
own book on the subject. As he
states on the inside flap, 'If the jacket
of this book attracts you, if its title
is clear and if it reflects accurately
the style and contents of the pages
within, then it is successful.'

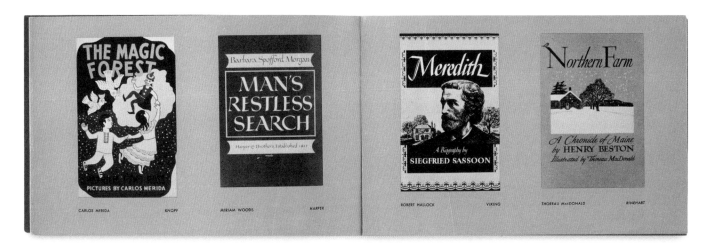

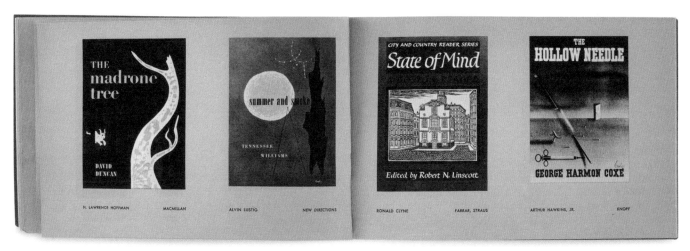

Second Annual Exhibition
Book Jacket Designers Guild
(New York) · 1949
140 × 420 mm · 5½ × 16½ in.

The short-lived Book Jacket
Designers Guild held annual
exhibitions of selected book-jacket
designs in the late 1940s and early
1950s. This 32-page catalogue was
for the show at the A-D Gallery, Room
309, 130 West 46 Street, New York.

Such scepticism about this nascent field of creative endeavour was clearly not uncommon despite the contribution of a number of outstanding artists, who were beginning to apply their talents in this direction. Among those doing so in the UK were Edward Bawden, John Piper, Barnett Freedman and Edward Ardizzone, while in the USA, jackets designed by N. C. Wyeth, Rockwell Kent, Arthur Hawkins, Jr. and Cleonike Damianakes were adorning some of the great works of literature. In fact, far from working to the 'fallacious doctrine that the loudest shout brings in the most customers',[5] these and other artists were contributing to the development of a new art form that the Book Jacket Designers Guild defined in terms of 'successful integration of concept with graphic means, taste in design and idea, and expression of the spirit of the book'.[6] The Guild had been formed in New York in 1947 by a group of graphic artists who were applying their talent to this field. They were keen to raise its profile and to gain wider recognition for designers and illustrators who were creating something a little more subtle than a squawking parrot.

More generally, the illustrated dust jacket as an integral aspect of the hardback book has been variable and patchy in its evolution around the world. In many cultures, including China and Japan, the jacket seems to have been something of a rarity. In Japan, the *obi*, a wraparound paper band much smaller and narrower than a full jacket, is used to give most of the textual information about the book, and folds over the printed boards, or sometimes over a jacket. Within mainland Europe there has been variation too, with some countries tending towards the use of illustrated stiff-card wraps as part of the binding, extended to form flaps that fold in and contain further information. For many years in France, certainly until the mid-1930s, the ubiquitous yellow paper jacket printed with black letterpress type prevailed. In Eastern Europe, the richly inventive graphic traditions were often applied in the form of printed, paper-covered boards rather than the detachable jacket. An exception was during the Weimar Republic. In that period, Germany, and Berlin in particular, was at the epicentre of avant-garde

Klassischer Journalismus
Egon Erwin Kisch
Rudolf Kaemmerer (Berlin) · 1923
188 × 125 mm · 7⅜ × 5 in.

Starting at a young age – his first
work was illustrating a fashion
catalogue in 1918 – George G.
Kobbe (Germany, 1902–1934)
became a busy commercial artist
and book illustrator in Berlin in
the 1920s. He designed jackets for
a number of publishers, including
Verlag Die Schmiede, where he
worked alongside George Salter.

Die Jungfrau von 18 Karat
Pitigrilli (Dino Segre)
Eden Verlag (Berlin) · 1927
185 × 125 mm · 7¼ × 5 in.

Willy Herzig (Germany, 1874–
1978) designed posters and covers
for sheet music and music albums,
as well as dust jackets. He worked
in the Art Deco style and later used
photomontage. This work shows
why German dust-jacket designers
of the Weimar period were called
Die Meister des Kleinplakats, or
'masters of the small poster'.

Die Stadt Oklahoma
George Milburn
Rowohlt (Berlin) · 1932
193 × 124 mm · 7⅝ × 4⅞ in.

Oklahoma Town had first been
published in America in 1931 and
the German edition with the design
by George Grosz (Germany,
1893–1959) appeared the following
year, prior to Grosz's emigration
to the US in 1933. The design was
repeated on both the cloth binding
and jacket.

experimentation in book art and design, with richly varied approaches, including photomontage, pictorial typography and painting.[7]

There is thus an inevitable bias in this overview towards the English language book. Though even here there can be found differences between British and American developments, as greater emphasis was placed on formatted series with consistent visual identity in Europe, whereas US publishers tended towards a more individualist approach to commissioning jacket designs. From the illustrators' perspective, the emergence of the dust jacket opened up a new source of freelance employment. It would be rare, however, for an artist to be seen as specializing in jacket design; most would need to work across many other areas of commercial art. Nonetheless, the critic Steven Heller has observed that jacket design in America in the late 1940s 'was still practiced by a small tight-knit group'. He quotes Ben Feder, one of the founding members of the Book Jacket Designers Guild, as recalling that, 'There were probably no more than thirty artists working on a regular basis.'[8]

In view of its origins as a plain protection to be discarded on purchase, and the relatively recent acceptance of the detachable jacket as an integral part of the book and its identity, it is ironic that for today's book collectors the jacket is key – the presence of an original jacket on a sought-after first edition now greatly adds to its value.[9] And if the design of the jacket is by a highly acclaimed artist, then that value will often increase further, at a time when awareness and appreciation of the book as a designed artefact is growing.

Before attempting to trace a brief history of the dust jacket, it might first be advisable to untangle the terminology, which has become confusing. The first 'jackets' were generally referred to as 'dust wrappers' and were exactly that, plain paper wrappings that protected the booksellers' wares from the dust and dirt of the city up until the point of purchase. At which time the buyer would immediately discard it in order to enjoy the often ornately decorated leather binding that it had protected.[10] The term 'jacket' specifically describes the detachable paper cover that wraps around the hardback book, extending beyond its overall length and folding in at either end. These 'flaps' hold the jacket in place and are usually printed with information relating to what the book is about. The jacket's role as a protector has diminished over the years as it has become primarily a form of display and promotion, a mini-poster that gives a taste of the contents, catches the eye and, once picked up, leads us to a 'blurb' about the author and perhaps advertisements for other titles from that author and/or the publisher. Although *book* jacket would seem the more proper term now for this object, *dust* jacket has clung on tenaciously in everyday language, long after its role in protecting the book from dust and dirt has become redundant. And although opinions vary among scholars, bibliophiles and the general public as to whether the jacket should be seen as part of the book itself or as an entirely separate, ephemeral addition, it would seem clear that the jacket is a historically important indicator of, and contribution to, contemporary graphic style and visual culture.

Although the almost universal early tendency to discard the jacket has hampered later scholarly research, it used to be generally accepted that the first printed dust jacket was for *The Keepsake of 1833* for the publishers Longmans in London. Until 2009, this was considered to be the earliest surviving example of a designed wrapper printed front and back, with a title design on the front (including border and decorative fleurons) and text on the back advertising other titles in print. Then a librarian at Oxford's Bodleian Library unearthed an example from 1830: a printed wrapper for a book called *Friendship's Offering*. However, in general through the nineteenth century publishers were slow to see the possibilities of the jacket as a promotional tool. The jacket itself became an increasingly common phenomenon as leather bindings were gradually superseded by cloth-covered boards, but most of them continued to be in the form of plain paper. Occasionally, transparent glassine coverings were supplied, which allowed a view of a pictorial binding. Plain jackets were also produced with die-cut 'windows', giving a glimpse of what was underneath.

By the early twentieth century jackets were becoming increasingly common but *design* tended to be limited to the addition of an image taken from the interior of the book or some form of random decoration. It was not really until the 1920s that the jacket as we know it today became a familiar sight in bookshops and the

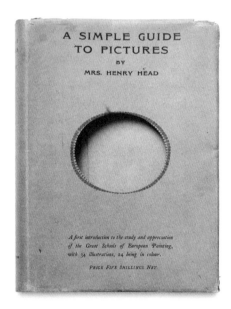

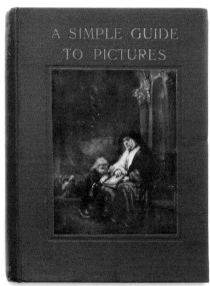

A Simple Guide to Pictures
Mrs Henry Head
Chatto & Windus · 1914
229 × 152 mm · 9 × 6 in.

This dust jacket from 1914 features
one of the typical die-cut 'windows'
that were in regular use at the time.
The oval is cut from a relatively
utilitarian protective jacket, but
most of the pictorial element of the
design is still hidden from view
at the point of sale.

art of book-jacket design became an important branch of the applied arts and
an area of opportunity for artists.

The process of arriving at a design for a book's jacket is and has always been
a collaborative one. Those involved include some or all of publisher, designer,
illustrator and printer. Once the brief for the work is agreed, accommodating
whatever house/series style or other ingredients are required, the design
begins. A jacket might be purely typographic or may combine typography and
image, photographic or illustrative. As indicated, this book is concerned with
the latter and aims to spotlight the high-quality pictorial art and design that
adorned the jackets of books through much of the twentieth century and, more
particularly, the contribution of the artists and illustrators who created that work.
Terminology is again an issue here and, happily, for a considerable portion of
the period under discussion, the words 'artist' and 'illustrator' were not quite
as irreconcilable as they are today. Some of the leading gallery artists of the time
engaged with the design of book jackets, particularly in the immediate postwar
years, notably John Craxton, John Piper, Graham Sutherland and Keith Vaughan.
In many instances 'artist' and 'designer' were one and the same person.

A well-designed jacket requires close synthesis between type and image. Some
of the best designs therefore have been by artists who were comfortable working
with type themselves, often in the form of hand-rendered lettering, or by artists
with an empathy for type and able to consider the overall balance of the design
in relation to the ideas of the typographic designer. As Steven Heller has observed,
'successful cover design requires the expertise of an artist, typographer, poster
designer and logo maker'.[11] For much of the period surveyed by this book, the
artists also needed to have a thorough grasp of the reprographic processes by
which their work would be transferred to paper if they were to achieve the best
results. Understanding and exploiting the limitations of, for example, letterpress
line-block separations or autolithography was a feature of the work of a number
of artists who became particularly influential in Great Britain, notably John
Minton, John Nash and Barnett Freedman.

The legendary American designer George Salter outlined some of the key
skills of the pictorial jacket designer in his article *The Book Jacket* in 1950:

> The question whether a jacket can be designed by one artist and lettered by another
> may be answered in various ways. As it is possible to use an old print or photograph
> for a certain function in a jacket it must also be possible to combine the work of two
> artists in one jacket. Both drawing and lettering are a means to an end: the jacket.

Salter goes on to make it clear that the design process must always come first and
that lettering and image must be considered in harmony from the outset. Equally
important is the artist's sensitivity to the text. An ability to absorb fully a book's
meanings and 'tone' is essential:

> Two elements not necessarily interrelated establish today the basic requirements
> for the makings of a good book jacket: graphic interpretation of the book's intrinsic
> character and the method by which the publisher wishes to promote the title.

And on the importance of reading the full manuscript rather than submitting to
publishers' instructions or designing on the basis of a plot synopsis, he is even
more unequivocal:

> It seems utterly paradoxical to think that a person who makes it his profession
> to promote reading should voluntarily claim exemption from it for himself.[12]

Salter was the chairman of the Book Jacket Designers Guild and he and his
fellow founders[13] were keen to counter the rise in sensationalist and titillating
pulp-fiction design. Salter's writings in the catalogues of the annual exhibitions
have a somewhat evangelical and at times puritanical tone, perhaps reflecting
the ongoing battle to gain acceptance of their work as a serious area of creative
endeavour. Eventually, however, the importance of maintaining a record for
scholars was acknowledged by the Library of Congress in the USA in the form
of an archive of almost every published example. In the UK, what is now called

Hazel Glen
M. E. Drewsen
Pickering and Inglis · Undated
185 × 130 mm · 7¼ × 5⅛ in.

Although undated, this Excelsior
Library edition for children was
published before 1925 and is an early
example of a coloured (letterpress
line-block separations) narrative
illustration as a promotional jacket.
A section of the image is extracted
and repositioned on the spine. The
artist is not credited.

The Love of the Foolish Angel
Helen Beauclerk
Collins · 1929
200 × 146 mm · 7⅞ × 5¾ in.

Edmund Dulac (France/UK, 1882–
1953) was born in Toulouse and
studied at the École des Beaux-Arts
in Paris before settling in London in
his twenties. He became one of the
leading artists of the so-called 'golden
age' of book illustration. This design
is highly stylized in the Art Deco
manner and the book features Dulac's
line decorations and illustrated
letterforms throughout.

The Hammering
Hal Martin
Faber and Faber · 1960
190 × 130 · 7½ × 5⅛ in.

Edward Bawden's prolific output
across many areas of the fine and
applied arts included the design of
numerous dust jackets through all of
the decades covered by this book. His
lino-cutting techniques informed his
colour-separation line work, where he
would often use a knife to scrape away
areas of black ink to create texture.

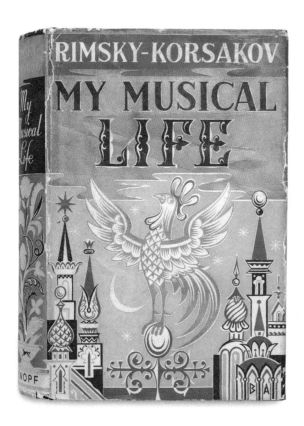

My Musical Life
Nikolai Rimsky-Korsakov
Alfred A. Knopf (New York) · 1942
245 × 170 mm · 9⅝ × 6¾ in.

Russian-born émigré Boris
Artzybasheff's unique visual
vocabulary was hired to adorn the
jacket of his fellow-countryman's
autobiography. In this instance,
the artist used Russian folk-art
iconography in red, blue and gold.

The Flight from the Enchanter
Iris Murdoch
Chatto & Windus · 1956
204 × 134 mm · 8 × 5¼ in.

In the 1950s, Edward Bawden's
work was sometimes more
abstracted, stylized and modernist
in nature than earlier in his career.
The jackets were sometimes
rendered in ink to give the
appearance of a lino-cut.

Decorative Art 1949
Edited by Rathbone Holme
and Kathleen M. Frost
The Studio · 1949
295 × 230 · 11⅝ × 9 in.

For this large-scale annual publication
Victor Reinganum made maximum
use of three colours to create a classic
period piece. The dramatic fusion
of highly stylized pictorial elements
and pattern reflected the growing
sense of optimism as the decade
came to a close.

the British Library Dust Jacket Collection had been started in the 1920s, initially in the form of a selection of jackets that were chosen on the basis of being of particular artistic interest.[14]

As in most areas of the commercial arts, the graphic style of dust jackets through the twentieth century generally mirrored the fashions and movements of the times, and some are outlined on the pages that immediately follow. However, in the case of the more pictorial, illustrative jackets featured in this book, an artist's unique personal visual vocabulary could often transcend fashion and in some instances lead to a long career. Artists such as Boris Artzybasheff, Edward Bawden and Victor Reinganum employed their instantly recognizable talents across many decades without needing to reinvent themselves artistically in order to accommodate changing graphic trends and motifs. But others came and went or cleverly developed multiple visual personalities that brought them commercial reward but perhaps less cultural, critical acclaim. What was clear as the century wore on was that the pictorial design of dust jackets was becoming an increasingly appealing and prestigious area of employment for the illustrator. Having your name on the dust-jacket flap (or perhaps even a discreet signature on the front of the jacket) could mean considerable exposure for the artist and, on occasion, close association in the public's mind with great works of literature. Conversely, for some authors it would be seen as a major boost to have the work of certain high-profile artists gracing their covers or jackets. Regrettably, many dust-jacket designs also appeared with no acknowledgment of the artist, with some publishers being more routinely guilty of this crime than others. Of course, ultimately, as the writer Jhumpa Lahiri observes in *The Clothing of Books*, 'What is the perfect book jacket? It doesn't exist. The great majority of covers, like our clothes, don't last forever.'[15] Nonetheless, I hope we can extend the lives of a few in this book.

Three Guineas
Virginia Woolf
The Hogarth Press · 1938
204 × 140 mm · 8 × 5½ in.

The dust-jacket designs of Vanessa Bell for Leonard and Virginia Woolf's Hogarth Press are instantly recognizable; the artist created an unmistakable 'brand' by means of simplified shapes and motifs.

Frolic Lady
S. B. P. Mais
Cassell · 1930
195 × 130 mm · 7¾ × 5⅛ in.

Signed 'Baird 30' this classic Art Deco design introduces a novel about the struggle of a poor young man to win and retain the affection of a capricious and beautiful woman brought up in luxury.

The Night Flower
Walter C. Butler
The Macaulay Company
(New York) · 1936
195 × 130 mm · 7¾ × 5⅛ in.

The dramatic use of light and dark by 'Ancona' (USA) immediately conveys the information that this is a mystery novel (one of only two written by Frederick Faust under this pseudonym) and echoes the film noir genre of the period.

The Isle of Auks
Nicholas Polunin
Edward Arnold · 1932
230 × 152 mm · 9 × 6 in.

This striking jacket for Nicholas Polunin's memoir of polar exploration is extremely rare. The artist, who is not credited and whose signature is barely legible, creates a dynamic Art Deco design that cleverly exploits the negative space of the white paper as a third colour. The title is kept at the bottom of the jacket in order not to interfere with the drama of the iceberg.

Brave Wings
Maud Diver
John Murray · 1931
175 × 110 mm · 6⅞ × 4⅜ in.

'Baird' uses pattern and contrasting geometric shapes to great effect in this design. The companion volume, *The Wild Bird*, another novel set in India in the imperial romance genre for which Diver was known, was issued by John Murray with the same jacket design but in different colours.

BLOOMSBURY, ART DECO & MURDER MYSTERY

The rapid rise of the pictorial dust jacket through the 1920s and 1930s coincided with the Art Deco period in contemporary design. Inevitably, the movement's ubiquitous dynamic, geometric motifs pervaded the covers of many books. Artists whose work displayed these stylistic idioms most prominently include Edmund Dulac, Rockwell Kent and, in his early career, Edward McKnight Kauffer. But many of the painter-illustrators ploughed their own artistic furrow, immune to such trends. At the Hogarth Press, Vanessa Bell's idiosyncratic designs for the covers of her sister Virginia Woolf's novels, and other publications, seemed out of step with the modes of the time but gave a highly distinctive identity to the output of the press. It had begun life in 1917 with a hand-printing press on a table at the Richmond home of Leonard and Virginia Woolf. Bell's sometime lover Duncan Grant also contributed a small number of designs.

In contrast, jacket designs within the increasingly popular genre of crime-fiction publishing were by and large suitably garish and melodramatic. However, many quality artists also contributed covers, including C. W. Bacon, Fritz Wegner and Victor Reinganum, notably for the Collins Crime Club editions. Unfortunately, this particular area of publishing suffered from a particularly high incidence of uncredited illustration.

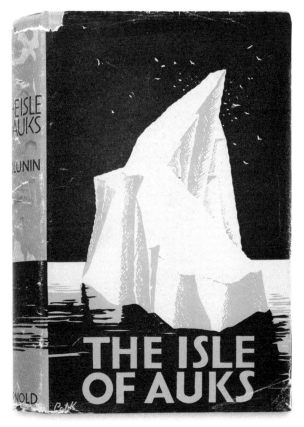

Appointment in Samarra
John O'Hara
Faber and Faber · 1965
200 × 130 mm · 7⅞ × 5⅛ in.

The modernist design by Alfred
Maurer (USA, 1868–1932) for
O'Hara's first novel, published in 1934
by Harcourt Brace in New York (and
Faber and Faber in London in 1935
– this copy is a later Faber edition),
sweeps the eye from left to right as the
car disappears into the unknown.

The Black Eye
Conyth Little
Collins · 1946
190 × 125 mm · 7½ × 5 in.

This Collins Crime Club title features
an intriguing uncredited jacket image.
The manner of the brushwork, the
faceless figure and the use of a broken
dotted line are highly reminiscent of
the work of Kenneth Rowntree.

The Penthouse Mystery
Ellery Queen
Grosset & Dunlap
(New York) · 1941
195 × 135 mm · 7¾ × 5½ in.

This jacket by an unknown designer
displays the typically brash stylization
of American pulp detective fiction that
has over time acquired period appeal.

The Spinster's Secret
Anthony Gilbert
Collins · 1946
190 × 125 mm · 7½ × 5 in.

One of many excellent yet uncredited
jacket designs for the popular Collins
Crime Club, this one depicts the
heroine of the story, Miss Martin, who,
the blurb explains, 'of small means and
delicate health, finds her chief interest
in sitting at the window of her single
room in Kensington and watching
the passers-by'.

Murder in the Mews
Agatha Christie
Odhams · 1937
190 × 130 mm · 7½ × 5⅛ in.

The architect Robin Halliday
Macartney (UK, 1911–1973) was
a friend of Agatha Christie and her
husband, the archaeologist Max
Mallowan. He designed some of
Christie's early dust jackets. This
one is highly effective in its use of
dramatic lighting and sensitivity
to architectural detail.

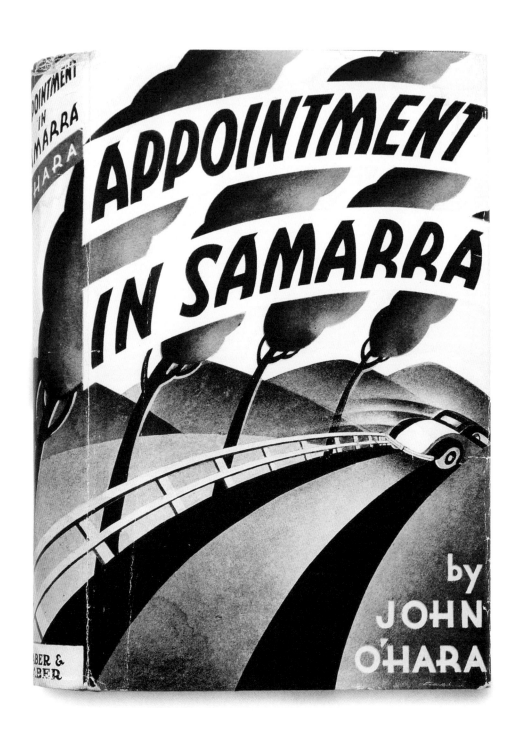

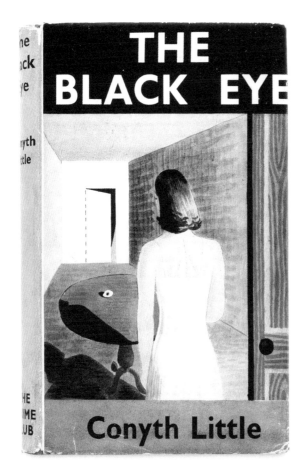

The White Hour
Neil M. Gunn
Faber and Faber · 1950
190 × 125 mm · 7½ × 5 in.

The jacket for this collection of Scottish writer Neil M. Gunn's short stories is sadly uncredited. It is beautifully conceived in a four-colour separation for letterpress line-block printing to convey the drama of the backdrop to the stories.

The Isle of Wight
Barbara Jones
Penguin · 1950
185 × 125 mm · 7¼ × 5 in.

The cover to Barbara Jones's *King Penguin* tour of the Isle of Wight is often assumed to have been designed by Jones herself, whose portrait of the island in words and pictures forms the content of the book. In fact, the designer was Clifford Barry, Jones's husband at the time.

The Long Walk Home
Peter Medd
John Lehmann · 1951
204 × 140 mm · 8 × 5½ in.

This wartime memoir tells of Peter Medd's 48-day walk down Italy to reach the British lines. The book was completed by his companion, Frank Simms, after Medd was killed in a plane crash in 1944. Bateson Mason (UK, 1910–1977) used geometric shapes and motifs of the period to evoke the drama and hardship of the journey.

Mani: Travels in the Southern Peloponnese
Patrick Leigh Fermor
John Murray · 1958
225 × 152 mm · 8⅞ × 6 in.

This design by John Craxton (UK, 1922–2009) for Leigh Fermor's *Mani* can be seen as one of the last examples of a jacket in the neo-romantic style. As a dedicated painter, Craxton's illustrative work was limited mainly to collaborations with close friends and acquaintances.

After the Second World War, Britain in the late 1940s and early 1950s saw the arrival of a mood of elegiac lyricism in the arts that became known as neo-romanticism. It was characterized by a sense of yearning for spiritual connection to the landscape and looked back for inspiration to the visionary paintings of Samuel Palmer and William Blake. It came and went rather quickly and by the mid-1950s was being replaced by the more forward-looking abstract expressionism.

Many of the so-called neo-romantic artists worked across a range of fine and applied arts. Most of the key figures illustrated books and/or contributed jacket designs, leaving us with a mini 'golden age' of book design and illustration. A key player was the publisher John Lehmann, brother of the novelist Rosamond Lehmann. Founded in 1946, his publishing house in London's Covent Garden survived for only eight years but during that time he published some of the most important illustrated books of the century and left a legacy of book-jacket design that has had a lasting influence. Keith Vaughan was his designer, as well as one of his regular illustrators, and among the other artists who contributed lavishly pictorial jackets were John Minton (by far the most prolific), Robert Medley, Edward Bawden, Edward Burra and Michael Ayrton. The lettering was frequently hand-rendered by the artist in a freewheeling, decorative manner. It is probable that none of these practitioners would have labelled themselves exclusively as illustrators, since each of them worked across the fine and applied arts. Vaughan himself did eventually devote himself entirely to painting.

Many other small firms contributed to this highly productive period of publishing beautifully packaged books, including Paul Elek, Hamish Hamilton, Rupert Hart-Davis, Cresset Press, Chatto & Windus, André Deutsch, Frederick Muller and, of course, Faber and Faber. From the mid-1950s, the mood began to change from poetic contemplation to one of assertive aspiration as technology and consumerism started to take hold.

Landscape into Art
Kenneth Clark
John Murray · 1949
229 × 152 mm · 9 × 6 in.

The choice of Graham Sutherland
(UK, 1903–1980) as jacket designer
of Clark's *Landscape into Art* was
a masterstroke. The artist's work
provides a perfect visual introduction
to the subject of the book.

Poems 1937–1942
David Gascoyne
Nicholson and Watson · 1943
210 × 155 mm · 8¼ × 6⅛ in.

Graham Sutherland was in many
ways seen as the elder statesman
of the neo-romantic movement. His
designs for *Poems* feature motifs and
approaches to letterforms that would
become much imitated in postwar
book design.

The Open Mind
Georges Bernanos
The Bodley Head · 1945
180 × 125 mm · 7 × 5 in.

James Holland (UK, 1905–1996)
was a major contributor to the 1951
'tonic to the nation', the Festival
of Britain. He worked as a painter
and illustrator and for many years
was also head of the Faculty of
Visual Communication Design at
Birmingham Polytechnic. This jacket
design is unusual in that it is printed
on both sides, featuring promotional
material for another George
Bernanos title on the reverse.

The Book of Woman's Hour
Ariel Productions · 1953
235 × 155 mm · 9¼ × 6⅛ in.

The BBC radio programme 'Woman's Hour' had a huge audience in 1950s Britain. This related book published by the BBC is filled with top tips for housewives. The cover artist, who would appear to have also been the originator of the playful interior illustrations, is not acknowledged.

Captain Caution
Kenneth Roberts
Collins · 1949
197 × 134 mm · 7¾ × 5¼ in.

This jacket for Roberts's historical novel features an impressive, highly stylized Art Deco inspired approach to figure painting, but the artist is not credited.

Adventures with Marmaduke
Elizabeth Chapman
Brockhampton Press · 1956
190 × 140 mm · 7½ × 5½ in.

Ferelith Eccles Williams (usually credited as 'Eccles Williams') illustrated numerous *Marmaduke* titles for Brockhampton Press. Her jacket designs, such as this example, have a carefree charm of a kind that is much imitated in current 'retro' illustration.

A Book of Mediterranean Food
Elizabeth David
John Lehmann · 1950
200 × 135 mm · 7⅞ × 5⅜ in.

Elizabeth David's books introduced the English-speaking world to the exotic and hitherto alien concept of Mediterranean cuisine. John Minton's brilliant designs perfectly complement the writing and form a highpoint not only in neo-romantic illustration but also in twentieth-century design as a whole.

Sweet William
Richmal Crompton
George Newnes · 1953
190 × 125 mm · 7½ × 5 in.

Thomas Henry (born Thomas Henry Fisher, UK, 1879–1962) learned his trade as a printer's apprentice in Nottingham but quickly found work as an artist on leading publications such as *Punch* and the *Strand* magazine. However, it is for his prolific illustrations for Richmal Crompton's ever-popular *William* books that he is best known. The prominent red of the covers makes them instantly recognizable, as with this 1953 reprint of a 1936 edition.

ANNUALS, CHILDREN'S & NON-FICTION

Through much of the twentieth century, many artists would not categorize themselves as specifically 'children's' illustrators. The ability to apply one's work to a range of age groups and across design, publishing and advertising gave the illustrator a far greater chance of earning a living, as is still the case. Children's annuals were a particularly fertile source of work for jobbing artists. Printed in vast editions, these books were a 'must' for the Christmas list and their heavyweight, course paper demanded a bold line-drawing style if the images were to be readable. The only use of full colour would often be on the cover boards and, if one was issued, the dust jacket. The latter were not common and relatively few survive the joyful battering the books received. As the concept of 'lifestyle' began to take hold in the 1950s, many non-fiction books targeted the feelings of optimism and aspiration by means of jackets that projected images of international travel and cuisine, and sophisticated home furnishing.

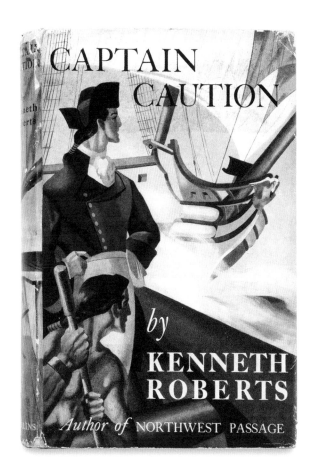

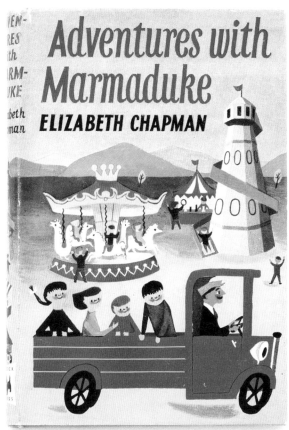

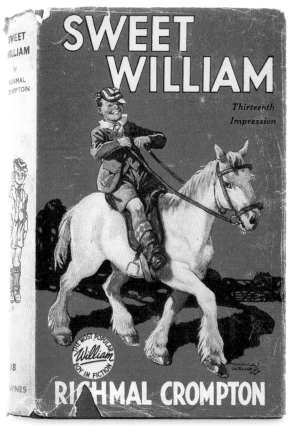

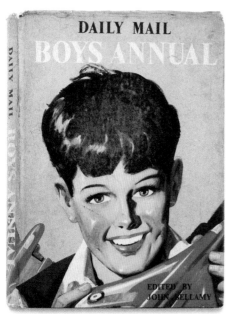

Flying the Atlantic
Manfred Reiss
Max Parrish · 1953
216 × 185 mm · 8½ × 7¼ in.

Manfred Reiss (Germany/UK,
1922–1987) wrote, illustrated and
designed this children's book. The
jacket conveys the growing sense
of prosperity and mobility of the
time. The free-flowing hand lettering
is embossed on the cover boards,
forming an attractive invitation
to explore the contents.

The Daily Mail Book for Boys
Edited by John Bellamy
Associated Newspapers · *c.* 1956
240 × 180 mm · 9½ × 7 in.

Undated and with no
acknowledgment for the artist, this
cover design projects an idealized
version of 1950s boyhood.

De Ark
Annie M. G. Schmidt
N. V. Amsterdamsche Boek-en
Courantmij (Amsterdam) · 1955
255 × 175 mm · 10 × 6⅞ in.

Jenny Dalenoord (The Netherlands,
1918–2013) illustrated over 180
children's books during her long
life. This beautiful three-colour
wraparound design demonstrates
total command of print processes
and type-image harmony.

Pinokkio
Carlo Collodi
Van Goor (Amsterdam) · 1969
255 × 175 mm · 10 × 6⅞ in.

The artist Willem Jacob Rozendaal
(The Netherlands, 1899–1971) worked
in many media, including stained
glass, but much of his output was print
based. This spectacular four-colour
design clearly draws on his particular
love of relief printing.

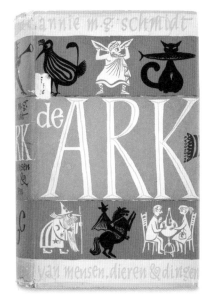

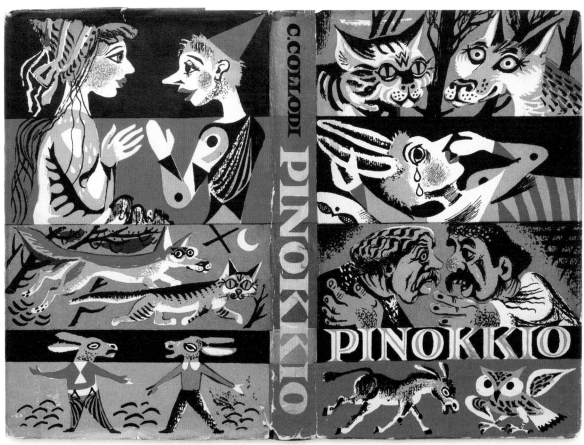

Glory of the Seas
Agnes Danforth Hewes
Cassell · 1935
190 × 125 mm · 7½ × 5 in.

N. C. Wyeth's image for this tale of
a young Boston shipping clerk's desire
to travel to California to find gold
was first used on the Alfred A. Knopf
edition in 1933. Wyeth's depth of
painterly understanding of land and
seascape meant that he was in great
demand to illustrate historical and
nautical drama.

Tender is the Night
F. Scott Fitzgerald
Charles Scribner's Sons
(New York) · 1934
188 × 130 mm · 7⅜ × 5⅛ in.

The unknown artist's design for the
jacket of Scott Fitzgerald's fourth
and final completed novel shows the
South of France backdrop to the story.
It has become one of the most admired
and instantly recognizable designs
of the period. Its presence on a first
edition greatly increases the value.

FROM REALISM TO MODERNISM IN AMERICA

The strong tradition of highly skilled 'realist' painting, as practised by artists such as Howard Pyle and pupils at his Brandywine School in Wilmington, Delaware, inevitably found its way into the field of dust-jacket design. Pyle's school gave its name to a movement, too, with 'Brandywine School' eventually becoming a term that was used to describe a particularly American form of narrative realism. Perhaps the best known of Pyle's pupils was N. C. Wyeth. He emerged in the early 1900s as photography was beginning to threaten the role of the realist painter.

Realist painting can have an uneasy relationship to illustration and does not always transfer comfortably to the art of dust-jacket design, where visual metaphor is often more effective than explicit representation in the distillation of text into image. And as the writer and academic Adam Sonstegard[16] has pointed out, there were other difficulties: many early illustrations to American literature were produced by artists who were not given the opportunity to read the complete book and were often having to make explicit visual representations of passages of text that were intended to be ambiguous or unstated, such as racial identities. In the emerging field of art direction, these shortcomings were no doubt not unique to the USA.

With the New Deal in the 1930s and later the postwar boom the strong presence of realist artist-illustrators such as Norman Rockwell, Walter Biggs and Dean Cornwall meant that such literal approaches continued to thrive. However, they co-existed with and sometimes were superseded by more design-based solutions as modernist artists created dynamic images that reflected wider developments in visual culture, including interior design and architecture. One of the first of this new generation was the American-born Edward McKnight Kauffer and, although he was based in England for much of his working life, his influence can be seen on artists such as Alvin Lustig and Paul Rand when they turned their attention to the dust jacket in the 1940s and 1950s. At the same time, a number of more graphic, gestural draughtsmen rose to prominence, including Ben Shahn, Leonard Baskin and David Stone Martin, with their powerful, sometimes more political, visual vocabularies.

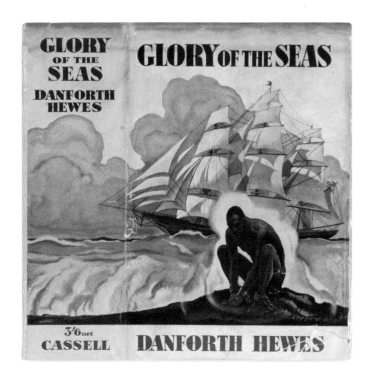

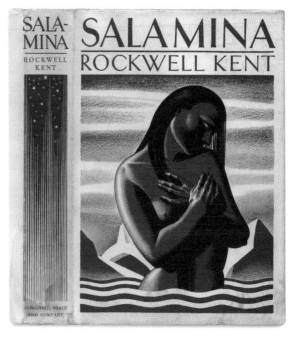

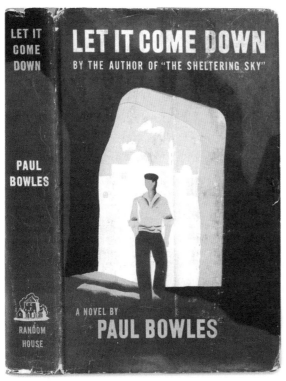

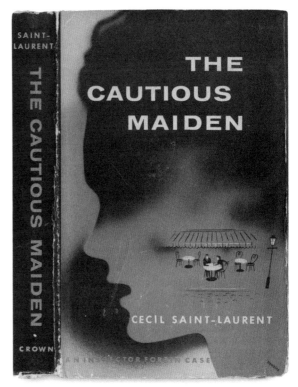

All Quiet on the Western Front
Erich Maria Remarque
Little, Brown (Boston) · 1929
195 × 125 mm · 7⅝ × 5 in.

The powerfully empty gaze of the
soldier on this most familiar and iconic
of Paul Wenck's designs leads the
reader into Remarque's classic First
World War novel.

Salamina
Rockwell Kent
Harcourt, Brace (New York) · 1935
222 × 159 mm · 8¾ × 6¼ in.

Rockwell Kent's account of his year
in a small village in north Greenland
includes twenty-three full-page tinted
woodcuts by the author as well as this
typically formalized jacket design.

Let It Come Down
Paul Bowles · Random House
(New York) · 1952
216 × 140 mm · 8½ × 5½ in.

The jacket for the first American
edition of Bowles's second novel
employs a technique informed by
Edward McKnight Kauffer's earlier
experience of stencilling or 'pochoir'.
Bowles's lead character, Nelson Dyar,
is depicted metaphorically entering the
dark underworld of Tangiers.

The Cautious Maiden
Cecil Saint-Laurent
Crown (New York) · 1955
210 × 130 mm · 8¼ × 5⅛ in.

Arthur Hawkins, Jr.'s mastery of the
airbrush is used to good effect on his
jacket design for this Inspector Forbin
case, which according to the blurb
alternates between 'the feverish world
of Paris's Left Bank and the brutal
realities of a police grilling room'.

FROM KITCHEN SINK TO GLAMOUR & INTRIGUE

The so-called 'Kitchen Sink' social realism that emerged in Britain in the late 1950s and early 1960s saw success for writers such as John Osborne, Alan Sillitoe, David Storey and Stan Barstow. Their 'angry young men' protagonists led a wave of novels, plays and films that swept away previous stereotypes of the life of the working classes. Jacket designs frequently reflected the relentlessly bleak tone of some of the writing, in contrast to the often sensationalist, exploitative marketing that can be seen in the posters of many of the films made from the books.

As the cultural and consumerist explosion of the 1960s expanded with all of its contradictions and paradoxes, glamour, romance, action and machismo were articulated visually through increasingly photographically referenced artworks. The use of the illustrator's new toy, the Grant Projector, a photographic projection device that facilitated tracing from photographs at different scales and from multiple sources, heralded an age of slick representational drawing of well-groomed models in static poses. The increasing reliance of illustration students on the device was later eloquently immortalized by the illustrator and author Raymond Briggs in the Association of Illustrators magazine in the late 1970s:

Our Enlarger,
Which art in College,
The Grant be Thy Name,
Thy light be on,
In Art as It is in Design.
Give us this Way our Easy Bread,
And Forgive us our Tracepapers,
As we Forgive Them
that Trace Off before us.
And Lead us not into Life Classes,
But Deliver us from Drawing;
For Thine is the Kodak,
The Polaroid and the Pentax,
For Agfa and Agfa.
Ah Me! [17]

Briggs' ironic version of the Lord's Prayer perfectly captures a period of growing infatuation with technology that would bring change to the craft of illustration and its relationship to drawing. This was followed by the inevitable swing back towards the craft's origins as the physicality of the book and its jacket reasserted themselves in the early twenty-first century.

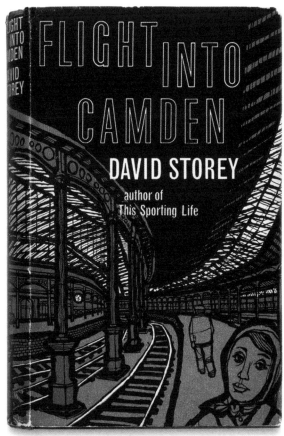

Lest We Lose Our Edens
Joan Kennedy
Valentine Romance Club · 1958
188 × 120 mm · 7⅜ × 4¼ in.

This Lovely Thing
Anne Hill
Valentine Romance Club · 1959
188 × 120 mm · 7⅜ × 4¼ in.

Kiss and Part
Caroline Fanshawe
Valentine Romance Club · 1957
188 × 120 mm · 7⅜ × 4¼ in.

Love is a Reckless Thing
Molly Seymour
Valentine Romance Club · 1958
188 × 120 mm · 7⅜ × 4¼ in.

The era of the role of 'housewife' and expectations that were clearly delineated by gender meant escapist romance and glamour were in great demand in the 1950s. Photographically posed jacket designs featured carefully shaped hair, coy glances and not-too-passionate embraces.

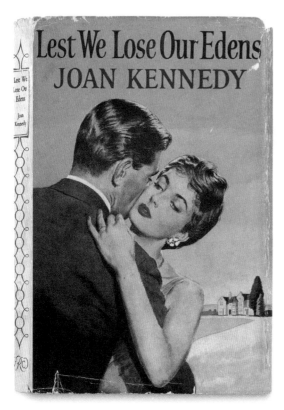

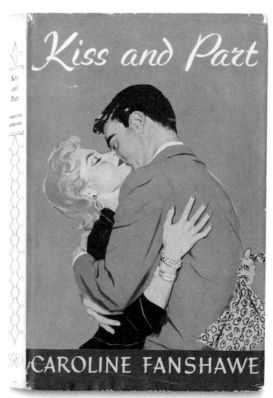

Very Like a Whale
Ferdinand Mount
Weidenfeld & Nicolson · 1967
195 × 130 mm · 7¾ × 5⅛ in.

As was common at the time, Alan Ball was a designer-illustrator in the 1950s and 1960s whose work ranged from the pictorial to the purely typographic. He taught for some years at Cambridge School of Art in the 1970s. This jacket is highly reminiscent of the heady late 1960s.

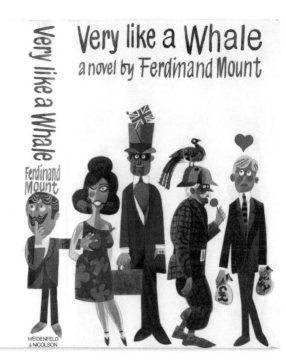

Recent Novels

FALL GIRL by Jill Neville

'. . . the author of the book's gimlet eye and caustic wit. Seldom have England's literary lice crawled more shamefully than under this antipodean microscope.' – Rivers Scott, *Sunday Telegraph*   18s

GAME IN HEAVEN WITH TUSSY MARX by Piers Read

'Now here's something to cheer about – a first novel which is outrageously funny and wickedly serious, and vibrates with talent on both planes.' – *Evening Standard*

'Piers Paul Read's first – and remarkable – novel exists on what a reviewer may justifiably call two levels: those of heaven and earth . . . marvellously comic, superbly inventive . . . Mr Read's is one of the most arresting British novels to have appeared in recent years.' – *The Times*   21s

THE NIGHTCLERK by Stephen Schneck

'What makes the book remarkable . . . is its exuberant eloquence, its glancing precision with the unexpected verb and epithet . . . there isn't a phrase that is not shapely and, however feverishly bright, under his complete intellectual control.' – Anne Duchene, *The Guardian*

'Schneck's original and vivid book . . . a mad humour as befits a mad world.' – Tony Tanner, *The Spectator*   21s

THE HOLIDAY by Dacia Maraini

'There is no doubt of her talent; the book is gracefully constructed and it bites like the east wind.' – Irving Wardle

'In its terse, observant, unspiritual way, it is a feat of incontestable brilliance.' – Christopher Wordsworth, *The Guardian*   21s

Weidenfeld and Nicolson

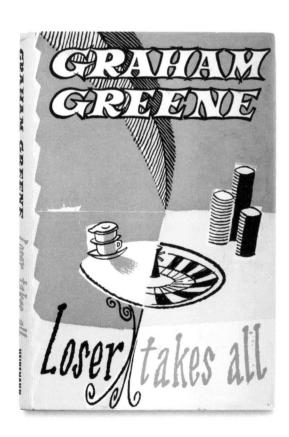

Loser Takes All
Graham Greene
Heinemann · 1955
190 × 125 mm · 7½ × 5 in.

The signature 'Stevens' is just visible on this jacket design for Greene's novella. The glamour of its Monte Carlo setting is evoked by the artist's stylish use of the graphic idioms of the period.

No Grave for a Lady
John and Emery Bonett
Michael Joseph · 1960
190 × 125 mm · 7½ × 5 in.

H. A. Grimley's jacket design aims for 1960s glamour and intrigue for the husband-and-wife writing team John and Emery Bonett (the pen names of John Coulson and Felicity Carter).

BELLS
IN
ENGLAND

TOM
INGRAM

FREDERICK
MULLER

The
WALL

JOHN
HERSEY

Hamish
Hamilton

Drugs
and
the
Mind

Robert
S. de
Ropp

FLOWER
of
CITIES

a Book of
LONDON

John
BETJEMAN

Elizabeth
BOWEN

E. Arnot
ROBERTSON

Nicolas
BENTLEY

Leonard
WOOLF

G.W. STONIER

William
SANSOM

And 15 other
Authors

Edward
BAWDEN

John
MINTON

Leonard
ROSOMAN

Ronald
SEARLE

Keith
VAUGHAN

And 8 other
Artists

PARRISH

Festival
at
Farbridge

J.B.
Priestley

Heinemann

EnGLI
FAIRS
MARKE

Willia
Addiso

BATSF

THE ARTISTS

Perhaps the twentieth century's most important and influential illustrator, Ardizzone has often been described as 'quintessentially English' in his depictions of everyday life, whether illustrating his own texts or those of others, for children or adults. His overall output was prodigious, from his very first illustrated book, the 1929 Peter Davies edition of Sheridan Le Fanu's *In a Glass Darkly*, through to *Ardizzone's Hans Andersen* (André Deutsch, 1978). This rather late start was due to an initial career as a clerk at the Eastern Telegraph Company in London, where he secretly drew and doodled on the job. His only formal art training was at evening life-drawing classes at Westminster School of Art, where he was taught by Bernard Meninsky (as were so many leading twentieth-century illustrators). This combination of formal and informal drawing education, alongside his own fascination with the visually anecdotal, seems to have been the key to Ardizzone's pictorial vocabulary. His departure from the job was facilitated by a gift of £500 from his father. He decided to use it to travel around Europe before setting out on a career as an artist.

Ardizzone's biographer, his brother-in-law Gabriel White, suggests that initially he 'eked out a precarious living by drawing book jackets'.[18] Although Brian Alderson's comprehensive bibliography[19] lists a 1934 jacket as the artist's first (*All in the Downs* by Frank Pollard, published by Constable), a number of jacket designs from the late 1920s exist including for *The Deep End* by Patrick Miller (Jonathan Cape, 1927), unrecognizable stylistically in its Art Deco/Rockwell Kent manner but signed 'E.J.I.A' (Edward Jeffrey Irving Ardizzone), and *The Midnight Bell: A Love Story* by Patrick Hamilton (Constable, 1929). Clearly though, it was not long before the supply of work became constant, in the form of illustrated books, dust jackets, advertising material, posters and prints.

Throughout this work over forty years runs a Chaucerian interest in the human condition. Every character described by Ardizzone's pen, whether central or incidental to the narrative, is entirely convincing as a living being, with aspirations, foibles, pretensions and insecurities. His was a semi-detached but affectionate eye. As the citation for his appointment as a Royal Designer for Industry put it in 1974: 'He was an unmalicious version of Thomas Rowlandson.' The text continued: 'His portrait of English life was an unruffled vision of town, beach and country populated by fubsy matrons, cooks like cottage loaves, dozy mongrels, pointy-feet children and men who in general seem to be off-duty.'

Many of Ardizzone's designs for dust jackets were executed for the books where he was either the author-illustrator or he illustrated them internally. But he was also regularly commissioned to design only the jacket, generally for books whose contents called for a visually garrulous artist. The 'hand-made' feel to the jackets, where type was usually hand-rendered and entirely integrated into the design, invariably formed a friendly invitation to enter the world within.

Hey Nonny Yes: Passions and Conceits from Shakespeare
Edited by Hallam Fordham
Saturn Press · 1947
140 × 110 mm · 5½ × 4⅜ in.

This pocket-sized book features two-colour autolithographic illustrations throughout, for which Ardizzone would have drawn each colour separately directly onto the lithographer's plate. Hallam Fordham selected various quotations from Shakespeare 'that touch or lie between the passions of Love and Hate'.

Showmen and Suckers
Maurice Gorham
Percival Marshall · 1951
220 × 140 mm · 8¾ × 5½ in.

Circuses, music halls, pantomimes
and fairgrounds formed the ideal
subject matter for Ardizzone's
pen. 'There's a streak of the
sucker in all of us, and part of the
showman's job is to bring it out',
the jacket blurb tells us. Ardizzone
and Gorham had been childhood
friends and they collaborated on
a number of titles. Gorham also
commissioned Ardizzone in his
role as art editor at *Radio Times*.

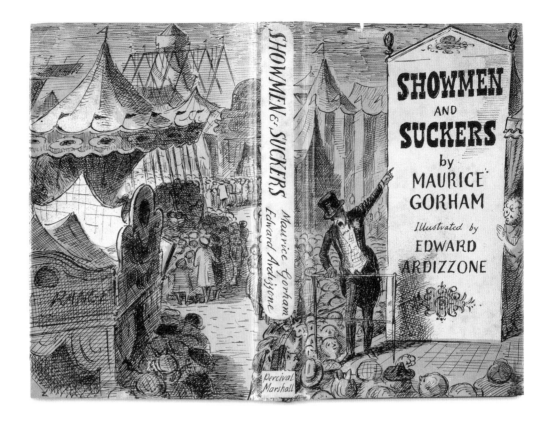

The Rose & the Ring
W. M. Thackeray (M. A. Titmarsh)
Guildford Press · 1948
220 × 140 mm · 8⅜ × 5½ in.

Ardizzone is at his most Victorian for
this repeated wraparound jacket, based
on the mood of Thackeray's originals
for the 1855 first edition.

The Cockney
Julian Franklyn
André Deutsch · 1953
220 × 140 mm · 8⅝ × 5½ in.

Ardizzone was the ideal choice
as jacket artist for Franklyn's
examination of the history and
culture of the London Cockney.

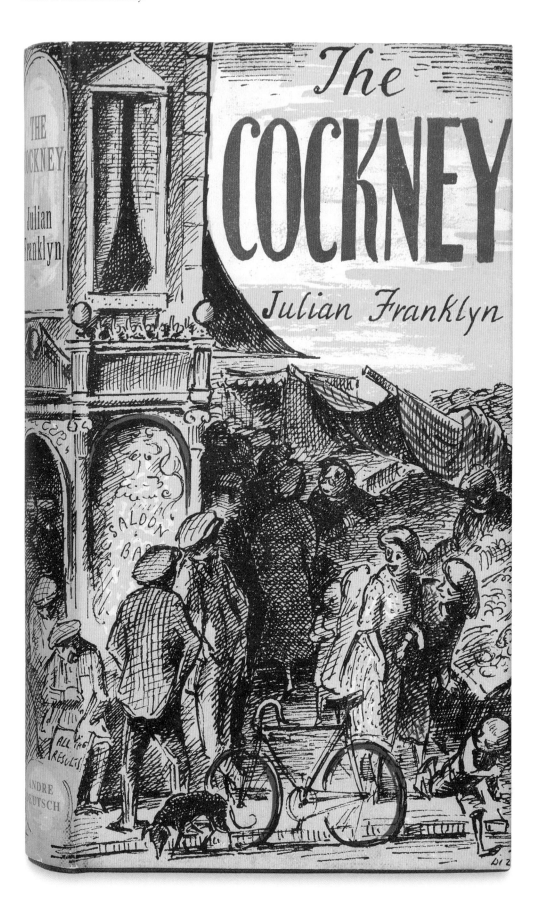

A Ring of Bells
John Betjeman
John Murray · 1962
220 × 146 mm · 8⅝ × 5¼ in.

Ardizzone's wraparound design
is repeated on the boards for this
volume of John Betjeman's poems
selected for young readers. The
artist uses an uncharacteristically
bold technique of brush drawing
here, along with three flat colours
as separations. The view is across
Hampstead Heath towards Highgate,
where Betjeman grew up.

Italian Peepshow
Eleanor Farjeon
Oxford University Press · 1960
210 × 159 mm · 8¼ × 6¼ in.

Farjeon and Ardizzone collaborated
on a number of titles over many
years. This design would no doubt
have been informed by the dozens of
observational drawings that Ardizzone
had made in Italy during his time as
an official war artist in the Second
World War.

The Growing Summer
Noel Streatfeild · Collins · 1966
204 × 140 mm · 8 × 5½ in.

Noel Streatfeild's novel for children
tells of a holiday in the south of
Ireland at the home of the redoubtable
Great Aunt Dymphna. The book
was published at the time full-colour
lithographic printing became the
standard. Ardizzone's typically fluid
line and watercolour technique are
on show here.

BORIS
ARTZYBASHEFF

USA · 1899–1965

Words such as 'idiosyncratic' or 'eccentric' do not begin to do justice to the extraordinary creations of Boris Artzybasheff. His was an art that defies categorization – one of elaborate compositions and constructions, rendered all the more surreal and disturbing by his intensely detailed techniques, in both colour and black and white. He was born in Kharkov, Ukraine, then part of Russia, and went to school in St Petersburg. He left Russia in 1919 and began a new life in New York, where he initially worked in an engraver's workshop but took various other jobs before beginning to establish himself as an artist. Artzybasheff's first illustrated book was *Verotchka's Tales* by Dmitrii Narkisovich Mamin-Sibiriak, published by Dutton in 1922. Book work continued to flow throughout the 1920s and the children's book *Gay-Neck* by Dhan Gopal Mukerji with his illustrations was awarded the Newbery Medal in 1928. As well as his highly decorative book illustrations, Artzybasheff is particularly known for his numerous covers for *Time* magazine, executed between 1941 and 1965. He created 215 of these in all. Many involved some sort of portraiture of leading figures of the period, but almost always included various other elements of fantasy, symbol or visual metaphor. He particularly favoured the anthropomorphism of man and machine, producing vast numbers of complex drawings of such hybrid constructions. They could loosely be described in terms of a fusion of M. C. Escher and Giuseppe Arcimboldo but with a highly individual dose of satire.

In 1954, Artzibasheff published a book of his work: *As I See* (Dodd, Mead). It is now highly sought after and features a classic Artzybasheff dust jacket in the form of an image of an elegant female hand holding two eyeballs with abundant eyelashes; the middle finger is gently curved downwards to form a face, a recycling of the central elements of his jacket design for the first edition of *The Incomplete Enchanter* (Henry Holt, 1941). *As I See* does not contain any textual commentary; the drawings form a language of their own that would probably be diminished by any attempt to explain them in words. However, the artist does include disembodied quotations and fragments of text including the following to introduce the section on 'Machinalia'. It is in the form of a letter to the nineteenth-century German poet and essayist Heinrich Heine in response to his tirade against the rise of the machine:

Dear Heinrich Heine
As many a poet, you are dismayed by the soulessness of machinery, then proceed to damn the obedient servant, which machinery is, for its master's own numscullery!…
I am thrilled by machinery's force, precision and willingness to work at any task, no matter how arduous or monotonous it may be. I would rather watch a thousand-ton dredge dig a canal than see it done by a thousand spent slaves lashed into submission. I like machines.
On the other hand, my dear Heinrich, you should never put a damp finger into a lamp socket.

Artzybasheff's dust-jacket designs generally display all of the theatrical, fanciful conceits of his wider body of work. He was most often commissioned to design for fantasy and crime fiction, where he could give full rein to his unique vision. He was usually responsible for all aspects of the design and typography.

As I See
Boris Artzybasheff
Dodd, Mead (New York) · 1954
292 × 216 mm · 11½ × 8½ in.

The jacket design for
Artzybasheff's own collection of
outlandishly surreal artworks and
metamorphoses recycles an idea
first used in the 1941 design for
The Incomplete Enchanter (below).

Land of Unreason
Fletcher Pratt and
L. Sprague de Camp
Henry Holt (New York) · 1942
210 × 146 mm · 8¼ × 5¾ in.

Eccentric and surreal collections
of animated, indeterminate beings
and objects regularly populated
Artzybasheff's designs and suited
fantasy novels like this one.

The Incomplete Enchanter
Fletcher Pratt and
L. Sprague de Camp
Henry Holt (New York) · 1941
210 × 146 mm · 8¼ × 5¾ in.

A typical Artzybasheff dust jacket
such as this one often involved
the assemblage of a range of
disembodied elements into a
composition that reads as something
else – in this instance, a face. The
book contained two fantasy novellas
and was the first volume in the
Harold Shea series.

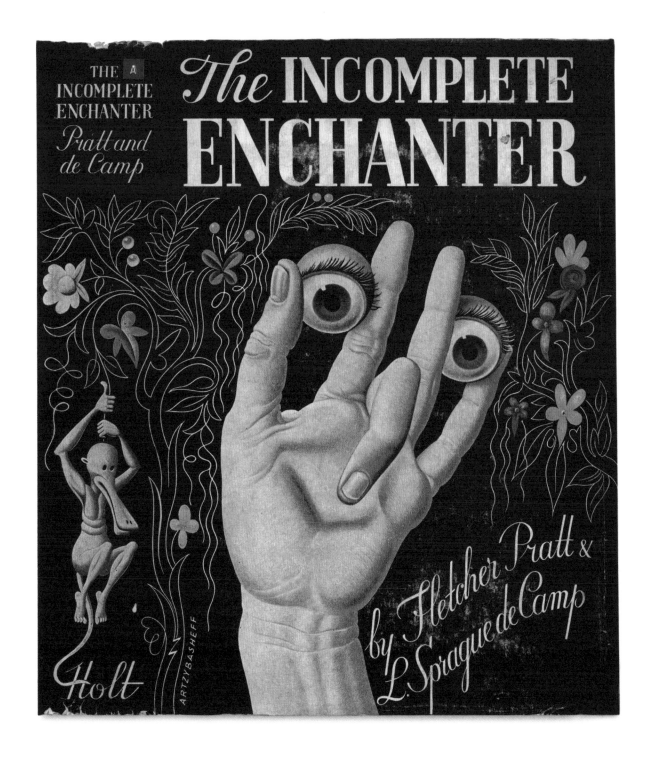

The Promise
Pearl S. Buck · Methuen · 1944
185 × 121 mm · 7¼ × 4¾ in.

Pavilion of Women
Pearl S. Buck · Methuen · 1947
190 × 125 mm · 7½ × 5 in.

C. W. Bacon's dust-jacket designs for
Pearl S. Buck's 1940s novels set in
the Far East feature intensely detailed
portraits of the main characters.
Despite bordering on the kitsch they
are totally compelling.

C. W. BACON
UK · 1905–1992

Cecil W. Bacon, or 'CWB' as he always signed his work, was
born in Battle, Sussex, where his father ran a tanning business,
and was educated at Sutton Valence School followed by Hastings
School of Art (1923–25). After that he joined a commercial art
studio in London and then worked both with an advertising agency
and as a freelance artist until 1941. Following a brief period in
the wartime RAF, Bacon was redirected from painting camouflage
for aircraft to working for the Ministry of Information. Here
he honed his illustration skills designing posters and leaflets.

After the war 'CWB' continued to build his career as a
freelancer, designing striking posters for London Transport and
other advertising clients, among them British Railways and the
Post Office Savings Bank, and regularly contributing black-and-
white illustrations for the *Listener* and *Radio Times*, including
memorable covers for the latter such as *Festival of Britain* (1951)
and *The Queen Returns* (1953). He produced innumerable
illustrations for children's books, particularly in the field of non-
fiction and information. Bacon was the consummate professional
who, though perhaps not regarded as highly as artists of his
generation such as Eric Fraser or Edward Bawden, could turn
his hand to any subject and always be relied upon to deliver. His
work was characterized by well-honed technical skills in a range
of different media. He was particularly adept with the medium
of scraperboard or 'scratchboard'. During the mid-twentieth
century, when the vast majority of illustration was reproduced
in black and white, this technique was in great demand for
advertising work. The process involved scraping away the black
surface of a specially prepared board to reach the white layer
below, giving an extremely crisp line quality that was excellent
for reproduction. Bacon authored a book on the technique for
Studio Publications in 1951: *Scraperboard Drawing* (number 41
in the *How To Do It* series).

C. W. Bacon's dust-jacket designs span his entire career, from
the mid-1930s through to the 1970s. His ability to create drama
by means of lighting made him particularly sought after in the
field of crime and horror fiction. As the crime-fiction specialists
John Cooper and B. A. Pike have observed:

> C. W. Bacon is unusual in that he continued to produce dust
> wrappers for crime fiction over several decades…Bacon was
> designing for Patricia Wentworth in 1933 and P. M. Hubbard
> in 1970. He was invariably stylish, whatever the mode in
> which he was working: thematic (as in Baynard Kendrick's
> *Death Knell* and Georgette Hyer's *Duplicate Death*); Pictorial
> (John Dickson Carr's *The Nine Wrong Answers* and Christopher
> Bush's *The Case of the Burnt Bohemian*); or stylized (Herbert
> Brean's *Hardly a Man is Now Alive*).[20]

Things Fall Apart
Chinua Achebe
Heinemann · 1958
190 × 125 mm · 7½ × 5 in.

One of the best-known and most
widely read novels by an African writer,
Achebe's classic tells of political and
social transition in Nigeria. Bacon's
powerful jacket design for this now
scarce first edition has contributed
to its desirability for collectors.

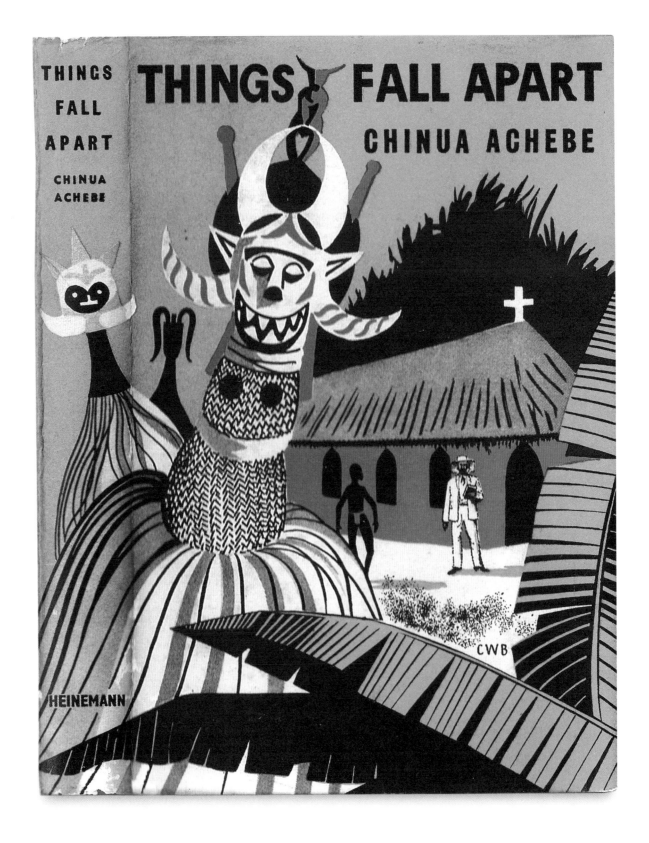

Reclining Nude
Maurice Watson
Cassell · 1960
190 × 125 mm · 7½ × 5 in.

Bacon's versatility as an artist allowed
him to tackle a wide a range of subject
matter including the more sensational
end of the crime-fiction genre.

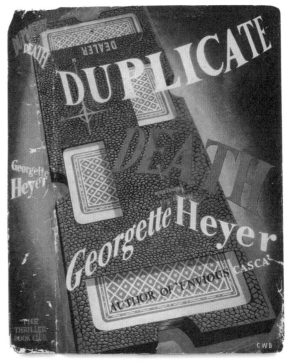

Death Knell
Baynard H. Kendrick
Methuen · 1946
190 × 134 mm · 7½ × 5¼ in.

First published by Morrow in the USA, the year before this Methuen edition, Kendrick's novel features the blind detective Captain Duncan Maclain, his 'seeing eye' dog and the femme fatale, 'gorgeous Try Singleton'. Bacon restricts his jacket design to the New York City backdrop.

Duplicate Death
Georgette Heyer
Thriller Book Club · 1951
190 × 130 mm · 7½ × 5⅛ in.

In this dust jacket, Bacon adopts a highly filmic idiom with floating typography evoking classic suspense. The book was first published by William Heinemann.

Patrick Butler for the Defence
John Dickson Carr
Hamish Hamilton · 1956
190 × 130 mm · 7½ × 5⅛ in.

Carr was a highly regarded American author who lived in England in the 1930s and 1940s. Many of his mystery stories have English settings. Against the background of London fog in Lincoln's Inn, Bacon depicts the strange man in the green fez whose murder poses a challenge for famed defence lawyer Patrick Butler.

Brazen Tongue
Gladys Mitchell
Michael Joseph · 1940
190 × 125 mm · 7½ × 5 in.

This novel is set in the fictional town of Willington in the early months of the Second World War. Bacon's dust-jacket design hints at the three mysterious deaths that pose the challenge to Mitchell's celebrated detective, Mrs Bradley. The book is scarce and the jacket even harder to come by, like many that were printed on fragile wartime paper stock.

STANLEY BADMIN

UK · 1906–1989

Stanley Badmin is known for his complete devotion over a long working life to representational, topographical painting of the English countryside, its everyday life and architectural heritage. The son of a Sydenham schoolmaster, he had something of a battle to persuade his parents to allow him to pursue what they considered an insecure career as an artist. However, once convinced of his passion and determination, they fully supported him as he gained a scholarship first to Camberwell School of Art and later to the Royal College of Art.

In the early years after graduation in the late 1920s, Badmin concentrated primarily on creating work for exhibition and initially flirted with the trends and styles of the time, such as stylized and elegant Art Deco figures and interiors. He had been taught etching at the RCA by Robert Austin, a noted printmaker, who introduced him to the Twenty-one Gallery, which specialized in etchings, where he was successful in selling prints. The intense detail and secure draughtsmanship of his work gradually began to draw attention in the form of press reviews that picked out his work for special mention from group shows. Publishing commissions began to follow, including one for the *Graphic* in 1927 and the *Tatler* in the following year. Badmin's first real breakthrough came in 1935 when his talents were spotted further afield and he was invited by *Fortune* magazine in America to cross the Atlantic and travel around the USA at the magazine's expense, making drawings and watercolours at specified destinations. Before returning to England, he exhibited his originals in New York.

Badmin is particularly known for his knowledge of, and ability to describe visually, trees. The publications he wrote and illustrated for Noel Carrington's Puffin Picture Books were extremely popular and were an important source of income for him. Carrington's Picture Puffin project was highly innovative in its use of autolithography – a process where artists would draw their colour separations directly onto the lithographic plate. Badmin's first such book was *Village and Town* (1942), followed by *Trees in Britain* (1943). Later, he illustrated *Farm Crops in Britain* (1955) in the same series, this time written by George Stapledon. Badmin's skills led to his involvement in the scheme for 'Recording the Changing Face of Britain' established by Kenneth Clark, then director of the National Gallery, at the beginning of the Second World War. Recording Britain employed artists on the home front, initially to capture the landscapes and areas that were under threat of invasion and bomb damage. Working in the great British topographical tradition, the scheme's artists produced over 1,500 paintings and drawings in the years 1940–43. Badmin contributed watercolours and drawings of Buckinghamshire, Kent, Northamptonshire and Suffolk.

Badmin's dust-jacket designs for the publishers B. T. Batsford exhibit all the intense clarity of architectural and botanical detail that one would expect from this artist. The original artworks are surprisingly small, not much bigger than the size at which they were reproduced. His typically understated 'S. R. Badmin' signature can usually be found somewhere on the image.

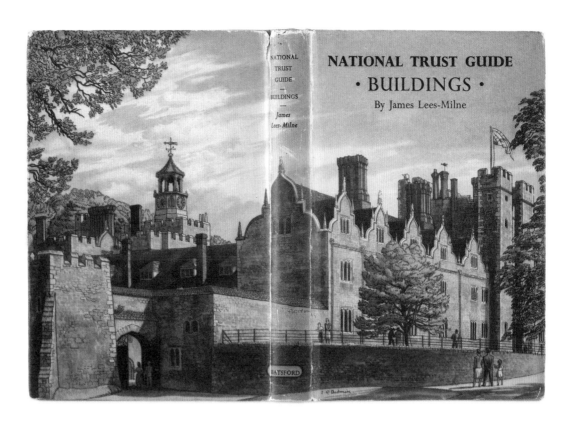

Local Style in English Architecture
T. D. Atkinson
B. T. Batsford · 1947
220 × 145 mm · 8⅝ × 5⅝ in.

This is a Badmin tour de force.
The wraparound design displays
all that is good about his work in a
quintessentially English scene that
seems to be an amalgam of several
places, including Long Melford in
Suffolk. The tower of the church is
cleverly positioned on the spine.

National Trust Guide: Buildings
James Lees-Milne
B. T. Batsford · 1948
190 × 125 mm · 7½ × 5 in.

Although typically representational
in execution, the jacket illustration
of Knole in Kent, the ancestral home
of the Sackvilles, is nevertheless
carefully composed in relation to
the type. Knole had passed to the
National Trust in 1947.

National Trust Guide:
Places of Natural Beauty
D. M. Matheson
B. T. Batsford · 1950
190 × 125 mm · 7½ × 5 in.

This idyllic autumnal panorama
is a view of Crockham Hill in Kent,
where Octavia Hill, co-founder
of the National Trust, lived and
is buried.

EDWARD BAWDEN

UK · 1903–1989

Along with his friend and contemporary Eric Ravilious, Edward Bawden can be seen as one of the key illustrator-designers of the twentieth century. And, as with Ravilious, in the early twenty-first century there has been a surge of interest in the artist's work as his contribution to British visual culture has been re-evaluated and increasingly appreciated.

Bawden was born in Braintree, Essex, the son of an ironmonger. At the age of 15, he was given permission by his teachers at Braintree School to travel one day each week on the bus to study at Cambridge School of Art. At that time it was one of the smallest of the provincial art schools that had been founded around the country in the 1850s with the Ruskinian aims of improving standards of art and design for industry. After a year as a part-time student, Bawden was able to study full-time there. He then won a scholarship to the Royal College of Art, where his own distinctive graphic language began to emerge under the tutelage of the painter Paul Nash and alongside a range of talented fellow students, including Barnett Freedman, Enid Marx and Edward Burra, as well as Ravilious.

Bawden's graphic work traversed multiple areas of the fine and commercial arts. His was a unique visual language that seemed to owe little to external influences. After a teenage infatuation with the work of Aubrey Beardsley, stylistic traces can perhaps be found in his early work of Edward Lear, Louis Wain and Claude Lovat

Fraser. He was known to admire the work of his brilliant young French contemporary Edy Legrand. However, it was Bawden's own dry, slightly detached humour and at times rather acid take on the world that powered his line illustration. He was by no means a proficient or natural draughtsman and as a student was inclined to avoid the life-drawing studio if at all possible. It was his experience as an official war artist in the Second World War, when he travelled extensively in North Africa, Ethiopia and the Middle East, that greatly enhanced his range of drawing skills. Bawden's thinking and drawing was constructed through the prism of design. He reinvigorated the process of lino cutting, a laborious printmaking method that perfectly suited this design-led approach. Writing in the *Penguin Modern Painters* series just after the war, J. M. Richards perceptively traced Bawden's focus of attention back to his choice of specialization at the Royal College of Art – writing and illuminating:

> These are subjects requiring control rather than dash; they are always subservient to the discipline of their materials, tools and purpose, and their practice is inseparable from the tradition of craftsmanship on which their slow evolution is based. Here may already be seen the germ of Bawden's interest in typography and book-making, of the calligraphic quality of much of his draughtsmanship and, perhaps, of his unfailing mastery over the tools and materials that he uses.[21]

Edward Bawden's interest in typography and book-making can be seen clearly in his designs for dust jackets over a period of fifty years, numbering well over a hundred in total. The jackets often featured his own hand-rendered typography and his designs always demonstrated a consideration of type as an integral aspect of pictorial design.

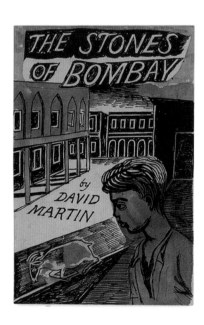
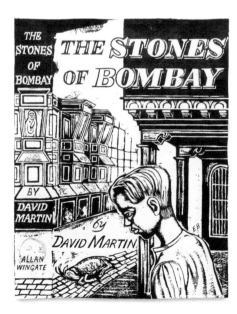
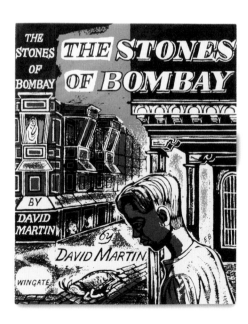

Gulliver's Voyages to
Lilliput and Brobdingnag
Jonathan Swift
Folio Society · 1948
210 × 135 mm · 8¼ × 5⅜ in.

This was an early Folio Society
publication. The subscription-based
company was founded in the previous
year with a mission to publish
handsomely produced illustrated
editions of classic literature. Few,
however, were clothed in dust jackets.
Bawden hand-lettered the titling, based
on eighteenth-century type, for this
typically formalized composition.

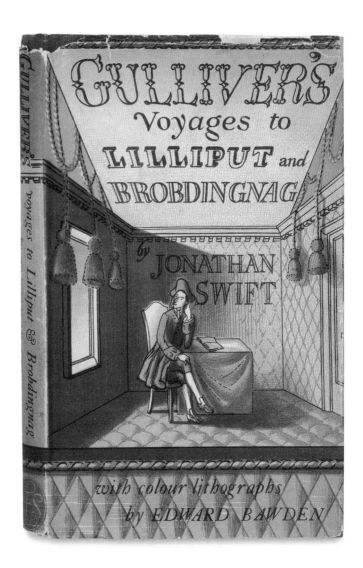

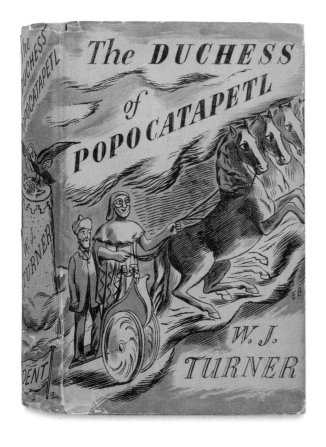

The Duchess of Popocatapetl
W. J. Turner
J. M. Dent · 1939
190 × 125 mm · 7½ × 5 in.

Bawden designed several jackets for
the novels of W. J. Turner during
the 1930s, all featuring integrated
illustration and hand-lettering created
as a single original artwork.

The Stones of Bombay
David Martin
Allan Wingate · 1950
190 × 125 mm · 7½ × 5 in.

Bawden's original design and final line
artwork are shown alongside the printed
jacket. Separate artwork would have been
supplied for each of the two additional
colours, to be printed letterpress.

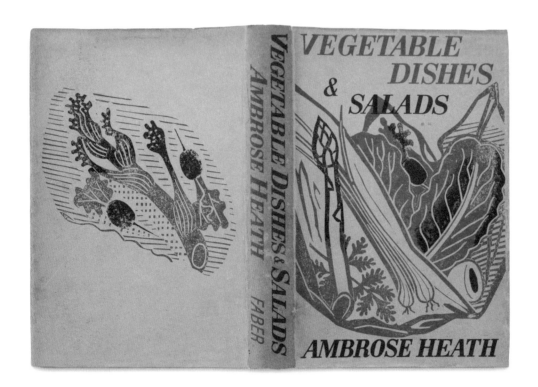

Vegetable Dishes and Salads
Ambrose Heath
Faber and Faber · 1938
197 × 125 mm · 7¾ × 5 in.

Good Potato Dishes
Ambrose Heath
Faber and Faber · 1938
197 × 125 mm · 7¾ × 5 in.

Ambrose Heath's cookery books
for Faber and Faber were extremely
popular. Bawden illustrated several
of the titles and designed jackets for
many more, with the same image
reproduced on the boards. The
jackets were printed on a sturdy,
utilitarian paper.

The Victim
Saul Bellow
John Lehmann · 1948
190 × 130 mm · 7½ × 5⅛ in.

One of only three dust-jacket
designs that Bawden produced
for the influential publisher John
Lehmann, this example shows
the artist in semi-Vorticist mode.
The Victim was Bellow's second
novel and the only one to deal
specifically with anti-Semitism.

The Sixpence that Rolled Away
Louis MacNeice
Faber and Faber · 1956
220 × 159 mm · 8⅝ × 6¼ in.

For MacNeice's foray into writing for
children, Bawden supplied a jacket,
five full-page interior illustrations and
six line drawings. The colour images
appear as if directly printed from lino
but presumably the individual linos
were converted into metal line blocks.

A Time to Laugh
Laurence Thompson
André Deutsch · 1953
190 × 130 mm · 7½ × 5⅛ in.

Bawden's two-colour design for
Thompson's comedy of the allied
forces in North Africa would no
doubt have been informed by his
own experiences as an official war
artist in that part of the world.

BBC Year Book 1947
BBC Publications · 1947
186 × 125 mm · 7⅞ × 5 in.

This exuberant, theatrical
design makes the most of a full
wraparound opportunity despite
being printed on rather flimsy
'war economy standard' paper.

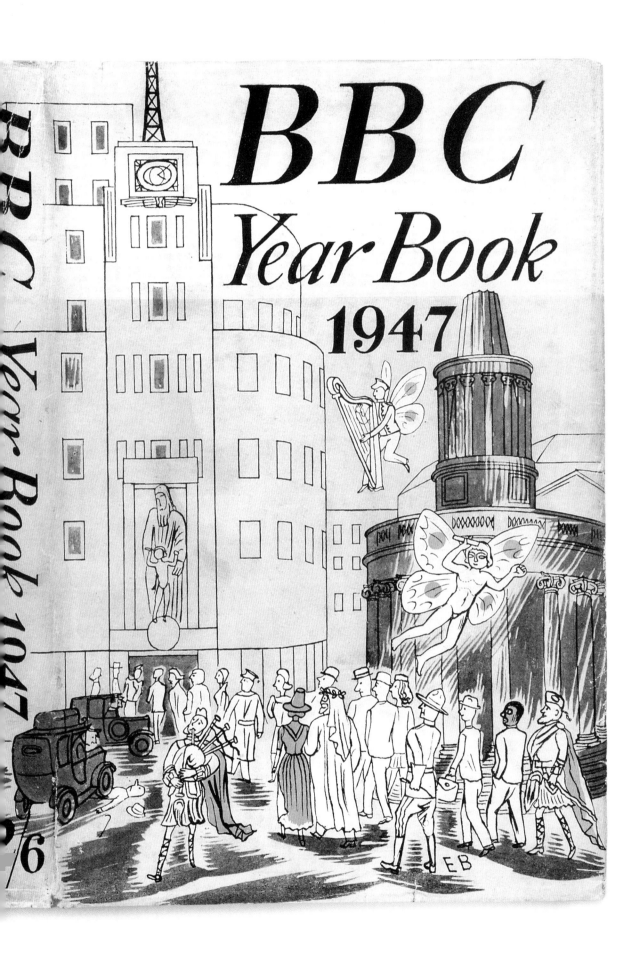

BBC
Year Book
1947

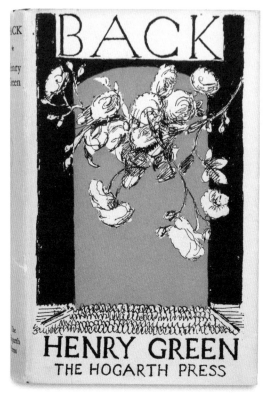

The Captain's Death Bed
Virginia Woolf
The Hogarth Press · 1950
204 × 125 mm · 8 × 5 in.

Despite the apparent crudity and
rather random nature of the image, the
sheer spiritedness of the mark-making
make Bell's design highly appealing.

Back
Henry Green
The Hogarth Press · 1946
190 × 125 mm · 7½ × 5 in.

This single-colour design sees
Bell in slightly more pictorial
but no less elegant mode for a
novel about a repatriated POW
in war-torn Britain.

The Years
Virginia Woolf
The Hogarth Press · 1937
190 × 125 mm · 7½ × 5 in.

Of the four designs on this page,
Bell's jacket for *The Years* is the most
resolved and substantial. It is also
one of the most iconic because of the
literary status of the book's contents.

To the Lighthouse
Virginia Woolf
The Hogarth Press · 1927
190 × 125 mm · 7½ × 5 in.

Some of Bell's Hogarth jackets
were almost entirely abstract or
decorative, others were more
descriptive or pictorial. This
design can be interpreted in many
ways in relation to the novel.

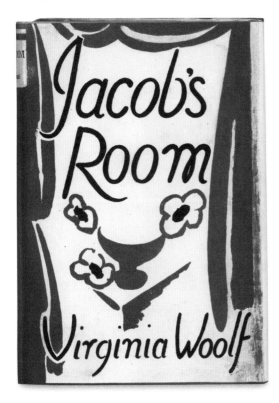

When looking at the broader world of illustrated dust jackets and the many accomplished, specialist artist-illustrators whose work appears in this book, the designs by Vanessa Bell for the Hogarth Press are difficult to place. Her daughter, the painter and writer Angelica Garnett, felt that Bell's designs shared 'the disarming simplicity' of drawings of her poodle and recalled the circumstances in which they were created at their home in Gordon Square:

> I associate them with moments when, her mind at ease, she sat before the stove with a sketchbook on her knee. If easel painting was a morning activity, conducted in the studio, designing for the page was destined for the lamp-lit evenings.[22]

Garnett went on to recount how her mother would express her irritation with Leonard Woolf if her designs were not well printed or if changes were made to the position of a word.

Leonard and Virginia Woolf first decided to produce a dust jacket on one of their publications in 1922. It was for *Jacob's Room*, the first of Virginia's novels to be published by their rapidly growing Hogarth Press. They quickly settled on Virginia's sister, Vanessa, as the artist. Her crude assembly of shapes in terracotta colour – curtains, flowers and bowl – with hand lettering in black, was ridiculed by the book-buying public. Although trained as a painter, Vanessa was unschooled in any form of printing or printmaking. Nonetheless, Virginia was insistent that she continue to design the jackets for all her novels and diaries, despite the disparaging comments from booksellers that regularly greeted each publication. Yet these simple, honest designs have come to be seen over time as classics and as inseparable from the writing of Virginia Woolf. Vanessa greatly enjoyed and appreciated her sister's writing. Her jacket designs never explicitly depicted the contents and often seemed to be only vaguely related on the basis of the titles, but they were the result of a good deal of trial and error in the sketchbook. Some were almost entirely abstract or decorative, in the form of favoured motifs of hoops, spirals and cross-hatching, others were more descriptive or pictorial. But the raw simplicity of the designs gave the books an enviable dose of what, in more recent parlance, would be described as 'brand identity'.

A Writer's Diary
Virginia Woolf
The Hogarth Press · 1953
225 × 146 mm · 8⅞ × 5¾ in.

The almost 'kitchen table' rusticity of Bell's designs for the writings of her sister have over time become some of the most instantly recognizable of all dust jackets.

Jacob's Room
Virginia Woolf
The Hogarth Press · 1922
190 × 125 mm · 7½ × 5 in.

This early Bell jacket is a typically minimal design. The apparently casually applied brushstrokes that describe both lettering and image are created as separations for brown and black printing.

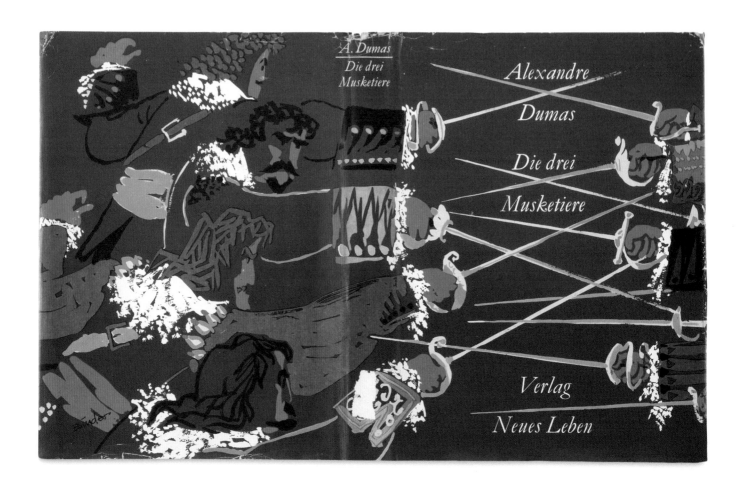

EBERHARD BINDER

Germany · 1924–1998

Had he not spent so much of his working life in the former East Germany (GDR), Eberhard Binder-Staßfurt (as he was also known) would surely have been more internationally known as a book illustrator of the highest order. As it was, Binder worked in a very particular publishing environment in Communist East Germany, as described by Professor Siegfried Lokatis of the University of Leipzig:

In the GDR book designers had, on the one hand, unquestionably less freedom than their West German counterparts: a rigorous process of vetting and censorship took place before a book could be published at all. Each design was thoroughly scrutinized and subject to strict restrictions, in the same way as was the actual content of the book. On the other hand, books in the GDR were extremely popular and were printed in long runs which often quickly sold out. Book designers were not under competitive economic pressure. So, unlike in West Germany, the designer was not subject to the constraints of the market and thus possessed, in this context, a high level of artistic freedom. This freedom is evidenced by the many special and beautiful book covers published in the GDR.[23]

It is perhaps surprising to find that several books issued in East Germany in the 1950s and 1960s are notable for high standards of production, often copiously illustrated and with decorative bindings, dust jackets and bound-in ribbon bookmarks. Operating within this culture of contradictions, Binder was a highly prolific illustrator and designer, producing many hundreds of illustrations for children's books and designing countless jackets for books for all ages. He also wrote and illustrated a number of picture books himself, a handful of which were published in English by Oliver & Boyd in Edinburgh.

Binder originally studied commercial art at Hildersheim and then graduated in 1952 from the Magdeburg College of Applied Arts. He quickly built a successful career in the commercial arts, helped by early acclaim for his illustrations to *The Adventures of Tom Sawyer* (Neues Leben, Berlin, 1954). He went on to illustrate other classics, including *Moby Dick* and *Gulliver's Travels*. In 1985, Binder was honoured with a National Prize of the GDR, in the category of Art and Literature. His illustration work is characterized by a combination of excellent design skills and an apparently effortless painterly approach to mark-making.

Die drei Musketiere
Alexandre Dumas
Verlag Neues Leben
(Berlin) · 1963
230 × 190 mm · 9 × 7½ in.

Binder built his reputation on
illustrating a number of the classics,
including this edition of *The Three
Musketeers*. As with many books
from East Germany at this time,
it is well produced, with embossed
illustration on the cover binding,
vibrant endpaper designs and line
illustration throughout.

Die leibhaftige Bosheit
Gustav Wied
Hirnstorff Verlag
(Rostock) · 1965
204 × 130 mm · 8 × 5⅛ in.

Traces of the influence of George
Grosz can perhaps be seen in this
wonderfully gestural, expressive
design. The book is a translation
of the Danish writer's ribald novel
Livsens Ondskab (*Life's Malice*)
of 1899.

Die drei Dickwänste
Juri Olescha
Verlag Kultur und
Fortschritt (Berlin) · 1962
195 × 125 mm · 7⅝ × 5 in.

The title translates as 'The Three Fat
Men' and Binder took a humorous,
almost slapstick, approach to the
allegorical text, which he illustrated
throughout as well as designing the
strikingly colourful jacket.

BRIAN COOK

UK · 1910–1991

In his foreword to *The Britain of Brian Cook* (1987), the artist Sir Hugh Casson recalled the impact of Brian Cook's highly distinctive dust-jacket designs when they first came out:

> Anyone who was around in the world of architecture and landscape during the 1930s will remember the remarkable Batsford publications and the work of their talented young designer, Brian Cook. You could spot them a mile off…not just because of the Englishness of the subject matter – villages, castles, churches, cottages, and the countryside, but through the instantly recognisable strength of Brian Cook's dust jackets – the careful drawings, the large areas of flat, bright colours, the slightly hairy paper.[24]

Cook was a member of the Batsford family on his mother's side and in 1946 changed his name to Brian Batsford. He became chairman of the family publishing firm in 1952 and later went into politics, becoming a Conservative Member of Parliament in 1958. He was knighted in 1974, the year he gave up the chairmanship of Batsford. In the early 1930s, however, Cook worked as designer of all the Batsford books for the then chairman, his uncle, Harry Batsford. The early 1930s was a time of austerity and in order to keep the company alive, Harry Batsford had taken the decision to dispense with the services of freelance illustrators and writers and produce everything 'in house'. Charles Fry was the principal editor and the three men were responsible for researching, writing, editing and designing the early Batsford guides, many published under various pseudonyms. They would even tour the country together in a Morris Oxford car to do research. In total, Brian Cook's artwork appeared on the jackets of over 130 editions of the guides and they have become extremely collectable as a series, comparable in status to the designs of Clifford and Rosemary Ellis for the Collins *New Naturalists* series.

The first of Cook's designs was for *The Villages of England* (with 'A. K. Wickham' as the author, actually Harry Batsford and Charles Fry), published in 1932, featuring a luminously coloured representation of the picturesque Suffolk village of Kersey. Cook designed the books in their entirety, contributing line drawings and researching photographic material for the interior. He was a master of the graphic representation of light through the juxtaposition of warm and cool colours. His best-known designs were created in flat colours, daringly formalized yet entirely readable in representational terms for the *British Heritage* series – around thirty jackets in total.

These wraparound designs give the impression at first sight of having been screen-printed, but were in fact rendered in opaque gouache paint. A key to the visual aesthetic of these jackets was the use of the Jean Berté process, named after the French printer who developed this technique. The method is similar to letterpress printing but uses plates that are made of rubber rather than metal, and employs water rather than oil-based inks. In an article on the Jean Berté process in the 1935 edition of *The Print User's Year Book*, Cook's jacket for *The Old Inns of England* [25] is handsomely reproduced through the same method, along with several other illustrations by Cook (including a rather racy 1930s 'bathing belle'), printed by Gibbs, Bamforth & Co. The accompanying text extols the virtues of the process with splendid hyperbole, outlining its 'considerable possibilities as a commercial process of strong aesthetic appeal to persons of good taste…designed literally to seize the beholder in a chromatic embrace and give him an unmistakable mental shake'.[26] If one is fortunate enough to find a pristine copy of one of these 1930s Batsford guides, the brilliance of the colour on Brian Cook's jacket design may indeed seize the beholder in a chromatic embrace. However, the water-based inks were highly prone to rubbing off and fading in sunlight over time.

Cook's love of the British countryside is clear to see in his designs. Strangely, it is said that he threw away the jackets of his personal copies of the books that he designed, before placing them on his shelves.

This reproduction of an early Brian Cook jacket in the *Print User's Handbook* of 1935 shows the intensity of colour of the original printed versions.

The Cathedrals of England
Harry Batsford
and Charles Fry
B. T. Batsford · 1934
216 × 140 mm · 8½ × 5½ in.

In the early 1930s, Batsford launched
a number of titles in the *British Heritage*
series covering the nation's building
types, land and customs, including this
volume, described in the book as 'intended
first and foremost as a pictorial review
of the cathedrals, with a brief account
of each, written as simply and concisely
as possible'.

Parish Churches of England
J. Charles Cox and
Charles Bradley Ford
B. T. Batsford · 1935
216 × 140 mm · 8½ × 5½ in.

Cook's compositions when dealing
with architectural imagery often featured
the use of dramatic, solid blacks in the
foreground, as here.

The Old Inns of England
A. E. Richardson
B. T. Batsford · 1934
216 × 140 mm · 8½ × 5½ in.

The luminosity of Cook's colours
as reproduced through the Jean Berté
printing process has not quite survived
the eight decades since it was printed.

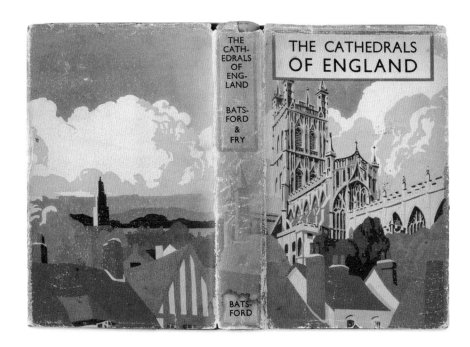

The English Castle
Hugh Braun
B. T. Batsford · 1936
216 × 140 mm · 8½ × 5½ in.

Solid blacks feature in the foreground
in this design, along with Brian Cook's
wonderful handling of billowing
clouds, providing a visual dialogue
between natural and man-made
shapes. The dust jacket demonstrates
clearly the graphic approach that led
to Cook being in demand as a designer
of travel posters for LNER.

THE
NGLISH
CASTLE

BRAUN

THE ENGLISH CASTLE

HUGH BRAUN

BATS-
FORD

BRIAN
COOK

CLEONIKE 'CLEON' DAMIANAKES

USA · 1895–1979

For an artist whose dust jacket designs have become synonymous with early editions of some of the great works of twentieth-century American literature, surprisingly little is known about Cleonike Damianakes. Her designs were usually signed 'Cleon' or other variations of her name, including 'Cleo' and 'Cleonika'. In later years she also used the name 'Wilkins' after her second marriage, to Ralph Wilkins.

Damianakes was born in Berkeley, California, of Greek descent, and studied at the University of California, Berkeley. After that, she lived in Hollywood until the 1940s, when she moved to New York. She was an etcher, painter and muralist, and exhibited widely during her career; her work is held in various private and public collections, the latter including the Smithsonian American Art Museum and the Art Institute of Chicago. She was active in both the Chicago Society of Etchers (the oldest in the US) and its California equivalent.

In the 1920s and 1930s, Damianakes designed dust jackets for the novels of, among others, Conrad Aiken, Ernest Hemingway and both Zelda and F. Scott Fitzgerald. The early designs were in the sensual Moderne style of the period. Steven Heller and Seymour Chwast described these heraldic, Hellenistic designs as 'romantic but emotionless' and as providing little insight into the content of the books.[27] Yet, as Leonard J. Leff has described, they clearly did the job intended by Hemingway's editor at Scribner's, Max Perkins, who was the key figure in commissioning Damianakes:

Perkins understood the value of an arresting cover, and on *The Sun Also Rises* he reached out to 'the feminine readers who control the destinies of so many novels.' On the face of the jacket was a Hellenic figure seated beneath a desiccated bush. Her head was bent to her shoulder, one hand draped over her knee, another holding an apple. Her robe billowed round her exposed thigh. Two apples dressed the title of the book. What Cecil B. de Mille's 'studies in diminishing draperies' had done for Hollywood, the artist Cleonike Damianakes had done for Scribners: 'Cleon' had made sex respectable. The design – the languor, the apple, the thigh – breathed sex yet also evoked classical Greece.[28]

In 1928, Perkins returned to Damianakes for the design of the jacket for Hemingway's *A Farewell to Arms*. This time, the process of commissioning went less smoothly. The artist's first submission was rejected. The publishers felt that the focus should be on the central love story; Damianakes' initial concept was seen as being too military, as if it were simply a 'war book'. Finally, after several false starts, a design was accepted. In similar style to that produced for *The Sun Also Rises*, the emblematic composition featured a semi-nude couple, reclining in classically posed manner, rendered in three colours. Hemingway himself was not impressed. He told his editor:

> The Cleon drawing has a lousy and completely unattractive decadence i.e. large misplaced breasts etc. about it which I think might be a challenge to anyone who was interested in suppressing the book…I cannot admire the awful legs on that woman or the gigantic belly muscles (on the man). I never liked the jacket on the *Sun* but side by side with this one the *Sun* jacket looks very fine now – So maybe this one is fine too –.[29]

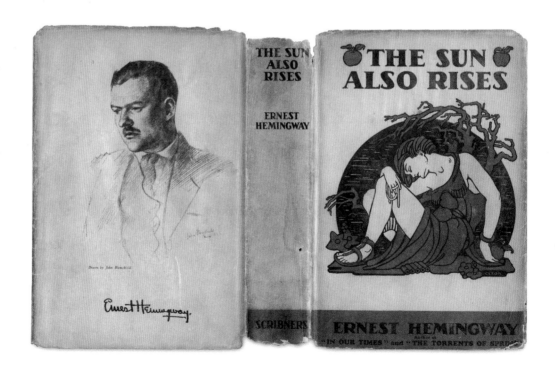

The Sun Also Rises
Ernest Hemingway
Charles Scribner's Sons
(New York) · 1926
197 × 134 mm · 7¾ × 5¼ in.

Hemingway was scathing in his criticism of the languidly erotic designs by 'Cleon' for his early novels, including this one.

A Farewell to Arms
Ernest Hemingway
Charles Scribner's Sons
(New York) · 1928
190 × 135 mm · 7½ × 5⅜ in.

After the rejection of her initial
design, Damianakes came up with
a less military concept, focusing
on the classical figure. However,
the views of the author were no
less dismissive.

Pandora
Arthur B. Reeve
Harper & Bros
(New York) · 1926
190 × 125 mm · 7½ × 5 in.

For Reeve's popular novel
featuring Detective Craig Kennedy,
Damianakes' jacket depicts a kneeling
Pandora pouring distilled ether into
her jar. As ever, the artist's manner is
one of formalized theatricality.

All the Sad Young Men
F. Scott Fitzgerald
Charles Scribner's Sons
(New York) · 1926
232 × 165 mm · 9⅛ × 6½ in.

A similar composition to that
employed on *Pandora* was used by
the artist for the jacket of F. Scott
Fitzgerald's third collection of
short stories.

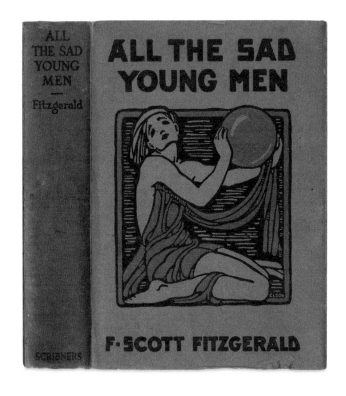

Pale Warriors
David Hamilton
Charles Scribner's Sons
(New York) · 1929
193 × 137 mm · 7⅝ × 5⅜ in.

A classic Art Deco representation
of the human figure features in this
sweeping design for a romance
about a woman without scruples.

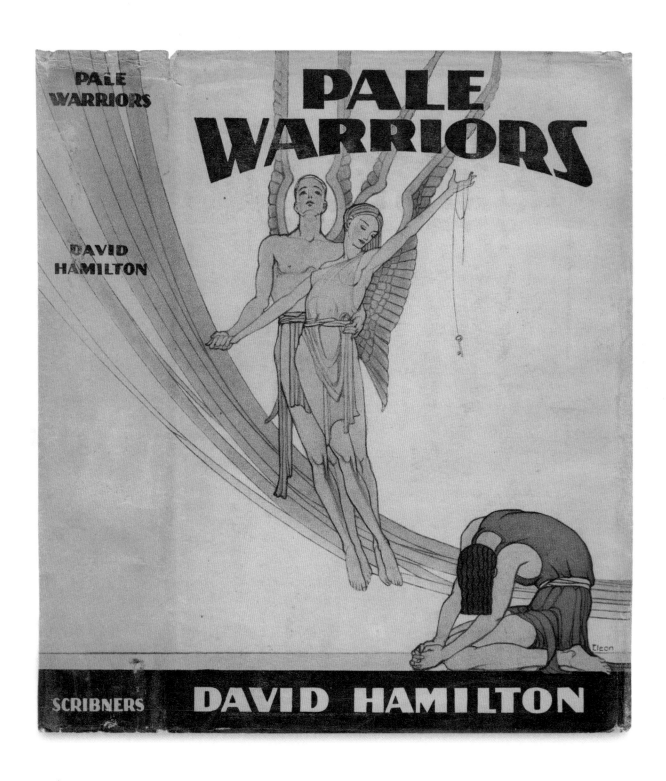

Great Circle
Conrad Aiken
Charles Scribner's Sons
(New York) · 1933
190 × 125 mm · 7½ × 5 in.

Aiken was perhaps best known as a
poet but he also produced five novels
and several collections of short stories
and criticism. His second novel, *Great
Circle*, is a psychological study of
a Harvard academic who relives a
childhood trauma. 'Cleon' represents
the eponymous circle through an
heraldic figure design.

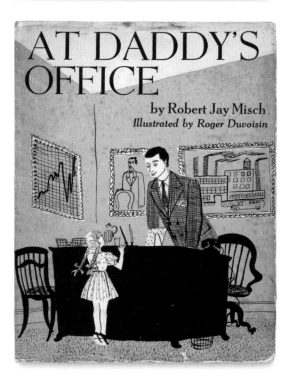

ROGER DUVOISIN

Switzerland & USA · 1900–1980

Duvoisin was widely known for his highly successful picture books featuring animal characters, such as *The Happy Lion* (written by his wife, Louise Fatio), and his own Petunia and Veronica characters, who appeared in numerous titles. However, Duvoisin's graphic work also appeared elsewhere, such as on numerous covers for the *New Yorker* and *Fortune* magazine from the 1930s to the 1950s. His dust-jacket designs include many for his own books, but throughout his long career he also produced a number of others for a range of writers and publishers.

Born in Geneva, Switzerland, in 1900 (though he sometimes gave 1904 as his year of birth), Duvoisin grew up in an artistic family. His father was an architect and his godmother a celebrated enamel painter who helped him with his drawing as a child. They both wanted him to follow their respective professions, but eventually he enrolled at the École Nationale Supérieure des Arts Décoratifs in Paris to study stage design. On graduation, Duvoisin's flair for pattern and decoration led to employment in mural design, scenery painting and textiles.

In the late 1920s he moved to New York to take a job at a textile firm, but the company ran into trouble, leaving Duvoisin, now married to Louise and with two young sons, needing to find work. Against the background of the Great Depression, he began to find freelance commissions producing dust jackets and general illustration for magazines and advertising while also working on his own children's book concepts. The various commissions as a 'jobbing' illustrator helped support him as he worked on his first book, *A Little Boy Was Drawing*, published by Charles Scribner's Sons in 1932. However, it was the next one, *Donkey-Donkey*, published by Whitman the following year, that was the breakthrough. The 1940 edition with full-colour illustrations has sold more than a million copies over the years and is still in print. Duvoisin became an American citizen in 1938.

A key characteristic of Duvoisin's graphic work is an apparently effortless charm and elegance. His drawing somehow manages to combine childlike awkwardness and good humour with adult sophistication. His designs often feature rumbustious groupings of characters in settings that flatten or abandon traditional perspective. He was a master of scale, too, frequently exploiting the contrast between human or animal characters and towering cityscapes, no doubt informed by his adopted home of New York. Many of the designs for dust jackets, both for Duvoisin's own books and those of others, feature his distinctive hand-rendered lettering, as used on the cover designs for his first two books, mentioned above. The lower-case 'joined up' handwriting perfectly complements the weight and quality of his line. Perhaps the struggles of supporting a young family in 1930s America contributed to the fact that Duvoisin continued to take on commissioned illustration long after his authorial work had achieved widespread acclaim and commercial success.

Amahl and the Night Visitors
Gian Carlo Menotti
McGraw Hill (New York) · 1952
235 × 155 mm · 9¼ × 6⅛ in.

Amahl was initially written by the Italian-American composer and librettist Menotti as a Christmas opera for TV and broadcast by NBC in 1951. The book is a narrative adaptation by Frances Frost that preserves the exact dialogue of the opera.

At Daddy's Office
Robert Jay Misch
Alfred A. Knopf
(New York) · 1946
255 × 204 mm · 10 × 8 in.

Duvoisin's illustrations were not universally admired when this book was first published, with one reviewer describing them as 'stilted and unappealing'.

The Man Who Could Grow Hair or Inside Andorra
William Attwood
Allan Wingate · 1950
190 × 125 mm · 7½ × 5 in.

This jacket has a typical Duvoisin melange of human life and manners. Attwood's book describing his adventures in postwar Europe was first published in the US by Knopf the previous year.

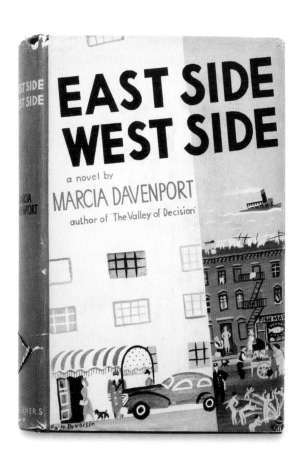

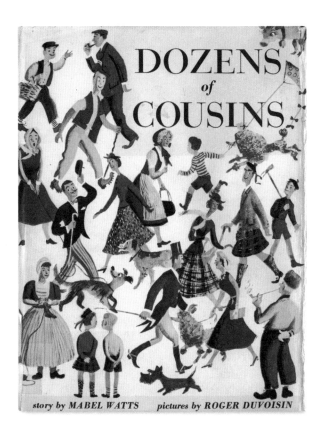

Dozens of Cousins
Mabel Watts
Whittlesey House
(New York) · 1950
229 × 180 mm · 9 × 7 in.

The slightly frenzied nature of this jacket design conveys the drama of the story that lies within. Benjy and his parents leave their Boston home and visit their cousins in Europe – in France, England, Scotland, Ireland, Holland and Switzerland – in search of great grandmother's china cat.

East Side West Side
Marcia Davenport
Charles Scribner's Sons
(New York) · 1947
216 × 145 mm · 8½ × 5¾ in.

Marcia Davenport's novel of contrasting life in New York – the upper class, café society and tenement dwellers – is captured by the fresh vision of the émigré Duvoisin.

*A Child's Garden of Verse*s
Robert Louis Stevenson
Heritage Press
(New York) · 1944
273 × 210 mm · 10¼ × 8¼ in.

Duvoisin illustrated Stevenson's
A Child's Garden of Verses for
a slip-cased, signed edition
published by the Limited Editions
Club in 1944. This trade edition
was issued in the same year.
The artist would have produced
artwork in the form of multiple
individual colour separations.

A CHILD'S GARDEN

OF VERSES

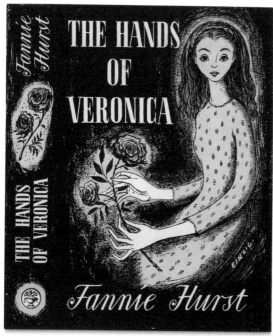

SUSAN EINZIG

UK · 1922–2009

Susan Einzig is best known for her jacket design and interior illustrations for Philippa Pearce's acclaimed Carnegie Medal-winning novel, *Tom's Midnight Garden* (Oxford University Press, 1958). However, she designed many other jackets and illustrated numerous books and magazines, as well as advertising material, over a number of years. Her line illustrations to advertise classic drama productions in *Radio Times* were equally influential. For much of her career, Einzig was also an extremely influential teacher of illustration, initially at Camberwell School of Arts and Crafts and later at Chelsea School of Art. In later life she concentrated mainly on painting and printmaking for exhibition.

Born Suzanne Einzig, she was one of the last of the children and teenagers to be brought out of Nazi Germany on the *Kindertransport* in the months running up to the outbreak of the Second World War. Having previously begun to study art at the age of 15 in Berlin (before the school was closed to Jews), she was able to enrol at the Central School of Art and Design in London, where she was the youngest student. After the war, Einzig was lucky enough to be offered some teaching at Camberwell. As well as the financial security this gave her, the contacts with other artist-teachers helped her to launch a freelance career as an illustrator. By far the most important and influential of these was John ('Jonny') Minton. Einzig soon fell under the mercurial, charismatic Minton's spell. They spent a great deal of time together in the full heady swing of postwar neo-romanticism. His own career was burgeoning and Einzig began to acquire commissions from many of his clients, including magazines such as *Contact*, *Our Time* and the popular *Lilliput*. Stylistically, her drawing was initially heavily influenced by Minton's, to the extent of being, on occasion, almost indistinguishable. Over time, however, Einzig's work began to assert its independence and her own particular brand of lyricism emerged. By the time of Minton's tragic decline and death in 1957, Einzig was well established in the field of book illustration. Of the commission to illustrate *Tom's Midnight Garden* in 1958, she later recalled:

> I had been to see the children's book editor at Oxford University Press, who had looked at my work and seemed very unsure about it. However, she gave me Philippa Pearce's manuscript to try and see if I could do it. I did two or three drawings and took them to show her, and then she asked me to do the book. She was rather surprised at the way it all turned out. It is astonishing that I was paid just £100 for the whole thing.[30]

Like many of the more sensitive illustrators, Susan Einzig never felt confident or secure in her draughtsmanship:

> The trouble is, once I'd got a job and taken it home, I always felt unfitted to do it, and that has remained with me to this day. Every drawing I have done is like a first drawing in which I have to discover how to do it – it's so difficult that I sometimes wonder how I've stuck at it.[31]

A Jade Miscellany
Una Pope-Hennessy
Nicholson & Watson · 1946
190 × 125 mm · 7½ × 5 in.

The jacket design for Pope-Hennessy's tour of the history and culture of jade was one of Einzig's first commissions as she began to forge a career after the war. Her experience in printmaking at the Central School, where she was taught by Gertrude Hermes, helped her to get the most out of the three-colour letterpress process used for this jacket.

The Hands of Veronica
Fannie Hurst
Jonathan Cape · 1947
200 × 165 mm · 7⅞ × 6½ in.

Set in Manhattan, the novel is about a woman who knows that she has a gift of healing in her hands. It was first published in America in 1947 by Harper & Bros. This proof of a design for Jonathan Cape appears not to have been used. The artist uses the same three colours as in her design for the jacket of *A Jade Miscellany*.

Tom's Midnight Garden
Philippa Pearce
J. B. Lippincott (Philadelphia) · 1958
210 × 140 mm · 8¼ × 5½ in.

Einzig will always be associated with
Pearce's classic of children's literature,
first published by Oxford University
Press in 1958 (the US edition is shown
here). The jacket with its flowing hand-
rendered lettering came at the end of
the neo-romantic period in painting
and illustration. The house is based
on Pearce's childhood home in Great
Shelford, Cambridgeshire.

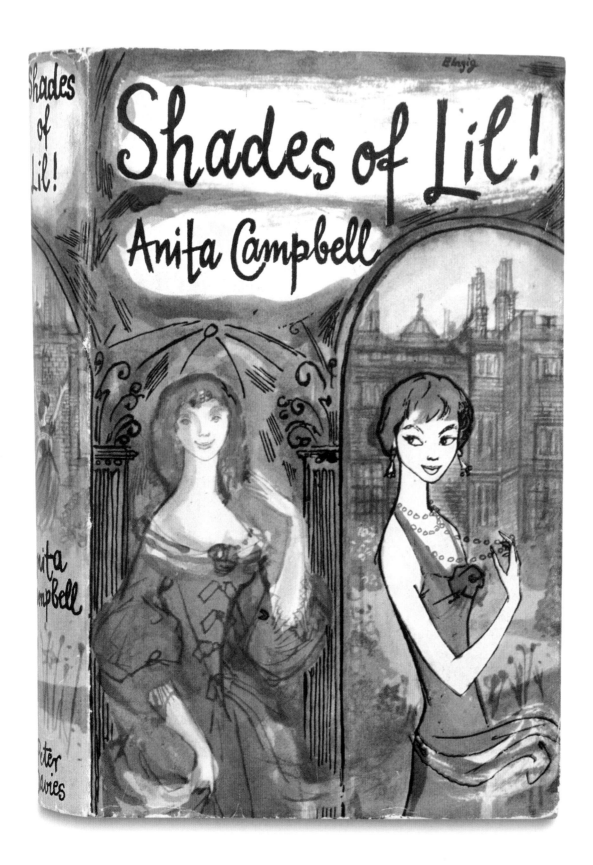

Shades of Lil!
Anita Campbell
Peter Davies · 1957
190 × 130 mm · 7½ × 5⅛ in.

In the late 1950s dust-jacket artists
were increasingly likely to have
four-colour lithographic printing
available to them, so designs could
be created as a single painting rather
than in separated overlays. For this
title, Einzig used her characteristic
hand-painted lettering.

Jo and the Skiffle Group
Valerie Hastings
Max Parrish · 1958
195 × 130 mm · 7⅝ × 5⅛ in.

The beat generation finds its way into
young adult fiction in this tale of Jo,
a school leaver at work in her mother's
coffee bar. Einzig overlays blue and
orange to create a fourth colour in this
vibrant design, which extended over
the spine and part of the back cover.

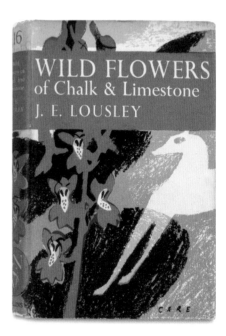

CLIFFORD & ROSEMARY ELLIS

UK · Clifford 1907–1989
Rosemary 1910–1998

The signature 'C & RE' was a familiar presence on the jackets of the Collins *New Naturalists* series over a period of forty years – in total the husband-and-wife team produced eighty-six designs for the books. As with other such marital collaborations (for example Alice and Martin Provenson, Beth and Joe Krush), the exact nature of the working relationship is unknown. Peter Marren and Robert Gillmor, who have written a book about the series, observed that Clifford and Rosemary respected each other's individual artistic preoccupations and directions but came together in a flexible creative partnership: 'The final artwork was only the last stage in a lengthy process of sketching and thinking, selecting and eliminating, and the creative impulse behind the design was, as they saw it, an equal joint effort. "C & R E" indicates a rare and complete fusion of creative thought.'[32]

Clifford Ellis was born into an artistic family; his father was a commercial artist and his grandfather a painter. As a youngster Clifford was also a keen naturalist, spending a great deal of time in the countryside and at London Zoo. He attended St Martin's College of Art and the Regent Street Polytechnic, where he soon became a member of the teaching staff. It was there that he met Rosemary, who was one of his students. She, too, was from an artistic family. They married in 1931 and during the 1930s they were important contributors to the thriving culture of commercial poster

design in Britain, alongside others such as Edward Bawden, Eric Ravilious and Paul Nash, at a time when leading artists were engaging with this area of design. Clifford and Rosemary created posters for many of the key commissioners including Shell-Mex BP, the General Post Office, London Transport and the Empire Marketing Board. It was in this period that their particular techniques were forged, in particular a building up of shapes through layers of non-linear colour, defining edges through negative space and cleverly using the white of the paper as a colour. They were also beginning to receive occasional commissions for dust-jacket designs.

The couple lived in Bath from the mid-1930s and from 1946 to 1972 worked full time at Bath Academy of Art, where Clifford was principal. Throughout these years they were working on the *New Naturalist* jackets as well as various other projects and commissions. Each of the books focused on a particular aspect of the natural world: groupings of species, habitats, landscape, etc. There was also a small series of 'monographs' studying individual species. The jackets were seen as highly innovative and 'artistic' at the time and not initially universally appreciated. But William (Billy) Collins, the chairman of the company, was a great supporter of their work.

The printing was done by the well-known lithographic printer Thomas Griffits at the Baynard Press. A slightly rough, matt paper was used, giving an organic feel to the finished product. The Ellises gave detailed instructions to the printer as to the order in which the separate colours should be printed, which was crucial to achieving the correct colour balance with overprinting and limited colour.

A particular feature of the *New Naturalists* jackets is the care the designers gave to the spines. They were always carefully considered in terms of how they would be 'read' independently of the front cover. The artists also designed the 'NN' logo used on the spine, each book having its own tiny colophon between the two initials, specific to the subject matter.

The Sea Shore
C. M. Yonge
Collins · 1949
220 × 159 mm · 8⅝ × 6¼ in.

The dismembered crab's claw lying on the shore is perhaps one of the darker of the Ellises' concepts.

British Mammals
L. Harrison Matthews
Collins · 1952
220 × 159 mm · 8⅝ × 6¼ in.

The visual dialogue between fox and rabbit brings narrative drama to this sweeping composition.

Wild Flowers of Chalk
& Limestone
J. E. Lousley
Collins · 1950
220 × 159 mm · 8⅝ × 6¼ in.

All of the Ellises' jackets were scrupulously researched and supported by sketchbook location studies. This bright and airy design incorporates the Westbury White Horse in Wiltshire.

The Folklore of Birds
Edward A. Armstrong
Collins · 1958
220 × 159 mm · 8⅝ × 6¼ in.

This had one short print run and is now one of the scarcest books in the *New Naturalists* series. Its subject matter was seen as slightly outside the series' remit, but it carries one of the Ellises' most dramatic designs – the image of the barn owl retaining basic realism but with ghostly overtones.

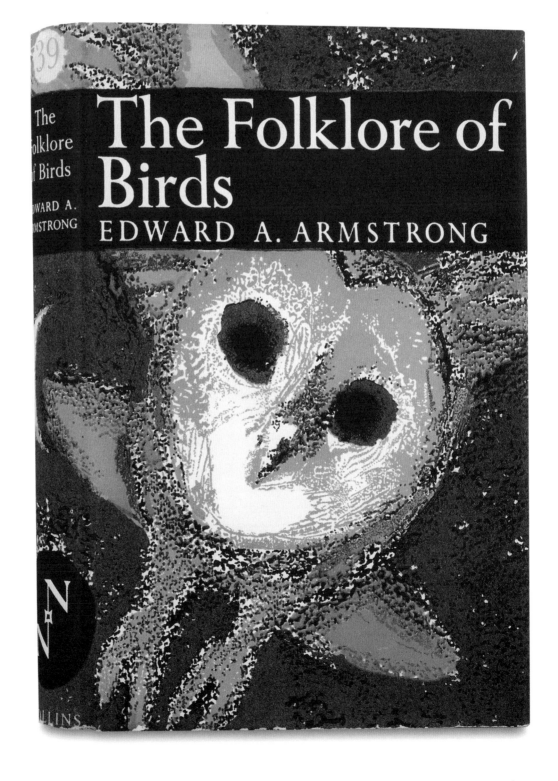

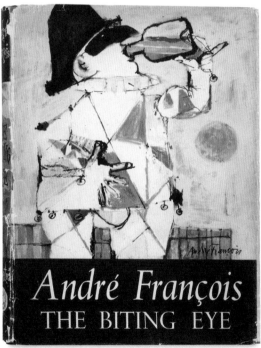

ANDRÉ FRANÇOIS
Hungary & France · 1915–2005

André François is one of those artists in whose work it is difficult to trace clear influences, his instantly recognizable graphic voice seeming to be unique. He studied at the École des Beaux-Arts in Paris and later under the great French poster designer Cassandre. In an interview with Wendy Coates-Smith that was conducted when he was well into his eighties, François elaborated on how he came to work with Cassandre:

> I managed to meet him and he said, 'Well, I am opening a school, and you can come to that school.' It was of course a private school and pretty expensive and what it cost to study was pretty much what I had for a living. I told him and he said, 'It doesn't matter, you don't pay!' But the school didn't last long because he would throw out the people who paid, and keep the people who didn't.[33]

It is hard to imagine a greater contrast than that between his teacher's highly formalized Art Deco designs and François's apparently clumsy, freewheeling draughtsmanship. Nonetheless, François claimed that, indirectly, the great man's influence was crucial: 'What I learned above everything else was rigour and precision.'[34] These qualities expressed themselves in a manner perfectly described by Claude Roy as 'adroitly awkward'.[35]

François was born André Farkas (he changed the surname, initially as a nom de plume for published cartoons, then formally on gaining French citizenship in 1939) in Timisoara in what was then Hungary (now Romania). His move to Paris in 1934 came after a year at the Academy of Fine Arts in Budapest. With the fall of France in 1940, François escaped to Marseille in the unoccupied sector and later to Savoie. After the liberation he returned to Paris and began to find commercial commissions for newspapers and magazines. He met Ronald Searle there in 1947 and they became friends. On visits to England he made contact with John Symonds at *Lilliput*, Malcolm Muggeridge at *Punch* and F. H. K. Henrion in the world of advertising. He was soon doing work for all of them, along with covers for the *New Yorker*.

In addition to his career as a cartoonist and illustrator, François was a painter, sculptor, designer for ballet and much more. But he did not see commercial design as in any way a lesser art. He said:

> I do not believe there is a clear line between working from commission and painting, though there is one great difference. In the first you are looking for a solution at somebody else's instigation and in the second you are delving inside yourself. As a result my approach to graphics has changed; I work best with a loose rein and a less fixed concept at the outset.[36]

This 'loose rein' is touched upon by Ronald Searle in his introduction to *The Biting Eye* in which he alludes to the idea of François's commercial work as a Trojan Horse with which to conceal his art.[37] François himself commented, 'You have to cheat by producing art at the same time as answering the brief…If you didn't, they wouldn't accept your ideas.'[38]

William Waste
John Symonds
Sampson Low · 1947
204 × 140 mm · 8 × 5½ in.

This very early dust-jacket design for Symonds's first novel predated the author and artist's later, frequent collaborations on picture books by several years. In this period François's line featured baroque decorative flourishes that were soon left behind in favour of a harder-edged graphic style.

The Biting Eye
André François
Perpetua Books · 1960
285 × 220 mm · 11¼ × 8⅝ in.

Perpetua Books was a publishing imprint set up by Ronald Searle in 1952 to publish his own work and that of acquaintances, such as his close friend François. This title was the first comprehensive collection of François's work.

André François'
Double Bedside Book
André Deutsch · 1952
255 × 195 mm · 10 × 7⅝ in.

François's apparently childlike yet
highly sophisticated graphic wit is
represented on the jacket in three-
colour letterpress separations, using
black, yellow and blue, with overlaying
of yellow and blue to give green.

ERIC FRASER

UK · 1902–1983

In the catalogue for the 1991 touring exhibition *Eric Fraser: An Illustrator of Our Time*, Pat Hodgson discussed the work of this distinguished artist and illustrator, who had a sixty-year career from 1923. For Hodgson,

> Fraser had the rare ability to catch the reader's attention and hold it, a skill which was particularly important for commercial artists, who had to compete with photographs on the printed page. Within the limitations imposed by commercial art, Fraser's personal vision transformed the subject matter into bold and dramatic images, which were sometimes curiously disturbing.[39]

Whether or not Fraser himself would have agreed with the idea that commercial art imposed limitations on his creativity is a moot point. It might be argued that it was within these apparent boundaries that his imagination was most fully liberated. But Hodgson perfectly describes Fraser's extraordinary, slightly peculiar and sometimes dark vision. The exhibition was sponsored by British Gas, for whom Fraser had designed the ubiquitous Mr Therm logo in the early 1930s.

Fraser was best known for his masterful black-and-white narrative illustration, in particular his work for the weekly *Radio Times* over a period of nearly fifty years. His skill when working in black and white can be attributed to a powerful sense of graphic organization. The dynamics of a composition were always of primary importance to him. He touched on this in a rare interview, given to fellow-illustrator Robin Jacques for his book *Illustrators at Work* (1963). After discussing the importance of thorough research, Fraser spoke about his method of making roughs and how he considered it important that they 'should be small…for it is thus easier to obtain a co-ordinated design. The eye can more easily assess the balance of masses, the continuity of line and the valuable repetition of shapes.'[40]

Fraser won a scholarship to Goldsmiths College, London, where he was taught illustration by the great E. J. Sullivan, whose work displayed aspects of Art Nouveau. Another important influence was the much younger teacher Clive Gardiner, who introduced students to more modern trends, such as Cubism and Futurism. Elements of both styles can be seen in Gardiner's striking posters for London Transport, which together with his stylized, sweeping descriptions of foliage clearly had an effect on the development of Fraser's own visual language. During the 1920s the motifs of the Jazz Age inevitably found their way into Fraser's designs. However, by never being particularly fashionable in his approach, Fraser achieved a longevity that would be the envy of many illustrators. His work extended to murals, including for the Empire Exhibition in Glasgow in 1938, the Festival of Britain in 1951 and the Brussels Expo in 1958, and stained glass. Dust jackets formed a significant aspect of his overall output and whether for fiction, non-fiction, children's books or those for adults, they were always produced to the same standard of care and professionalism.

Man Against Aging
Robert S. de Ropp
Scientific Book Club · 1960
220 × 152 mm · 8⅝ × 6 in.

Fraser designed numerous dust jackets for books that were Scientific Book Club publications. His ability to convert complex scientific concepts into imaginative visual outcomes was unparalleled. This was the second book by the biochemist de Ropp.

A Tale for Midnight
Frederic Prokosch
Secker & Warburg · 1956
204 × 134 mm · 8 × 5¼ in.

This novel, set in late sixteenth-century Italy, is based around the case of Beatrice Cenci, who plotted with her brother and stepmother to murder her abusive father. All three were later executed.

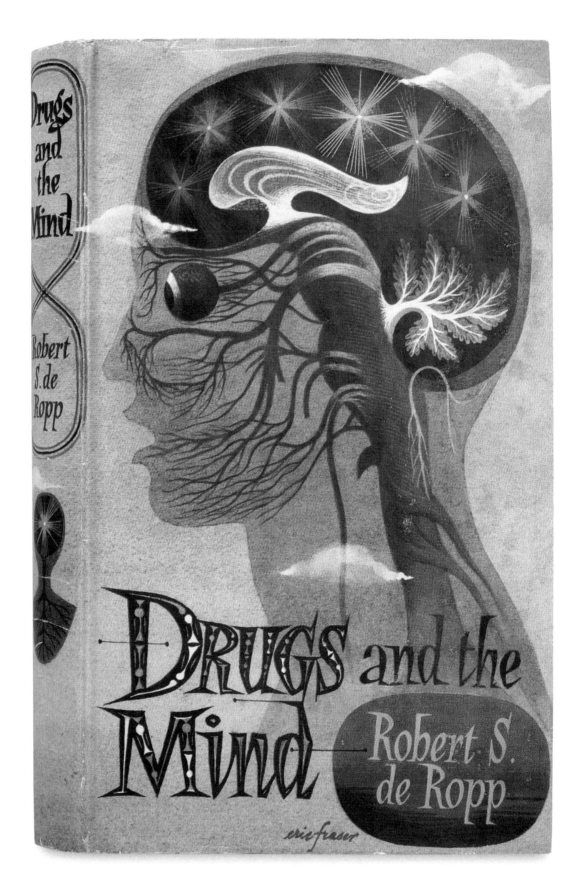

Drugs and the Mind
Robert S. de Ropp
Scientific Book Club · 1957
204 × 134 mm · 8 × 5¼ in.

This jacket is one of Fraser's
most strikingly original designs. Dr de
Ropp's first book introduced readers to
the joys and mental tortures of ancient
herbs and modern drugs.

Festival at Farbridge
J. B. Priestley
Heinemann · 1951
190 × 125 mm · 7½ × 5 in.

This wraparound jacket is one of
Fraser's most spectacular designs,
in contrast to the rather poor quality
paper and production of the book
as a whole. It clearly draws on the
artist's experience as a mural
painter and features integrated
hand-rendered lettering. Priestley's
light-hearted novel set in an English
village was published to coincide
with the Festival of Britain.

Last Laugh, Mr Moto
John P. Marquand
Robert Hale · 1943
190 × 130 mm · 7½ × 5⅛ in.

The dust jacket of Marquand's story
of violence, intrigue and romance
on a lonely Caribbean island features
a highly stylized tableau-style
composition. This was Marquand's
fourth Mr Moto mystery with
a Japanese detective hero.

Inventors of our World
Joachim G. Leithäuser
Scientific Book Club · 1958
220 × 145 · 8⅝ × 5¾ in.

First published in Germany in 1954, the book was issued in the UK by Weidenfeld & Nicolson in 1958 and was a Scientific Book Club selection. Fraser employed many of the technology-inspired motifs, such as Sputnik and spirals, that were so prevalent in 1950s design.

The Twelve Days of Christmas
Miles and John Hadfield
Cassell · 1961
260 × 175 mm · 10¼ × 6⅞ in.

The authors of this potpourri of Christmas lore wanted the book to be as lively as a symbolic Christmas tree; Fraser's dust jacket admirably matches their ambition. The front board design is repeated on the back.

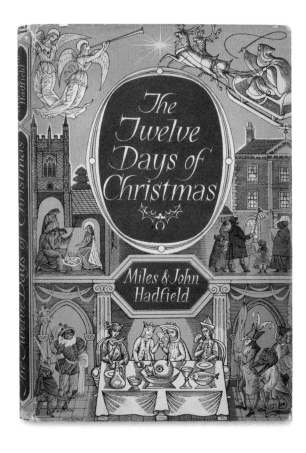

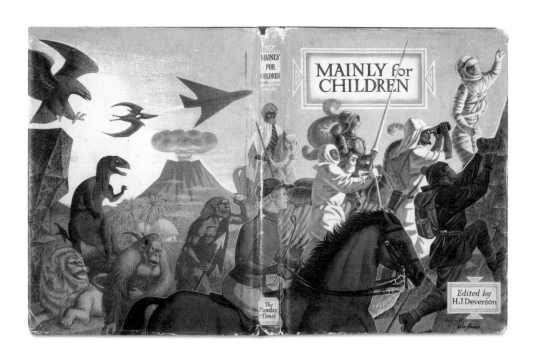

Mainly for Children
Edited by H. J. Deverson
The Sunday Times · 1960
270 × 220 mm · 10⅝ × 8⅝ in.

This is a collection of factual articles for young people, reprinted from the 'Mainly for Children' column of the *Sunday Times*. The artist gives full value for money in his jacket design for this large-format publication.

BARNETT FREEDMAN

UK · 1901–1958

One of the finest illustrator-designers of the twentieth century, Barnett Freedman worked for a range of commercial clients, including London Transport, the General Post Office, Shell-Mex BP, Ealing Films and Wedgwood. His dust jackets, many for the publishers Faber and Faber, constitute some of his best work. He is particularly celebrated for his achievements and influence within the field of lithography, where his work was driven by an interest in light and tone.

The son of Jewish immigrants from Russia, Freedman was born in the East End of London. As a child, he suffered poor health, and from age 9 to 13 spent time in hospital, where he learnt to draw and paint, among other educational pursuits. His affinity for letterforms may have originated in his teens when he worked as a draughtsman for a monumental mason, followed by a stint in an architectural practice, when war memorials and their associated lettering were in demand after the First World War. For five years he took evening classes at St Martin's School of Art and eventually, thanks to William Rothenstein, the principal of the Royal College of Art, won a scholarship that enabled him to study full time at the RCA from 1922.

On leaving the Royal College, Freedman devoted himself to painting, but despite some success, he was unable to make a living. Early commissions from the publishers Faber and Gwyer (the name changed to Faber and Faber after Sir Maurice and Lady Gwyer departed in 1929) provided some income, together with teaching at the RCA, but it was not until Faber commissioned him to illustrate a deluxe edition of Siegfried Sassoon's *Memoirs of an Infantry Officer*, published

in 1931, that his career really took off. In addition to producing numerous line drawings, some of them full page and coloured lithographically, he created a wraparound design for the cover boards and dust jacket with integrated typography, as well as dramatic designs for the endpapers or 'pastedowns'. This was a tour de force of complete design. Such all-round skills caught the attention of publishers and other agencies and Freedman was soon in great demand. Apart from dust-jacket commissions, he designed posters, pattern papers, postage stamps, all kinds of advertising material, including packaging, trade booklets and pamphlets, as well as narrative illustration to classic literature for the Limited Editions Club of New York. He worked particularly closely with key printing houses of the time, including the Baynard Press, Curwen Press and Chromoworks. As a genial man of humble Cockney origin he was readily accepted by the craftsmen at these companies.

Freedman's subtle use of graded tones emerged from this close involvement with print. Initially, as in *Memoirs of an Infantry Officer*, tonality was achieved primarily through cross hatching – the use of varying densities of parallel lines, overlaid at different angles to each other. But he developed a technique of using chalks on textured paper, giving the illusion of continuous gradation of tone, while only ever using solid black. The result gave the impression of lithographic printing but through the cheaper process of letterpress line block.

In the Second World War, Freedman was appointed an official war artist, documenting and interpreting wartime life, initially travelling to France in the spring of 1940 with fellow-appointees Edward Ardizzone and Edward Bawden to record the work of the British Expeditionary Force. Ardizzone described him as having 'an enormous voice, a fund of good stories, the cheek of the devil and a great charm of manner'.[41] He returned to France following the D-Day landings.

After the war Barnett Freedman's wide-ranging commercial work continued where it had left off, including many more jacket designs and other publicity material for Faber. Sadly, his delicate health led to an early death at the age of 56.

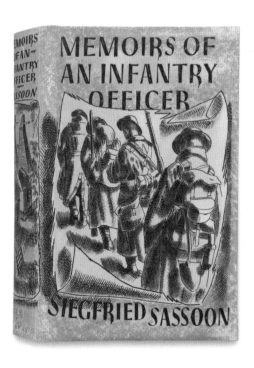

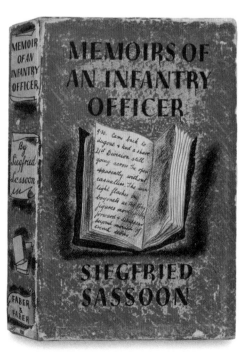

Memoirs of an Infantry Officer
Siegfried Sassoon
Faber and Faber · 1931
230 × 150 mm · 9 × 5⅞ in.

Freedman's illustration and all-round design make this one of the key illustrated books of the twentieth century. The book was issued with a dust jacket and 320 copies were produced with a slipcase and signed by author and artist, of which 300 were for sale. This was Freedman's first major work of illustration. The dust jacket demonstrates his meticulous concern for the synergy of type and image, as well as his careful consideration of the spine, making it work both as part of and independently of the overall design.

Art and Understanding
Margaret H. Bulley
B. T. Batsford · 1937
280 × 220 mm · 11 × 8⅝ in.

Freedman produced a striking
three-colour repeat design over
plain black boards for this large-
scale publication. Before the
Second World War, Freedman
designed some thirty dust jackets.
This was one of the few that was
for a publisher other than Faber
and Faber.

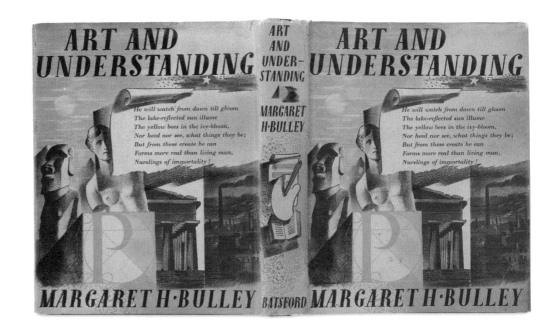

The Looms Are Silent
Maxence van der Meersch
Cassell · 1934
190 × 125 mm · 7½ × 5 in.

Van der Meersch's tale of the human
consequences of industrial strife
in a French textile town is elegantly
represented by the jacket design
on this scarce title.

The Wall
John Hersey
Hamish Hamilton · 1950
220 × 150 mm · 8⅝ × 5⅞ in.

Hersey's novel tells the story of the
Jews in Warsaw from 1939 to the
ghetto's destruction in 1943 through
the fortunes of a group of individuals
from three families. Freedman's
jacket design floats key elements
of the book's narrative against the
background of the ghetto wall.

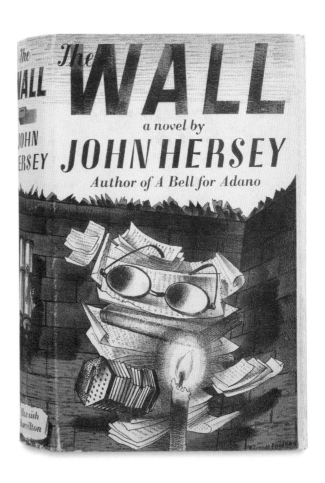

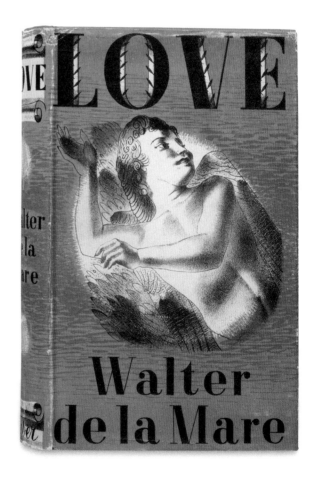

*Tribute to Walter de la Mare
on his 75th Birthday*
Faber and Faber · 1948
220 × 150 mm · 8⅝ × 5⅞ in.

Freedman's original ink and wash
sketch for the angel design is shown
here alongside the printed jacket. The
rough sketch contrasts with the artist's
meticulously exacting lithographic
technique. The image was also used
as the book's frontispiece.

Love
Walter de la Mare
Faber and Faber · 1943
220 × 145 mm · 8⅝ × 5¾ in.

A barely discernible third colour
of pale blue is used sparingly in the
design for de la Mare's collection of
writings on the subject of love. The
cherub motif is repeated on the title
page and Freedman also provided
black-and-white illustrations for
the interior.

The Complete Nonsense of Edward Lear
Edited by Holbrook Jackson
Faber and Faber · 1947
232 × 165 mm · 9⅛ × 6½ in.

Freedman lays his hand-rendered
lettering over Lear's own nonsense
drawings that illustrate the book.
The three-colour design is repeated
on the back of the jacket and on the
cover boards.

The Faber Book of Children's Verse
Edited by Janet Adam Smith
Faber and Faber · 1953
204 × 140 mm · 8 × 5½ in.

Many of Freedman's book jackets
were cleverly designed to repeat the
front image on the back seamlessly.
This example shows the artist at his
best. The design is also repeated
on the cover boards.

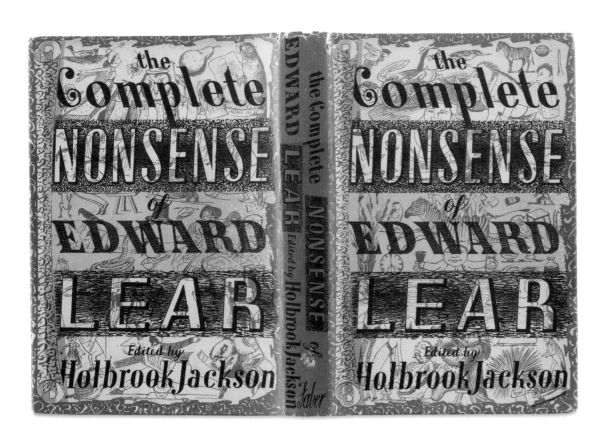

John Ruskin:
The Portrait of a Prophet
Peter Quennell · Collins · 1949
220 × 146 mm · 8⅝ × 5¼ in.

Freedman based his full-length
portrait of John Ruskin on a painting
by John Everett Millais in the
Ashmolean Museum. The design
is repeated on the reverse and a
vignette design of paper and books
is used on the spine.

Readings from Dickens
Emlyn Williams
Folio Society · 1953
220 × 150 mm · 8⅝ × 5⅞ in.

Byron in Italy
Peter Quennell · Collins · 1941
230 × 150 mm · 9 × 5⅞ in.

Here are two other portrait-based designs
using two colours and conceived to
repeat on both sides of the jacket. The
Folio Society publication of *Readings
from Dickens* also includes Freedman's
decorated endpapers. It was lithographed
at the Curwen Press.

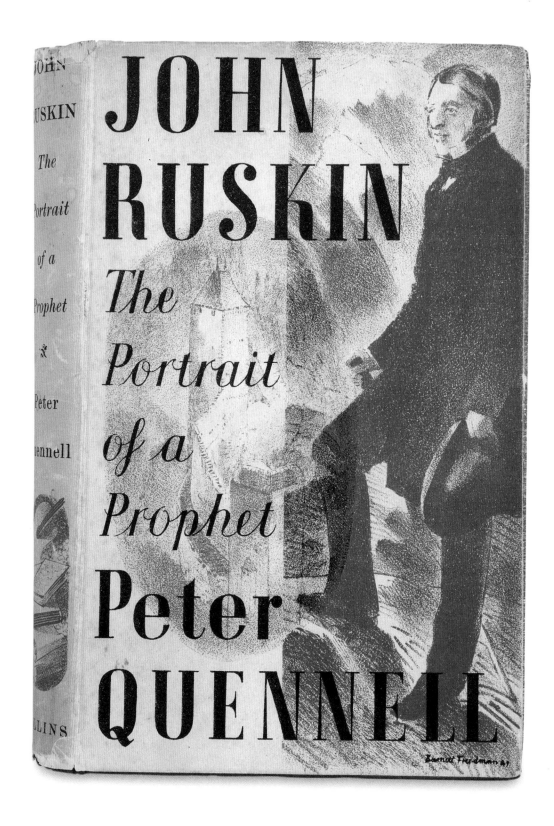

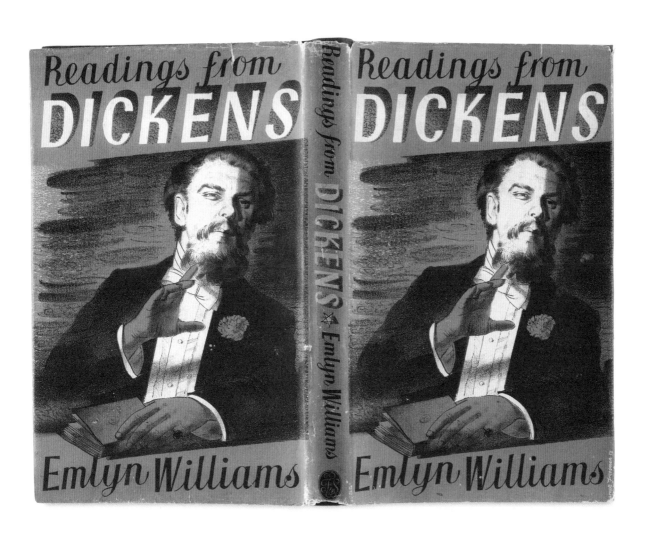

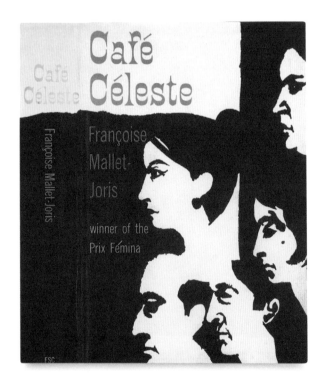

MILTON
GLASER
USA · b. 1929

For Milton Glaser, as a consummate communication designer and all-round visual thinker, the lines between illustration and pure design have perhaps become blurred. It is fair to say that he is one of the most influential designer-illustrators of the last sixty years, responsible for several of the most iconic images and logos of his generation. Among Glaser's most well-known designs are the poster that was packaged with Bob Dylan's 'Greatest Hits' LP of 1967 and the 'I Love NY' logo of 1976, which was credited with playing a significant role in the rejuvenation of the city.

Glaser was born to Hungarian Jewish immigrant parents in New York and studied at the Cooper Union art school there. He subsequently won a Fulbright scholarship to the Academy of Fine Arts in Bologna, where Giorgio Morandi taught him printmaking. In 1954, upon his return from Italy, he joined three fellow graduates from Cooper Union, Seymour Chwast, Edward Sorel and Reynold Ruffins, to set up Push Pin Studios. Glaser and Chwast directed the company for over twenty years and it became enormously influential in the world of graphic design; its work from that period is now seen as a reference point for the highest quality design. The studio's standing in the world of art and design was confirmed by the award of an exhibition at the Louvre's Musée des Arts Décoratifs in 1970.

Glaser himself has had one-man shows at the Museum of Modern Art in New York (1975) and the Centre Georges Pompidou in Paris (1977). He left Push Pin in 1975 to pursue work in a wide variety of design disciplines. This has ranged from newspaper and magazines (his company, Milton Glaser, Inc. has been responsible for the complete redesign of a number of international newspapers) to architectural and interior design, including supermarkets, restaurants and museums. He has personally designed hundreds of posters. A concern for ethics and sustainability has characterized all Glaser's work and he has retained a keen interest in design education, having been an instructor and board member at the School of Visual Arts in New York since 1961 and is a board member at Cooper Union. In 2009, President Barack Obama presented Glaser with the National Medal of Arts, the first time that this award has been bestowed on a graphic designer.

As with all his work, Glaser brings to the design of dust jackets a depth of visual and conceptual intelligence that, even when employing diverse techniques, makes the work instantly recognizable.

Café Céleste
Françoise Mallet-Joris
Farrar, Straus and Cudahy
(New York) · 1959
216 × 146 mm · 8½ × 5¾ in.

Mallet-Joris's prize-winning novel (it won the Prix Fémina in 1958) deals with the various motivations and emotional shortcomings of the habitués of a Montparnasse café. Glaser's jacket graphically reflects the psychological intensity of the text.

The Assistant
Bernard Malamud
Eyre & Spottiswood · 1959
204 × 134 mm · 8 × 5¼ in.

The cramped immigrant experience in 1950s Brooklyn, New York, was explored in Malamud's second novel, where the protagonist is an assistant to a grocer. Glaser's understated jacket design was first used on the US edition, published two years earlier by Farrar, Straus and Cudahy, but with a purple-coloured background.

The Electric Kool-Aid Acid Test
Tom Wolfe
Farrar, Straus and Giroux
(New York) · 1968
216 × 140 mm · 8½ × 5½ in.
....

It is difficult to imagine a more
appropriate choice than Glaser for the
jacket design of Tom Wolfe's account
of late-1960s psychedelic drug culture
through the experiences of Ken Kesey
and the Merry Pranksters.

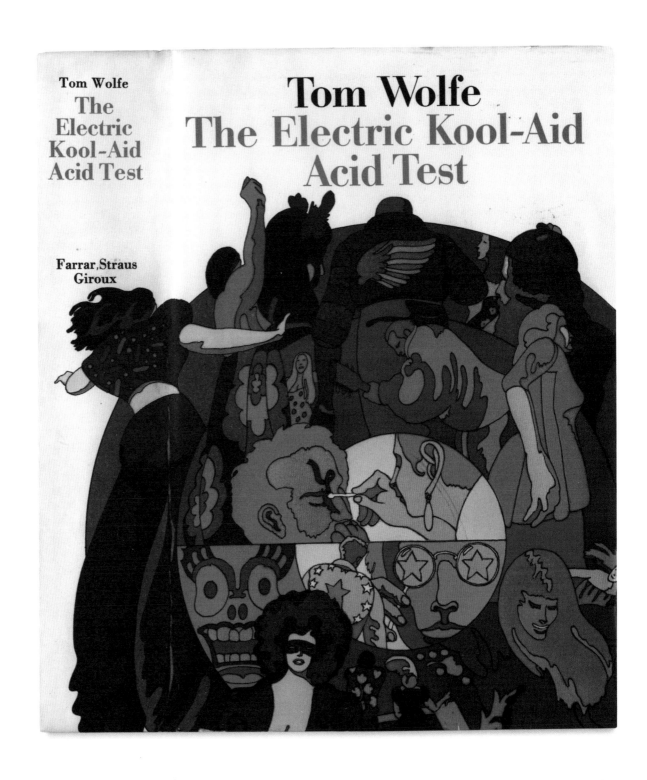

A Seizure of Limericks
Conrad Aiken
Holt, Rinehart and Winston
(New York) · 1964
185 × 134 mm · 7¼ × 5¼ in.

In addition to the jacket design,
Glaser's drawings accompany the fifty
limericks in the book's interior. It was
published in the UK the following year
by W. H. Allen with the same jacket.
The collection was the product of time
Aiken spent in a Savannah hospital
after suffering a heart attack.

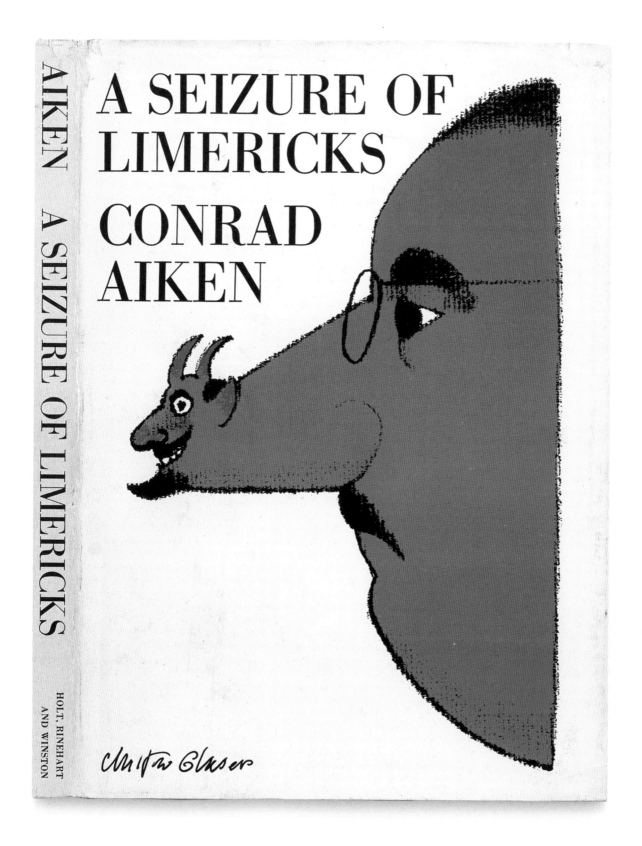

Keep the Aspidistra Flying
George Orwell
Harcourt, Brace
(New York) · 1956
204 × 140 mm · 8 × 5½ in.

Although first published in
England in 1936, Orwell's
semi-autobiographical story
of a poor young man who works
in a bookstore by day and spends
his evenings trying to write in
his squalid rented room was not
published in the US until this
edition in 1956. Glaser's design
visualizes Orwell's sarcastic titular
reference to the middle classes.

The Magic Barrel
Bernard Malamud
Farrar, Straus and Cudahy
(New York) · 1958
216 × 140 mm · 8½ × 5½ in.

The problem of how to design
the jacket of a book of varied short
stories is cleverly resolved by
Glaser's use of formalized shapes
that give glimpses of the lives of
those whom Malamud chronicles.
This first collection of Malamud
short stories won the US National
Book Award for Fiction in 1959.

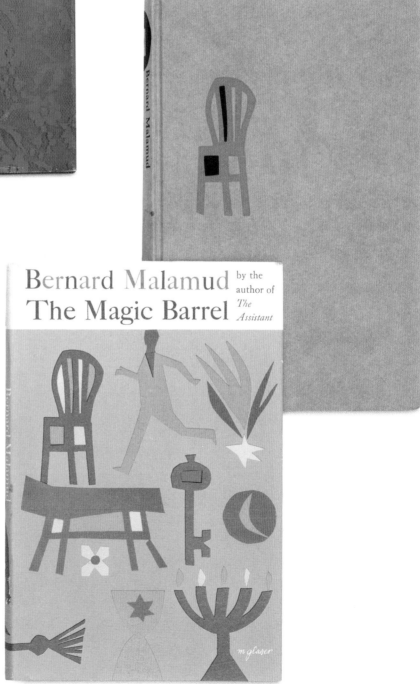

EDWARD GOREY

USA · 1925–2000

In a conversation with his friend the artist Clifford Ross in 1994, Edward Gorey expanded on many of his artistic preoccupations and influences and how he would 'cheerfully sell my soul to draw like some people'. Invited to elaborate, he stated, 'Actually, the person I most wish I could draw like is someone you've probably never heard of named Edward Bawden, who's probably dead by now…he's got a black and white technique that I'd kill for.'[42] He cited another quintessentially English artist and fellow cross-hatcher, Edward Ardizzone, as a further inspiration. These influences may have contributed to the myth that Gorey was English. In fact, he was born in Chicago and was educated at Harvard, and his unique voice as an artist and book-maker was informed by a thorough knowledge of design history and wide-ranging interests in art, literature, music and dance. In the books he wrote, his fusion of the Edwardian parlour and small-town American Gothic provided a backdrop for dark goings on, many of which were only vaguely suggested as happening 'off stage' and entrusted to the febrile imagination of the reader.

As with many of the artists featured in this book, Edward Gorey's dust-jacket designs may be regarded as only a relatively minor part of his *oeuvre*. Yet this aspect of his work played a significant role in the development of his graphic vocabulary. After graduation from Harvard, he remained in Cambridge, Massachusetts, trying to write a novel while working in a bookshop and beginning to pick up commissions to illustrate book jackets. Gorey was eventually persuaded in 1953 to take a full-time job in the art department of Doubleday Anchor Books in New York as artist and typographer. He continued there until 1959 when he spent two years as an art director and editor at the newly established Looking Glass Library, a short-lived publishing venture aimed at producing classic children's books for a modern audience.

The jackets and covers that Gorey designed over this period, and indeed subsequently, are characterized by an intense understanding of the texts, flair for symbolic interpretation and a clear concern for all aspects of the design, including typography (he usually referred to himself as a 'freelance illustrator and book designer'). Many of the designs feature his own hand-rendered typography, often arrived at through a process of tracing fonts from old printers' typeface manuals.[43] Throughout his time as an employee, Gorey was working in the evenings on his own book concepts and as these gained increasing acclaim and sales he was able to give up his post and choose his own projects. However, his experience of thorough immersion in all aspects of book design, illustration and production would inform his later output. Working on his own allowed him to control the overall aesthetic of the book, integrating and synthesizing the design of jackets, cover boards, endpapers, etc. as his increasingly eccentric vocabulary of motifs and indeterminate creatures continued to evolve.

Quake, Quake, Quake
Compiled by Paul Dehn
Hamish Hamilton · 1961
190 × 125 mm · 7½ × 5 in.

Published in the same year by Simon and Schuster in New York and Hamish Hamilton in London and using the identical jacket concept, *Quake, Quake, Quake* afforded Gorey the opportunity to design a full wraparound jacket, an embossed motif on the cover boards and illustrated endpapers as well as illustrations to Dehn's droll verse. The author was best known for his many film screenplays.

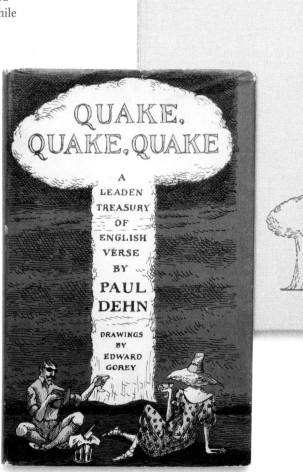

Men and Gods
Rex Warner
Looking Glass Library
(New York) · 1959
190 × 125 mm · 7½ × 5 in.

This wraparound design for jacket
and boards packages Warner's
retelling of Greek legends. Gorey's
animals display the sense of sinister
intent that are familiar from his
own titles.

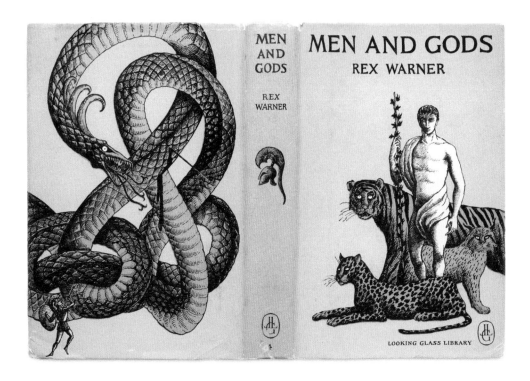

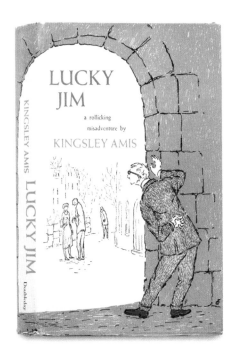

The Christmas Bower
Polly Redford
E. P. Dutton (New York) · 1969
190 × 125 mm · 7½ × 5 in.

Gorey's jacket design and illustrations
for this publication were the product
of a long-standing pact between writer
and artist to the effect that they would
one day collaborate on a book. The
two had been high-school classmates.
The resulting jacket is a masterpiece
of fully integrated pictorial and
typographic design.

Lucky Jim
Kingsley Amis
Doubleday (New York) · 1954
190 × 125 mm · 7½ × 5 in.

One of Gorey's early jackets while
working at Doubleday was this one
for *Lucky Jim*, Amis's first novel,
which was published in the UK by
Victor Gollancz the same year. Gorey
uses the three colours cleverly and
sparingly in his design overall and
for the evocation of the lead character,
Jim Dixon, said to be inspired by
the poet Philip Larkin, to whom the
book is dedicated.

The War of the Worlds
H. G. Wells
Looking Glass Library
(New York) · 1960
204 × 125 mm · 8 × 5 in.

Gorey's jacket design and illustrations
for this edition of Wells's science-fiction
novel have been described by Steven
Heller as 'a slight detour' from the
artist's emerging style.[44] It is, however,
considered highly collectable.

Hauntings: Tales of the Supernatural
Edited by Henry Mazzeo
Doubleday (New York) · 1968
220 × 143 mm · 8⅝ × 5⅝ in.

The visual language perfectly
matches the subject matter of this
book, a collection of seventeen ghost
stories with an element of the gothic
by some of the acknowledged masters
of the genre, such as M. R. James and
Henry James. Each story is prefaced
by an illustration by Gorey.

The Web and the Rock
Thomas Wolfe
Grosset & Dunlap
(New York) · undated
204 × 125 mm · 8 × 5 in.

A somewhat brooding design hints at
the struggle of the protagonist George
Webber – a novelist from North
Carolina – to establish himself
as a writer in New York. Wolfe died in
1938 and this novel was first published
by Harper & Bros the following year.
Gorey's jacket on this edition by
reprint publishers Grosset & Dunlap
is probably from the early 1950s.

You Can't Go Home Again
Thomas Wolfe
Grosset & Dunlap
(New York) · undated
204 × 125 mm · 8 × 5 in.

This was Wolfe's final novel,
published posthumously by Harper
& Bros in 1940 as a sequel to *The
Web and the Rock*. Gorey's poignant
figure looking out to sea chimes
with the book's title. The novelist
Webber travels to London and
Berlin, but realizes how he has
changed and that he cannot go back
home. This reprint probably dates
from the mid-1950s.

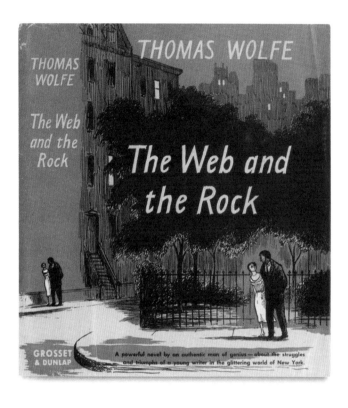

The Haunted Looking Glass
Ghost Stories Chosen
by Edward Gorey
Looking Glass Library
(New York) · 1959
204 × 125 mm · 8 × 5 in.

For this title, Gorey chose the
stories, provided one full-page
illustration at the beginning of each
of the tales and designed the jacket.

Olivia · Olivia
The Hogarth Press · 1949
210 × 140 mm · 8¼ × 5½ in.

The autobiographical story of an
English schoolgirl spending a year
in a French school was originally
published anonymously. Now
regarded as a lesbian classic, it was
actually written by Dorothy Bussy,
Duncan Grant's cousin and one
of Lytton Strachey's sisters, and
dedicated to Virginia Woolf. Grant's
design was perhaps influenced by his
own experiences of Paris in 1906.

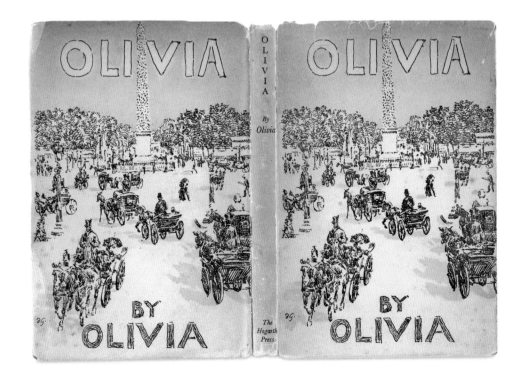

DUNCAN GRANT
UK · 1885–1978

Inevitably, Duncan Grant's designs are compared to those
of Vanessa Bell, given their close relationship, personal and
artistic, over more than forty years, much of it living and
working under the same roof. There are of course similarities.
They shared a passion for the spontaneous, unruly hand-made
and a belief in a democratic approach to art. As well as in
painting, this ethos embraced a wide range of decorative and
applied arts to which they happily turned their talents and
which, for both of them, fell within their very broad definition
of 'art'. Alongside book-jacket design, these activities included
ceramic, fabric, costume and theatre design, posters (Grant and
Bell were each commissioned by Jack Beddington to produce
a poster for Shell-Mex BP and also created prints for the
Contemporary Lithographs series), commercially commissioned
murals for private and publicly owned spaces and, famously,
decoration of furniture and interiors. Just as they declined
to see the edge of a canvas as the point at which a painting
ended, they refused to see the gallery as a boundary for what
is generally considered to be art. This attitude was at least
partly instilled by the artist and critic Roger Fry, whose Omega
Workshops both Bell and Grant had become closely involved
with. It would continue throughout Grant's long life, and even
at the age of 90 he was producing lithographs for sale through
the *Observer* newspaper.

Grant was born into a well-connected family in Aviemore,
Scotland, but spent much of his early childhood in India and
Burma where his father was posted as a major in the army.
Educated in England, he lived for a time in his late teens

with his uncle and aunt, Sir Richard and Lady Strachey, who
encouraged his artistic ambitions and helped him to enrol at
Westminster School of Art. While there he was particularly
influenced by the French painter Simon Bussy, who married
his cousin Dorothy Strachey. He had further spells of study
in Paris and at the Slade in London, and became involved with
the Bloomsbury Group. Thanks to Roger Fry, he obtained
one of his earliest commissions, in 1911, to decorate the dining
rooms of the Borough Polytechnic in south London, on the
theme of 'London on Holiday'. During the First World War
Grant was a conscientious objector and it was at that time that
he and Vanessa Bell started to live at Charleston Farmhouse
in Sussex.

Later commissions included designs for the First Class
main lounge of Cunard's new liner, RMS *Queen Mary*,
launched in 1936. For the best part of a year, Grant created
large murals, carpet and textile designs, only for his entire
work to be rejected as unsuitable at a very late stage.

Over the years Grant designed a handful of dust jackets
for a range of publishers. These included, of course, the
Hogarth Press, but also Hamish Hamilton, Gerald Duckworth,
Harvill Press, William Heinemann and Hamish Hamilton.
One of his finest designs was for the cover boards of *Duncan
Grant* in the *Living Painters* series, which was published by
the Hogarth Press in 1923, with an introduction by Roger
Fry. Angelica Garnett, Grant's daughter with Vanessa Bell,
compared his approach to such commissioned work to that
of her mother:

His drawings were witty, calligraphic and light hearted,
delighting his many literary friends. His inspiration was
more closely related to the text than Vanessa's, less poetic
but more lively – a vitality that lost a little of its vivacity
in the printing since he found it more difficult than she did
to accept the flatness of the printer's block.[45]

O Pale Galilean
Paul Roche
Harvill Press · 1954
190 × 130 mm · 7½ × 5⅛ in.

One of Grant's most striking dust-jacket designs was for this novel by his close friend and lover Paul Roche. He also designed chapter vignettes for the interior of the book, which is now extremely scarce.

Monkey
Wu Ch'eng-en
George Allen and Unwin · 1942
222 × 152 mm · 8¾ × 6 in.

In deference to its Chinese origins, the jacket of *Monkey* was printed in reverse format, with what we normally regard as the back cover placed at the front.

AUBREY HAMMOND

UK · 1894–1940

The stylish and stylized artwork of Aubrey Hammond was a familiar feature of the advertising and publishing worlds of the 1920s and 1930s. His graphic language is instantly recognizable through his use of sweeping curves and arches, described with a bold line and large areas of flat colour, often featuring a daring and skilful use of solid areas of black. At its most angular and severe, his work could be said to be influenced by the Vorticists of the early twentieth century.

Hammond was born in the seaside town of Folkestone, Kent. After studying at the Byam Shaw School of Art and then in Paris at the Académie Julian, he worked in the commercial arts in the UK, notably in the areas of poster design, book illustration and design for the theatre. He also taught design and illustration at Westminster School of Art. His London Transport posters are some of the best of the period.

Hammond's dramatic and theatrical approach to graphic representation of the human figure also lent itself particularly well to the theatre. He designed sets for Shakespeare plays at Stratford-upon-Avon and two of his studies for costume designs are held at the Victoria and Albert Museum. These comprise a watercolour and a pencil design for Fay Compton as The Lady in Ashley Dukes's play, *The Man with a Load of Mischief*, performed at the Haymarket Theatre in London in 1925.

Hammond illustrated widely for magazines and advertising during his relatively short life, and his drawings were always beautifully conceived and elegantly executed. However, it is for one particular dust jacket that he is probably most universally recognized and remembered. Thea von Harbou's novel of her screenplay for her husband Fritz Lang's film *Metropolis* was published in 1927 and Hammond's colour wraparound jacket design has become as iconic as images from the black-and-white film. The futuristic themes of automation and industrialization are strikingly conveyed in classic Art Deco style.

A Christmas Book
Compiled by
D. B. Wyndham Lewis
and G. C. Heseltine
J. M. Dent · 1928
190 × 120 mm · 7½ × 4¾ in.

Hammond's fusion of hand-rendered lettering and image form a striking introduction to this collection of all things Christmas-related, including quotations, music and recipes.

On Straw and Other Conceits
D. B. Wyndham Lewis
Methuen · 1927
190 × 120 mm · 7½ × 4¾ in.

This elegant and stylish jacket suggests 1920s hedonism in introducing a selection of the author's columns in the *Daily Mail* that ranged from Jane Austen and Aesop to red hair, fat men and milk.

Word of the Earth
Anthony Richardson
Heinemann · 1923
195 × 125 mm · 7¾ × 5 in.

Billowing clouds and trees were
recurrent motifs in Hammond's
highly formalized designs. This
first book by Richardson was not
a novel, but subtitled 'Conversations
Between Fictitious Characters',
who included a poet, a physicist
and a shepherd.

Metropolis
Thea von Harbou
Readers Library · 1927
169 × 106 mm · 6⅜ × 4⅛ in.

One of the stand-out dust
jackets of the twentieth century,
Hammond's design juxtaposes
delicate colour harmony with
nightmarish vision.

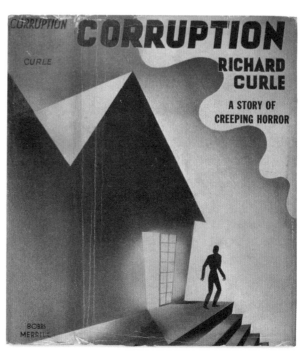

Kept Woman
Viña Delmar
Harcourt, Brace
(New York) · 1929
190 × 125 mm · 7½ × 5 in.

Delmar's novel was a follow up to
her risqué debut of the previous year,
Bad Girl, which became a bestseller.
Kept Woman explores similarly
provocative themes and Hawkins's
Art Deco jacket design is clearly
influenced by the burgeoning visual
culture of Hollywood movies.

Corruption
Richard Curle
Bobbs-Merrill
(Indianapolis) · 1933
190 × 125 mm · 7½ × 5 in.

Hawkins was a master of sensation
and suspense. The sickly green light
that here flowed from his airbrush
perfectly complements the jacket
blurb's description of the book as
a 'murder mystery of terror and
"creeping horror".'

Barron Ixell: Crime Breaker
Oscar Schisgall
Longmans, Green & Co.
(New York) · 1929
190 × 125 mm · 7½ × 5 in.

For this collection of stories
featuring the intrepid international
sleuth Barron Ixell, Hawkins's highly
theatrical design is repeated to
create a full wraparound jacket.

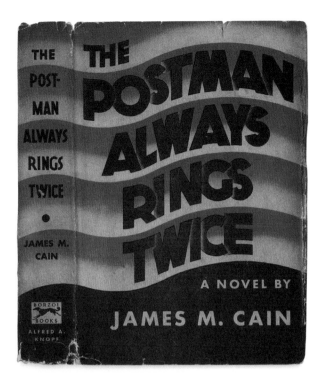

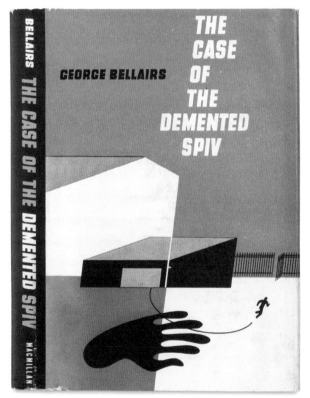

ARTHUR HAWKINS, JR.

USA · 1903–1985

An unmistakably eerie air pervades the pictorial dust-jacket designs of Arthur Hawkins, Jr. He produced an extraordinary number of these for over twenty years from the late 1920s, totalling around 1,500 overall. Some of them were primarily typographic, such as his best-known one, for the first edition of James M. Cain's *The Postman Always Rings Twice* (Alfred A. Knopf, 1934), later to be filmed with Lana Turner and John Garfield in the starring roles. Even this jacket, with its titles taking up the whole front panel and floating against ribbons of tonally graded red, somehow evokes the darkness and despair of the book's contents.

Hawkins was born in Cumberland, Maryland, the son of a surgeon, and graduated from the University of Virginia in 1925. He then rapidly established himself in New York as a designer-illustrator of dust jackets. Many of his early designs were done in the strongly geometric manner of the period, often executed with airbrush and stencil. During this time, Hawkins's rather flamboyant curlicued signature stood out clearly in contrast to the artwork itself. As a freelancer, he was in great demand to design for murder-mystery novels. He was member of the Book Designers Guild and was president of the New York Art Directors Club in 1945–46, and was toastmaster at their galas for many years.[46]

Hawkins gave up designing dust jackets because he felt the fees were not acceptable but carried on with some freelance assignments from publishers for promotional material. He continued to work in design but found employment in the fields of advertising and art direction. In his later years, Hawkins collaborated with his wife, Nancy, to produce a number of cookery books, specializing in American regional cuisine.

Arthur Hawkins's son Gil, a sculptor, has many memories of his father and his work. He recalls that he would commute two or three days each week into New York from his home and studio in suburban Leonia, New Jersey, to do a circuit of the major publishers. At each one he would either pick up a new commission or deliver completed jackets, or both. His absolute professionalism meant that he always read the books, sometimes one a night. He created dummy books with blank pages as facsimiles so that publishers could see the jacket designs *in situ*. Gil Hawkins also recalls his father telling him that, when starting out, he worked for weeks practising that famous signature hundreds and hundreds of times. It was a signature that would become instantly recognizable and admired throughout the industry. Some time after his father's death, Gil found himself in a bookstore in Englewood, New Jersey. The proprietor spotted him perusing the outfacing spines of books:

> I explained that my dad's work was so distinctive to me that all I needed was a brief scan of the spine to recognize one of his jackets among all the other books. Curious, he asked me who my dad was. To my surprise, he knew [his] work and scorned, 'I bought more bad mysteries because your dad's covers were so good!'[47]

The Postman Always Rings Twice
James M. Cain
Alfred A. Knopf (New York) · 1934
188 × 125 mm · 7⅜ × 5 in.

This is perhaps the most instantly recognizable of Hawkins's many designs for dust jackets. Unlike much of his work at the time, it was purely typographical and unsigned. The book's racy contents, both in the sense of its speedy telling and undercurrents of sadomasochism, ensured its success and notoriety.

The Case of the Demented Spiv
George Bellairs
Macmillan (New York) · 1950
195 × 130 mm · 7¾ × 5⅛ in.

Created at the end of Hawkins's career as a dust-jacket designer, this composition for Bellairs's Inspector Littlejohn crime novel shows him adopting modernist techniques with an angular construction of image and text.

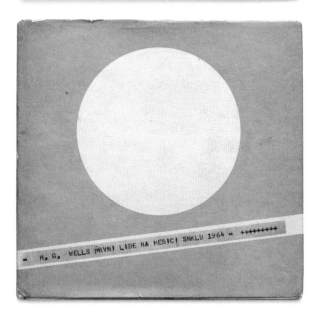

ADOLF HOFFMEISTER
Czechoslovakia · 1902–1973

The extraordinary imagination of Adolf Hoffmeister was employed in the field of book arts, both commercial and experimental (often simultaneously) across several decades of the mid-twentieth century. He was born into a middle-class Prague family and grew up to become a left-wing intellectual and creative powerhouse whose breadth of interests resist classification or labelling. He was an artist who applied his work to painting, caricature, illustration, journalism / art criticism and stage direction. In addition, he was an author, editor, playwright, translator, diplomat and professor of art.

As an 18-year-old in 1920, Hoffmeister was a founder member and first secretary of the Czech avant-garde art society that was opaquely named Devìtsil (Czech name for the 'butterbur' plant, literally 'nine forces') and which came out of the Café Union in Prague as Czechoslovakia itself was emerging from the Austro-Hungarian empire. It has been suggested that Devìtsil's rich but haphazard mixture of Surrealism, Dadaism, Constructivism and other European movements was fuelled by the intoxication of newfound freedom. Devìtsil eventually ran out of steam in 1931, having survived rather longer than most such groups manage. Hoffmeister had begun to travel through Europe some years earlier and his ties to the group loosened. He sent back articles for Czech journals and magazines, including interviews with artists and other cultural figures. These were illustrated with his drawings and caricatures. He met and interviewed James Joyce and collaborated on a translation into Czech of *Finnegans Wake* (1932). In 1928–30, Hoffmeister edited one of the leading Czech newspapers and in 1930–32 the main literary magazine. In the 1930s, he set up the anti-fascist magazine *Simplicus* after the German satirical magazine *Simplicissimus* came under attack from the Nazis.

In 1939, Hoffmeister fled to France, but with the Nazi occupation was interned before escaping to Lisbon and then New York in January 1941. After the war he returned to Czechoslovakia and became Director of International Cultural Relations at the Ministry of Information and a member of his country's delegation to the General Assembly of UNESCO. He welcomed the Communist takeover in 1948 and was appointed ambassador to France, but as the regime became more Stalinist he took up a professorship at the Academy of Applied Arts in Prague in 1951. He was instrumental in developing a department that specialized in children's illustration. In the late 1950s Hoffmeister began to use collage in a sytematic way in his work, and his jacket and illustrations for Jules Verne's *Around the World in Eighty Days* (1959) demonstrate this interest.

With the Soviet invasion in 1968 and quashing of the 'Prague Spring' Hoffmeister went to France once again and taught at the University of Vincennes. An exhibition of his portraits and collages was held at the Palais des Beaux-Arts in Brussels in 1969. The following year he returned home, but was considered a 'non-person' by the regime and died three years later in Eastern Bohemia.

Cesta Kolem Světa za Osmdesát Dní
(*Around the World in Eighty Days*)
Jules Verne
SNKLU (Prague) · 1959
245 × 170 mm · 9⅝ × 6¾ in.

Hoffmeister focuses on the American West in this design for Jules Verne's classic. Using collage, he somehow manages successfully to balance imagery of widely differing graphic origin as well as the ornate type, which echoes the strong reds in the profile of the Native American.

První Lidé na Měsíci
(*The First Men in the Moon*)
H. G. Wells
SNKLU (Prague) · 1964
200 × 210 mm · 7⅞ × 8¼ in.

For the jacket of this Czech edition of Wells's *The First Men in the Moon* (1901), Hoffmeister reduces the imagery to the simplest possible moon motif. The lettering imitates the now-forgotten script of a telegram or teleprinter, giving the sense of a news flash from outer space.

Pohádky (*Fairy Tales*)
Jiří Wolker
SNKLU (Prague) · 1964
245 × 170 mm · 9⅝ × 6¾ in.

This dust jacket employs geometric
simplicity and features organic and
mechanical textures. Hoffmeister's
playfully collaged typography
floats engagingly within the central
yellow circle.

Neobyčejná dobrodružství Julia Jurenita
(*The Extraordinary Adventures
of Julia Jurenita*)
Ilya Erenburg
Odeon (Prague) · 1966
245 × 170 mm · 9⅝ × 6¾ in.

Hoffmeister merges abstract painting
and typographic design in this dust
jacket. The book also features six full-
page and twelve double-page colour
collages by Hoffmeister, as well as
collaged endpapers.

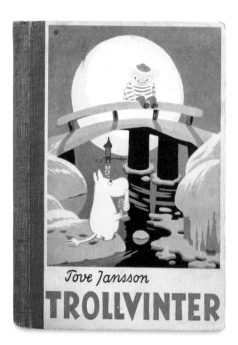

It is perhaps inappropriate to attempt to apply any normal criteria of design to the appreciation of the dust jackets of Tove Jansson's *Moomin* books. Her creative vision was so uniquely idiosyncratic that the illustrations and designs essentially follow their own form of visual grammar. Jansson's genius has been acknowledged by writers and critics the world over and she is appreciated by readers of all age groups. In 2014, the centenary of her birth was celebrated widely in her native Finland and around the world through exhibitions and events, including a major show at the National Gallery in Helsinki, which travelled to Japan. Jansson's world resonates with readers from different cultures and backgrounds. This is nicely exemplified by the British writer Frank Cottrell Boyce: 'I lived on this great big housing estate in suburban Liverpool, from a working class background, and somehow this bohemian, upper middle-class, Finnish lesbian eccentric felt like she was speaking directly to me.'[48]

Jansson grew up in an artistic, Swedish-speaking household in Helsinki. Her father was a sculptor and her mother an illustrator. Her childhood was therefore spent learning at her parents' side. Drawing and storytelling became as one, sometimes in sequential image form, sometimes in a combination of words and pictures. Jansson said that the first Moomin drawing appeared in response to an argument with one of her brothers about the philosopher Immanuel Kant. She had wanted to draw the ugliest possible creature in the role of Kant and place him on a WC. Kant gradually evolved into a Moomin.

In the years just before the Second World War Jansson studied at art school in Stockholm and Helsinki, then in Paris and Rome. She returned to Helsinki just before the outbreak of hostilities. The war affected her profoundly and it is said that the first Moomin book was greatly influenced by the anxieties that she was experiencing at the time. The original Finnish edition of *The Moomins and the Great Flood* (*Småtrollen och den stora översvämningen*) was published in 1945, followed by *Comet in Moominland* (*Kometjakten*) the following year and *Finn Family Moomintroll* in 1948. The first Moomin book had little impact initially but after the second and third were published things took off, and those were the first to be translated into English, in 1951 and 1950 respectively. In tandem with the Moomin books, Jansson continued working as an illustrator and cartoonist for the Swedish language satirical magazine *Garm*, to which she had first contributed in her teens. In 1954, she accepted an invitation from the *Evening News* in London to do a daily *Moomintroll* comic strip, which she drew until 1959.

The huge international popularity of the Moomin brand is now controlled from the Helsinki offices of Oy Moomin Characters Ltd, whose creative director and chairman of the board is Tove's niece, Sophia Jansson. It is one of Finland's most successful creative export industries.

The original Finnish editions of the Moomin books were not issued with dust jackets but with illustrated paper-covered boards. There have been various versions of the dust jackets for the English editions that were first published by Ernest Benn.

Trollvinter
Tove Jansson
Helsingfors Gebers
(Stockholm) · 1957
185 × 124 mm · 7¼ × 4⅞ in.

Moominland Midwinter
Tove Jansson · Ernest Benn · 1958
200 × 130 mm · 7⅞ × 5⅛ in.

With Jansson's novels issued in so many language co-editions there have been multiple versions of her cover and jacket designs. Shown here are the illustrated paper-covered boards of the original edition of *Trollvinter* (above) and its adaptation for the English edition, published the following year.

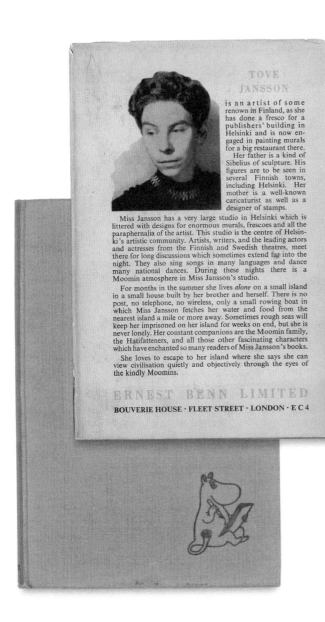

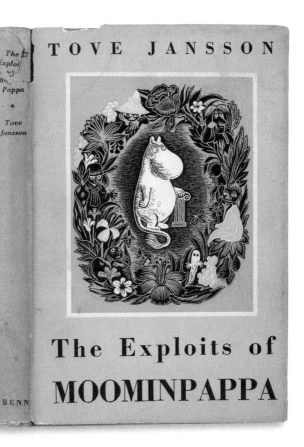

The Exploits of Moominpapa
Tove Jansson · Ernest Benn · 1952
188 × 124 mm · 7⅜ × 4⅞ in.

Finn Family Moomintroll
Tove Jansson · Ernest Benn · 1950
188 × 124 mm · 7⅜ × 4⅞ in.

These English editions, published
by Ernest Benn in the early 1950s,
featured Moomin motifs printed on the
front of the binding with the colours
repeated on the respective jackets. *Finn
Family Moomintroll* was the first of the
books to be published in England.

Comet in Moominland
Tove Jansson
Ernest Benn · 1975
216 × 140 mm · 8½ × 5½ in.

The dust jacket of the first English
edition in 1951 was produced by
Tove Jansson in three-colour separation
form. The second and subsequent
editions, from 1959, featured this full-
colour lithographic design.

Tales from Moominvalley
Tove Jansson
Ernest Benn · 1963
204 × 134 mm · 8 × 5¼ in.

The literal translation of the original
Swedish title (*Det osynliga barnet och
andra berättelser*) of this sixth book
in the *Moomin* series is 'The Invisible
Child and other stories'. Unlike the
previous books, all novels, this one
was in the form of nine short stories.

BARBARA JONES
UK · 1912–1978

Barbara Jones was a pioneer. Through her tireless and wide-ranging activities as an artist, illustrator, muralist, writer and curator she challenged accepted notions of hierarchies within art and design. She was an inveterate collector of popular everyday man-made objects and delighted in their qualities, whether hand- or machine-made. Jones combined everyday 'jobbing' illustration work with writing on her favourite topics of architecture and curiosities of popular culture, and she curated important national exhibitions on these subjects.

Jones was born in Croydon, Surrey, where she attended Coloma Convent Girls' School and Croydon School of Art. She went on to the Royal College of Art where she initially studied engraving but soon found the high level of technical detail unsuited to her more spontaneous nature and she transferred to the department of mural decoration. Although she only graduated in 1937, Jones became involved with Kenneth Clark's wartime Recording Britain project, sponsored by the Pilgrim Trust. Commissions and self-generated projects followed at a feverish pace. After the war, she was invited to contribute a lithograph – *Fairground* (1946) – to the first series of Brenda Rawnsley's ambitious School Prints scheme, whereby well-known artists created colour lithographs for classroom walls to give children an introduction to contemporary art. Jones's choice of subject matter was a natural one and her fascination with all of the vernacular detail of the fairground rides is evident in its execution.

An early authorial project was the book *The Isle of Wight* (see p. 21) produced for the *King Penguin* series in 1950. As with John Piper's *Romney Marsh* and Kenneth Rowntree's *A Prospect of Wales* in the same series, the book features an initial essay on the region in question followed by a series of colour reproductions of paintings by the artist. After *The Isle of Wight* came one of Jones's most important and influential books, *The Unsophisticated Arts* (Architectural Press, 1951). Reissued in 2013 as a facsimile (Little Toller Books), the book examines every possible kind of informal, untrained artistic endeavour, including cake decoration, tattooing, pub signs and fairground art. Also in 1951, Jones was heavily involved with the Festival of Britain. As well as designing the Seaside section of the festival, Jones curated the Whitechapel exhibition 'Black Eyes and Lemonade', causing something of a stir with her presentation of popular art and craft, much of it from her own collection. The substantial *Follies and Grottoes* book followed in 1953 (Constable), and once again Jones was able to indulge her passions, this time hunting down eccentric or extravagant architectural conceits through the ages. The more modest *English Furniture at a Glance* (Architectural Press) followed in 1954.

Many of these books featured dust-jacket designs and interior illustrations by Jones herself. Alongside these demanding projects, she took on other commissions, designing around a further thirty dust jackets. When referring to picture making that was not commissioned, Barbara Jones always preferred to describe herself as a 'painter' rather than as an 'artist'.

The Consul at Sunset
Gerald Hanley
Collins · 1951
204 × 130 mm · 8 × 5⅛ in.

The dominant warmth of the yellow and the use of simple, symbolic objects evoke the heat and intrigue of the African desert under British rule, as told in Gerald Hanley's novel.

Follies and Grottoes
Barbara Jones
Constable · 1953
216 × 146 mm · 8½ × 5¾ in.

Jones's fascination for architectural eccentricity is given full rein in this tour of buildings that serve no purpose, other than to give pleasure to those who dreamed them up.

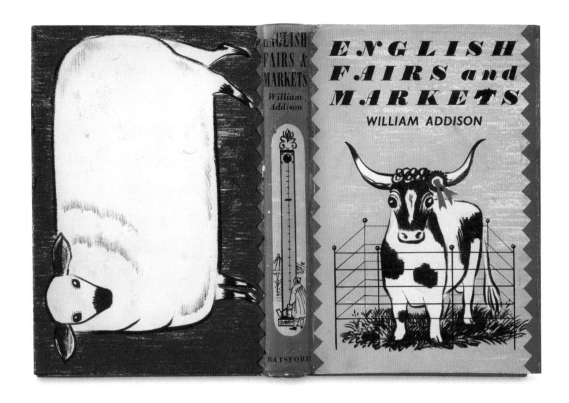

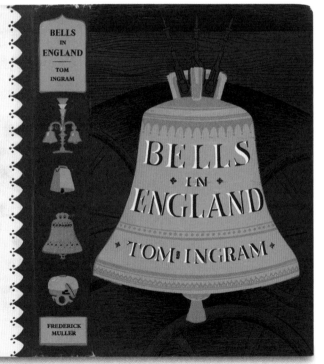

English Fairs and Markets
William Addison
B. T. Batsford · 1953
170 × 108 mm · 6¾ × 4¼ in.

Jones was an inspired choice to
illustrate this title. As well as the
characteristically eye-catching cover,
she produced a number of richly
coloured full-page interior lithographs
and black-and-white line drawings, all
of which, as the jacket blurb explains,
'have a wit and gaiety which is in
active sympathy with their subject'.

Bells in England
Tom Ingram
Frederick Muller · 1954
222 × 142 mm · 8¾ × 5⅝ in.

'Bells exert their curious magic over
us all', the blurb reminds us in this
very specialized book. Barbara Jones's
jacket and interior illustrations are
clearly driven by empathy for the
subject. Unusually, the line drawings
of bell-ringers were sketched directly
from observation.

Flower of Cities: A Book of London
Studies and Sketches
by twenty-two authors
Max Parrish · 1949
230 × 152 mm · 9 × 6 in.

In this book, leading writers and
artists (including Jones) describe in
words and pictures various aspects
of London and London life. In
designing the jacket, Jones suffered
the indignity of having to list
herself on the spine as one of the
'8 other Artists'.

Banns of Marriage
Tom Ingram
Constable · 1956
190 × 125 mm · 7½ × 5 in.

Sparing use of the white of the paper
to isolate and describe the shawl of
the central figure gives the artist an
extra 'colour' in this unusual design.
This was Ingram's first novel.

The Unsophisticated Arts
Barbara Jones
Architectural Press · 1951
255 × 197 mm · 10 × 7¼ in.

Jones's dust jacket for her own
book is one of the most memorably
idiosyncratic designs of the
twentieth century. The existence
of an early rough with the title
English Vernacular Art suggests
some dialogue with the publisher.

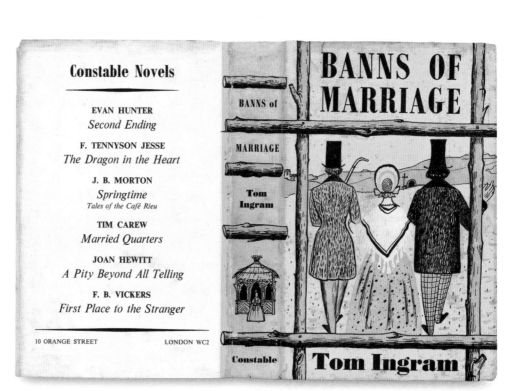

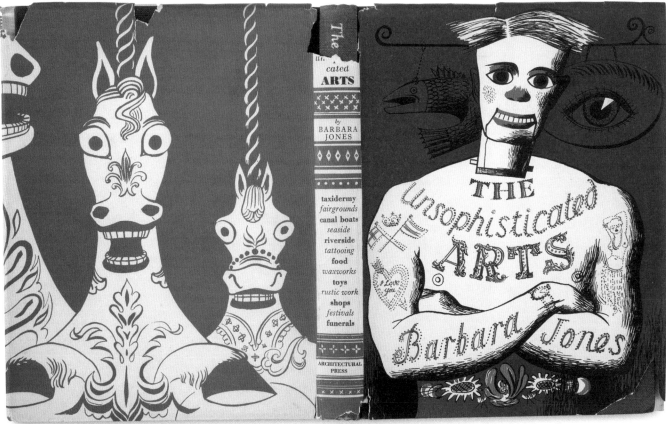

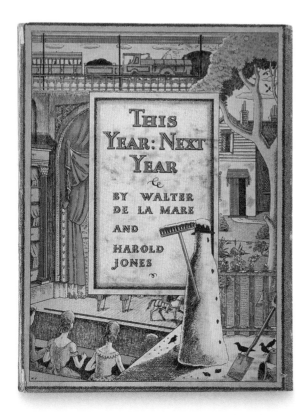

HAROLD JONES
UK · 1904–1992

The vast majority of Harold Jones's output as an illustrator sat within the field of children's literature. As well as his many designs for dust jackets, notably for the adventure stories of M. E. Atkinson, he was perhaps best known for the anthologies of poetry and nursery rhymes that he illustrated and decorated in picture-book form. The first of these made his name: *This Year: Next Year*, a collection of Walter de la Mare poems published by Faber and Faber in 1937. *Lavender's Blue*, a book of nursery rhymes compiled by the noted librarian Kathleen Lines (Oxford University Press, 1954) was another highly acclaimed collaboration. Jones also wrote and illustrated a number of books himself and took on several projects with religious themes. A common feature of all the books is Jones's complete overview of the design and decoration of the page. In an interview with Susan Varley for *Books for Keeps* magazine in 1986, he spoke about the role of illustration for him:

> I have a very positive idea of what is meant by illustration and a lot of the illustrated books I see don't fulfil that idea. I think that an illustration has to be more than just a representation of facts and things. I think it also has to perform the function of decoration.[49]

A substantial archive of Jones's work and correspondence in this field is held at Seven Stories, The National Centre for Children's Books in Newcastle upon Tyne.

In addition to his children's books, Jones designed a number of dust jackets for important works of fiction for adults. There is no real change of style from his work for children; the distinctively geometric approach to composition, often employing isometric perspective, remains a key feature, along with the mechanical cross-hatching with which he builds up tone. The tableau-like organization of many of his designs was touched on in the same interview with Varley: 'Whenever I've drawn pictures for illustration I've always thought of them as mural decorations.'[50] Jones sits firmly within the British tradition of decorative British book illustration with many of his designs for dust jackets featuring intricately patterned borders.

Harold Jones was born in London and began his artistic training in 1920 with evening classes at Goldsmiths College, where he was taught by, among others, Albert Rutherston. The stylistic influence of Rutherston on his later work is clear. He went on to Camberwell School of Arts and Crafts before gaining a scholarship to the Royal College of Art, where he studied printmaking processes – etching, engraving and lithography – rather than illustration. The influence of these exacting technical processes can be clearly seen in Jones's work, the apparent simplicity of which belies a compelling undercurrent of the surreal and slightly sinister.

This Year: Next Year
Walter de la Mare
Faber and Faber · 1937
250 × 190 mm · 9¾ × 7½ in.

This was Harold Jones's first major picture book and it is now extremely desirable for collectors. The dust jacket repeats the design on the paper-covered boards. It is a typically ordered and meticulously rendered Jones design.

Bless This Day:
A Book of Prayer for Children
Compiled by Elfrida Vipont
Collins · 1958
235 × 185 mm · 9¼ × 7¼ in.

A well-known Quaker and author of books for children, Vipont selected prayers from the whole range of Christian literature, Catholic and Protestant. The book was illustrated throughout by Jones, including endpapers and pictorial boards.

Going Gangster
M. E. Atkinson
The Bodley Head · 1940
204 × 140 mm · 8 × 5½ in.

Many of the novels for children by
M. E. Atkinson were dressed in jackets
by Harold Jones. This title is fully
illustrated with his black-and-white
drawings and features his two-colour
decorative endpaper designs.

The Croquet Player
H. G. Wells
Chatto & Windus · 1937
195 × 125 mm · 7¾ × 5 in.

Jones's early dust-jacket design for
Wells's short ghost story of ancestral
Neanderthals already exhibits his
careful attention to decorative detail
and all aspects of image and text. Jones
designed the jacket for another H. G.
Wells title with Chatto & Windus, *The
Brothers*, in the following year.

A Ring of Tales
Compiled by Kathleen Lines
Oxford University Press · 1958
210 × 155 mm · 8¼ × 6⅛ in.

Published the same year as *Bless
This Day*, Kathleen Lines's collection
of stories and poems is based around
themes of nature and the seasons.
Jones's jacket design is rendered in
three colours with a characteristic
decorative border.

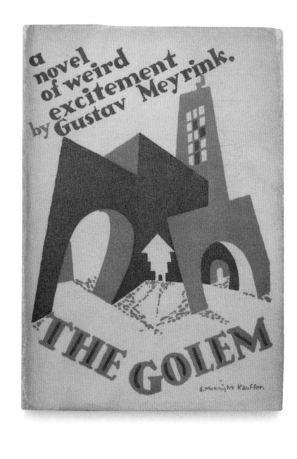

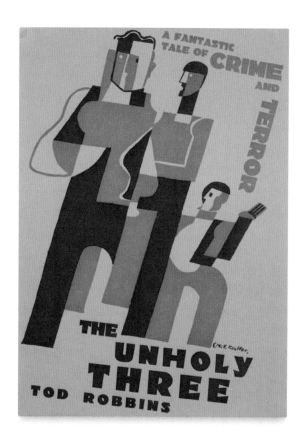

Eminent Victorians
Lytton Strachey
Chatto & Windus · 1921
190 × 125 mm · 7½ × 5 in.

Through the use of the lamp,
sword, book, and the rosary and
cross Kauffer references the four
subjects of Strachey's biographical
essays: Florence Nightingale,
General Gordon, Thomas Arnold
and Cardinal Manning. Strachey's
text reassessed the Victorians'
pretensions to moral superiority and
was immediately successful when first
published in 1918. This early Kauffer
design is reminiscent of Hogarth
Press jackets in its rustic simplicity.

The Unholy Three
Tod Robbins
Victor Gollancz · 1928
190 × 125 mm · 7½ × 5 in.

Robbins's tale of three freakish
carnival castaways who wage
war on society was said to be the
inspiration behind the controversial
Hollywood fear film *Freaks* of
1932. Kauffer avoids sensationalist
imagery in his jacket design, instead
constructing a dynamic formal
composition of type and image
in two colours.

The Golem
Gustav Meyrink
Victor Gollancz · 1928
195 × 135 mm · 7½ × 5⅜ in.

This was the first English edition
of the expressionist horror story
of the Prague ghetto, initially
published in German in serial form
in 1913–14. Kauffer's angular
jacket design was printed in two
colours on poor quality paper
stock. It is now very scarce.

EDWARD McKNIGHT KAUFFER

USA · 1890–1954

Given his status as one of the most highly respected and influential designers of the twentieth century, it is something of a mystery that Edward McKnight Kauffer was not more widely appreciated during his own lifetime in his native America. He was born Edward Kauffer in Great Falls, Cascade County, Montana. He adopted the name McKnight later in life in honour of his mentor, Joseph E. McKnight. Kauffer's early childhood had not been happy and he grew up an introspective boy, spending much of his time drawing. He moved to San Francisco in 1910, worked for a bookseller and art dealer and studied at the Mark Hopkins Institute of Art. While there, he met McKnight, a professor of elementary education at the University of Utah, whose patronage allowed him to set off for Europe to study in Paris.

On the way, he spent several months in Chicago in 1912–13, where he enrolled at the Art Institute and saw the groundbreaking Armory Show. The 643 works in the exhibition, in the words of Kauffer's biographer Mark Haworth-Booth, 'introduced America in one blow to almost everything of major importance in European painting from Delacroix to Marcel Duchamp'.[51] Kauffer later remarked that, although he could not fully process or articulate what he was seeing at the time, it registered profoundly. Certainly, the influence of Cubism and Modernism (and later Vorticism) could be seen in the designs for which he was to become famous.

After he arrived in Europe, Kauffer travelled in Germany, where he saw Ludwig Hohlwein's poster masterpieces in Munich, and attended the Academie Moderne in Paris. With the outbreak of war in August 1914, he was obliged to leave France and arrived in England with just enough money to get back to America. He decided to stay, in part, as he later explained to Frank Zachary, because in England he 'felt at home for the first time'.[52] Kauffer struggled to make a living as a painter in the early war years until he met the renowned poster artist

John Hassall, who introduced him to Frank Pick at London Transport. Pick commissioned him to design posters featuring rural destinations within reach of London that the public might be encouraged to visit. The first Underground posters came out in late 1915 and it was the beginning of a successful twenty-five-year partnership. Kauffer's designs were rendered in water-based paint and used flat areas of colour to create simplified landscapes. He believed strongly in the importance of the formal geometry or dynamics of shapes to capture attention.

To begin with Kauffer still considered himself a painter and was loosely connected with the Bloomsbury Group (his jackets would later adorn their books) but soon saw the futility of attempting to paint while trying to succeed in the world of advertising. Such was his succees in that profession that in the 1930s he was described as the 'Picasso of Advertising Design'.[53] In the late 1920s his work showed the influence of Modernist photomontage from Germany and Russia and in the 1930s he began to use the airbrush to achieve a streamlined effect. Although he is best known for his posters, Kauffer designed many book jackets, which he thought of as mini-posters.

When the Second World War broke out Kauffer returned to the USA as he did not want to be a burden to his adopted country, but was never able to adjust to the world of advertising in New York. Nonetheless he produced some fine dust jackets for American publishers in this period.

There are many contradictions in the work of Edward McKnight Kauffer. Some have put this down to his 'mid-Atlantic' status. In some respects he was a stylistic chameleon, moving freely between abstraction and realism. Yet whichever method was used, a clear and consistent voice emerges that is underpinned by observation and rigorous simplification to the point of austerity.

Quack, Quack!
Leonard Woolf
The Hogarth Press · 1935
180 × 118 mm · 7 × 4⅝ in.

As also shown in his design for the jacket of Herbert Read's *Art Now* for Faber and Faber, Kauffer was as comfortable with constructivist photo-collage as he was with the hand-drawn image. Here a photograph of the eye-bulging Hawaiian war god Kukailimoku is juxtaposed with those of the bellicose dictators Mussolini and Hitler.

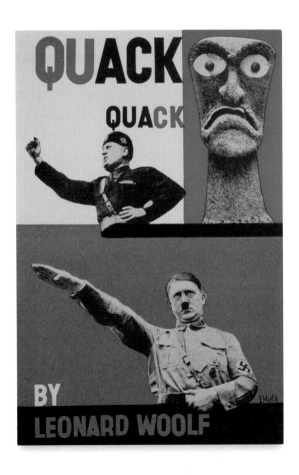

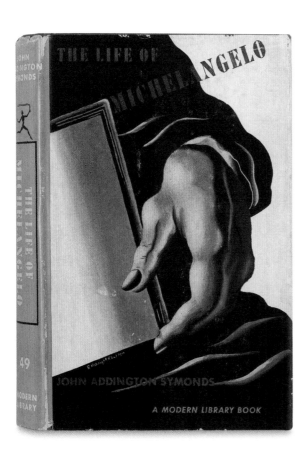

Art Now
Herbert Read
Faber and Faber · 1933
207 × 142 mm · 8⅛ × 5⅝ in.

By the time Kauffer was commissioned
to design the jacket for this influential
book by the art critic Herbert Read,
his visual vocabulary was becoming
increasingly confident in its formalized
use of space. Later editions used the
same design but with red instead
of blue.

The Life of Michelangelo
John Addington Symonds
Modern Library
(New York) · 1941
185 × 125 mm · 7¼ × 5 in.

Kauffer combined Renaissance
realism with Futurist typography in
Random House's Modern Library
edition of Symonds's biography,
first published in 1883.

Intruder in the Dust
William Faulkner
Random House
(New York) · 1948
210 × 140 mm · 8¼ × 5½ in.

Faulkner's novel explores racial
tension in Mississippi through the
story of a black farmer accused of
killing a white man. Kauffer's almost
oppressive visual tension between
symbolism and realism provides
an appropriate way into the book.

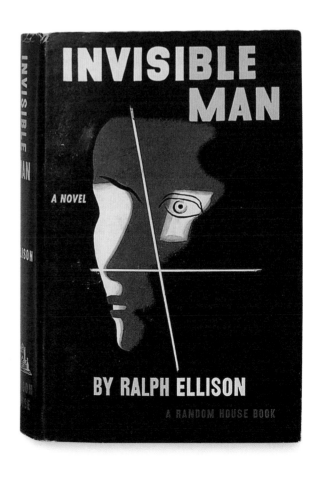

Looking Backward
Edward Bellamy
Modern Library
(New York) · 1942
184 × 125 mm · 7¼ × 5 in.

Bellamy's enormously influential
utopian novel was first published in
1888 and set in the distant year of
2000. Kauffer designed many jackets
for the Modern Library series.

Invisible Man
Ralph Ellison
Random House
(New York) · 1952
210 × 140 mm · 8¼ × 5½ in.

This is one of the most widely known of
Kauffer's designs through the popularity
of the novel, narrated by an unnamed
black man. The jacket features a clever
solution to the problem of 'how to
make invisibility visible'. *Invisible Man*
won the US National Book Award for
Fiction in 1953.

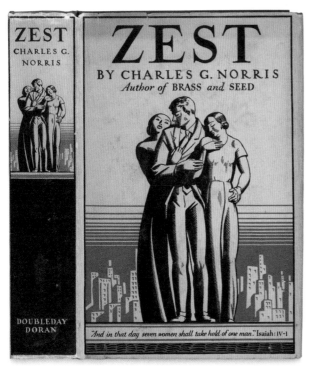

ROCKWELL KENT
USA · 1882–1971

Moby Dick
Herman Melville
Random House (New York) · 1930
220 × 114 mm · 8⅝ × 4½ in.

There was a resurgence of interest in *Moby Dick* in the early 1920s and Rockwell Kent's illustrated edition (initially in three volumes published by Lakeside Press in Chicago, followed by the Random House one-volume trade edition) is thought to have been a factor in the recognition of the book as one of the great American novels. Such was Kent's reputation at this point that his name is prominently displayed on the jacket and Melville's does not appear at all. The dynamic design for the spine is especially impressive.

Zest
Charles G. Norris
Doubleday Doran
(New York) · 1933
216 × 140 mm · 8½ × 5½ in.

Kent's design for *Zest* has strong overtones of figurative sculpture. The classically posed, static figures are picked out in black against the brown cityscape. The design is reproduced on the brown cloth binding beneath. The figure grouping alludes to the novel's exploration of a man's feeling that he needs more than one woman in his life to touch all aspects of his personality.

A key factor in the range and quality of Rockwell Kent's output as an artist is the length and depth of his education. He was born in Tarrytown Heights, New York, and began his artistic training as a schoolboy at the elite Horace Mann School in New York City. Kent studied painting under William Merritt Chase at his summer school in Shinnecock, Long Island, while he was an architecture student at Columbia University; but the lure of painting was such that he dropped out of Columbia before his senior year and enrolled at the New York School of Art, where one of his teachers was the painter Robert Henri. He was later apprenticed to the naturalist and painter Abbott Handerson Thayer in New Hampshire. Kent's subsequent work as an architectural draughtsman and carpenter may have played a role in developing a strong sense of three-dimensional form as well as empathy with, and understanding of, graphic processes.

In 1906, he purchased land on Monhegan Island, Maine, and was profoundly influenced by his time there. He was inspired and awed by the forces of nature, and landscape formed the subject matter of much of his acclaimed painting and printmaking. He was also affected by living in the artistic community on the island and by the lives of the local people, which contributed to his political activism later in life. Kent and his growing family went to Newfoundland in 1914, and over the next twenty-five years he made trips to Alaska, Tierra del Fuego, France, Greenland, Copenhagen, Puerto Rico and Rio de Janeiro. These travels not only resulted in paintings and drawings, but also books that Kent wrote and illustrated, such as *Wilderness* (G.P. Putnam's Sons, 1920) and *Salamina* (Harcourt, Brace, 1935; see p. 29). He also drew on these experiences when illustrating other books, such as an edition of Herman Melville's *Moby Dick* (Random House, 1930).

In the 1920s and 1930s, Kent was one of the leading book illustrators in America. Writing in the *Studio* in 1931, F. J. Harvey Darton analysed his skill: 'Whoever his chosen author, he gets inside his skin. He is that author, for the moment, expressing in pictures, with all the power and range which modern methods permit, what the writer has said in words.'[54] Kent's work in this period also included government commissioned murals and advertising. Influenced by the Symbolists and German Expressionists, he is often grouped with the American Social Realists of the 1930s. Graphically, Kent's work seems to stem from the English tradition, stretching back to William Hogarth and William Blake.

During his early, stellar career, Kent was generally acknowledged to be an artist of genius. However, changing artistic taste from the 1940s onwards and his left-leaning political views and support of radical causes caused a fall in his popularity, particularly during the era of McCarthyism in the early 1950s. In 1950, his passport was revoked by the State Department and was not reinstated until 1958, at which point he started travelling again to Europe and the Soviet Union. He donated a number of his paintings to the Soviet Union, which were divided among four Soviet museums, and in 1966 he was elected to the Academy of Arts of the USSR. Kent always denied being a Communist.

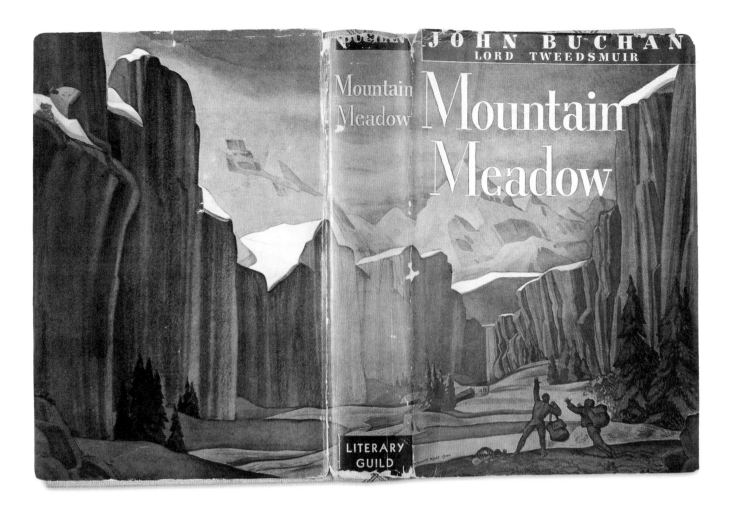

Mountain Meadow
John Buchan
Literary Guild of America
(New York) · 1941
216 × 146 mm · 8½ × 5¼ in.

The artist's lifelong preoccupation
with the drama and beauty of landscape
is given full rein in this spectacular
wraparound design. The exaggerated,
almost heroic, posing of the foreground
figures suggests the influence of Soviet
Realism. Buchan's adventure story
(published the year after his death)
follows Sir Edward Leithen as he travels
in the Canadian Arctic to investigate
a man's mysterious disappearance. No
doubt Kent's own experiences in Alaska
helped him to capture the feel of the
novel's locale. The jacket first appeared
on the Houghton Mifflin (Boston) edition,
published in the same year.

The Decameron
Giovanni Boccaccio
Garden City (New York) · 1949
240 × 162 mm · 9½ × 6⅜ in.

Alongside this trade edition, the
publishers issued a limited two-volume
edition of 1,500 copies signed by Kent
and presented in a slipcase. Both editions
featured thirty-two full-page illustrations
plus headpieces. Although Kent's
popularity was waning by this time, his
name is larger than that of the author's
on this jacket.

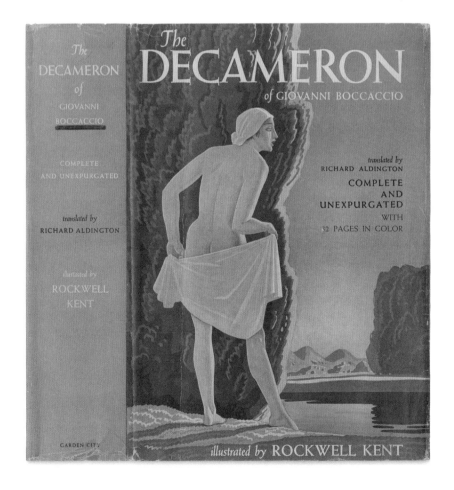

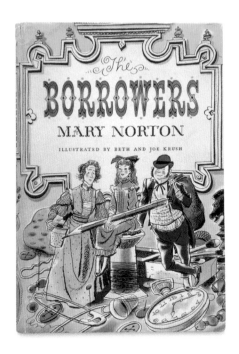
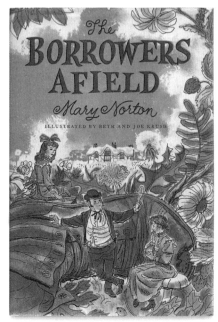
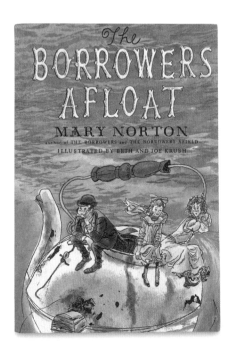

BETH &
JOE KRUSH

USA · Beth 1918–2009 · Joe b. 1918

While there have been a number of husband-and-wife writer-illustrator teams in children's literature down the years, there have not been too many such partnerships purely in the field of children's illustration. The Provensens – Alice and Martin – spring to mind and Leo and Diane Dillon. In all instances, the first question is 'who exactly does what?' And almost always the teams are coy about this aspect of their collaboration. Collective responsibility is key. Even when we have examples of the work done by each person individually, as is the case with the Krushes, we cannot be sure of the nature of the division of labour. In a letter written in 2017, Joe revealed something of their method: 'We utilized our own strong points. Only one person was responsible for the finished artwork in the book. Incidentally, I was responsible for all lettering.'[55]

Joe was born in Camden, New Jersey, and Beth in Washington, DC, and they met on their first day as students at Philadelphia College of Art. They married during the Second World War and from 1948 lived in Wayne, Pennsylvania, on the Main Line. Joe worked as a graphic designer for the Office of Strategic Services, the forerunner of the CIA, in the war and subsequently attended the Nuremberg trials in 1945–46; the sketches he made were published in magazines of the time. He was also responsible for drawing the leaves that became part of the universally recognized United Nations logo.

The couple had not initially intended to work as a team, as Beth explained in a 1988 interview: 'I had my work, my clients, and Joe had his. He did album covers for RCA and I worked for children's magazines. And then we started to help each other, to get the work done.'[56] Gradually, it seems, their work became fused into one. Looking at early commissions attributed to each of them individually, for example Joe's illustrations to *Huon of the Horn* by Andre Norton (Harcourt, Brace, 1951) and Beth's for *The Shoe Bird* by Eudora Welty (Harcourt, Brace, 1964), it is clear that there is a stylistic congruence. Notwithstanding the fact that the two publications are separated by more than a decade, one might argue that Beth's slightly more fluent, confident line is marginally the dominant force. However, considering Joe's jacket design and interior illustrations for Welty's *The Ponder Heart* (Harcourt, Brace, 1954), the drawing and hand-lettering has become indistinguishable from Beth's.

The most familiar of the Krushes' collaborations are their illustrations for the American edition of Mary Norton's classic, *The Borrowers*, along with the four further titles in the series. In the same 1988 interview, Joe explained how they set to work:

> We both read the story separately and we both usually have our own ideas about [it]…Then we sit down together and arrive at the better of the ideas and try to set up the characters. You cast your characters and you set your stage. It's like being a theater director; the only thing you can't do is give it sound and action.[57]

Both Joe and Beth found time to teach illustration, Joe at their alma mater, the Philadelphia College of Art, and Beth at Moore College of Art and Design, the only visual arts college for women in the United States, also in Philadelphia.

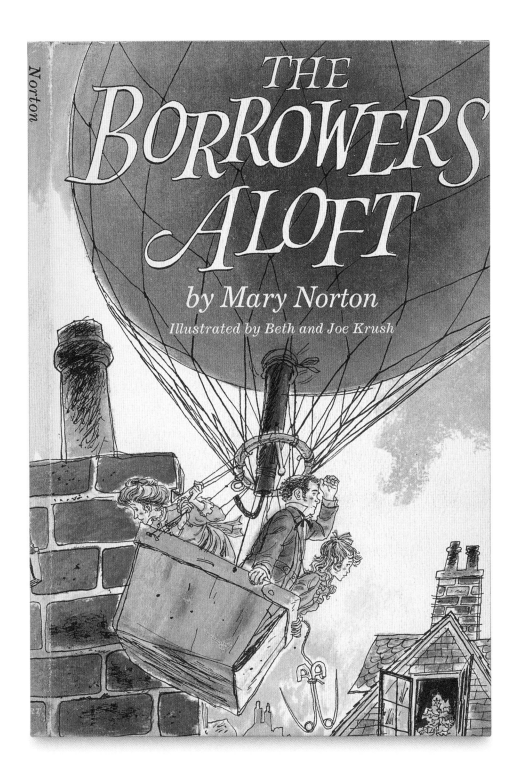

The Borrowers
Mary Norton
Harcourt, Brace and World
(New York) · 1953
210 × 140 mm · 8¼ × 5½ in.

The Borrowers Afield
Mary Norton
Harcourt, Brace and World
(New York) · 1955
210 × 140 mm · 8¼ × 5½ in.

The Borrowers Afloat
Mary Norton
Harcourt, Brace and World
(New York) · 1959
210 × 140 mm · 8¼ × 5½ in.

The Borrowers Aloft
Mary Norton
Harcourt, Brace and World
(New York) · 1961
210 × 140 mm · 8¼ × 5½ in.

Mary Norton's *The Borrowers* series
has been a major factor in bringing the
work of Beth and Joe Krush to a wide
audience. The creative partnership
of the two artists has resulted in
jacket and interior illustrations for
the series that feature highly adept
draughtsmanship and composition
combined with vibrant colour. In their
hands the quintessentially English
setting and tone of Norton's text is
given an unmistakably American
flavour – a visual equivalent perhaps
of Dick Van Dyke's Cockney accent
in the screen adaptation of P. L.
Travers's *Mary Poppins*.

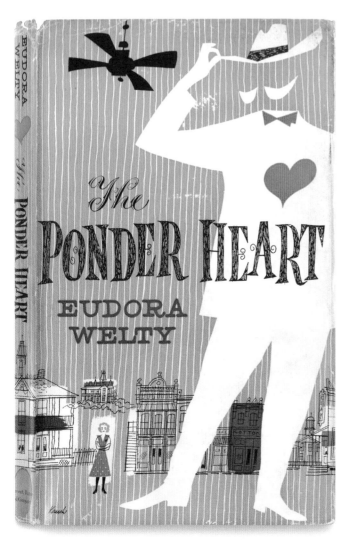

The Ponder Heart
Eudora Welty
Harcourt, Brace (New York) · 1954
210 × 135 mm · 8¼ × 5¼ in.

This early jacket design credited to
Joe Krush, who also produced line
illustrations for the interior, suggests
a slightly more graphic, shape-based
approach to illustration than when
working in partnership with Beth. The
comic generosity of Eudora Welty's
Uncle Daniel character first appeared
in the *New York Times*.

The Shoe Bird
Eudora Welty
Harcourt, Brace and World
(New York) · 1964
235 × 157 mm · 9¼ × 6¼ in.

Eudora Welty's only book written
specifically for children was
illustrated throughout by Beth
Krush, who also designed the
jacket. The use of overprinting to
maximize colour separations and the
cleverly integrated titles make this
a particularly pleasing design.

Return to Gone-Away
Elizabeth Enright
Heinemann · 1962
200 × 135 mm · 7⅞ × 5⅜ in.

This novel by the American children's author (and niece of the architect Frank Lloyd Wright) Elizabeth Enright was a sequel to her successful *Gone-Away Lake*, also illustrated by the Krushes. It follows the summer adventures of Portia and Foster Blake as their family restores a Victorian mansion near the ghostly Gone-Away Lake. The subtle overlaying of available colours and clever use of negative space to accentuate the fall of light from the window are features of this design. The book was first published by Harcourt, Brace and World in the US in 1961.

Miracles on Maple Hill
Virginia Sorensen
Harcourt, Brace and World · 1956
204 × 140 mm · 8 × 5½ in.

Awarded the Newbery Medal in 1957 'for the most distinguished contribution to American literature for children', Virginia Sorensen's uplifting human story is one of the Krushes' best-known collaborations. The jacket design delicately balances line, flat colour and a half-tone screen for the grey.

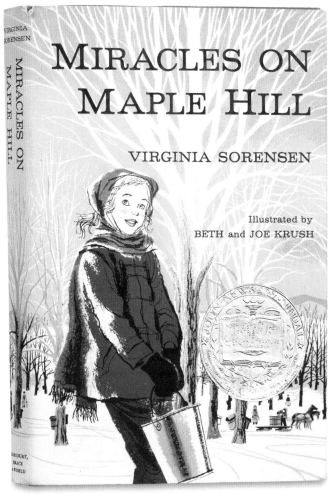

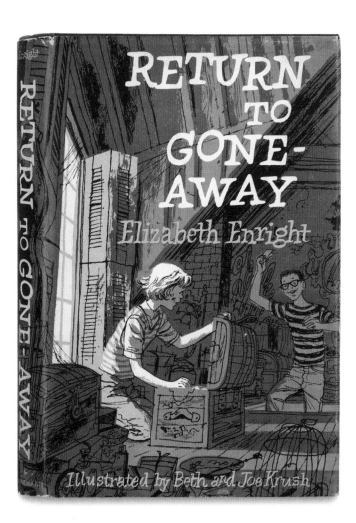

The Sheltering Sky
Paul Bowles
New Directions
(New York) · 1949
213 × 146 mm · 8⅜ × 5¼ in.

Lustig's first jacket for a New
Directions book was for Henry
Miller's *Wisdom of the Heart* (1941).
James Laughlin, the founding
publisher of New Directions,
continued commissioning dust jackets
from Lustig until the designer's
early death in 1955. Lustig's highly
conceptual approach to design brought
an instantly recognizable 'branding'
to the publications.

A Handful of Dust
Evelyn Waugh
New Directions
(New York) · 1945
185 × 125 mm · 7¼ × 5 in.

James Laughlin wrote in *Print*
magazine in Oct/Nov 1956 that
'opening each envelope from Lustig
was a new excitement because the
range of fresh invention seemed to
have no limits'. Lustig took a slightly
more literal, pictorial approach than
usual when designing the jacket
for this edition of Waugh's semi-
autobiographical novel.

The Wanderer
Alain Fournier
New Directions
(New York) · 1946
232 × 170 mm · 9⅛ × 6⅝ in.

Lustig's jacket design for Alain
Fournier's only novel (first
published in France as *Le Grand
Meulnes* in 1913) suggests the book's
theme of search for the transient and
unobtainable through the motif
of the leaf.

A Season in Hell
Arthur Rimbaud
New Directions
(New York) · 1945
184 × 125 mm · 7¼ × 5 in.

It is worth comparing Keith
Vaughan's design for the 1949 John
Lehmann edition of *A Season in Hell*
(p. 183) to this one by Lustig. There
is a marked contrast between Lustig's
minimalist amalgam of pictorial
symbol and text and Vaughan's
grittily textured neo-romanticism.
Each design helped to build a clear
visual identity for the literary
ambitions of the publisher.

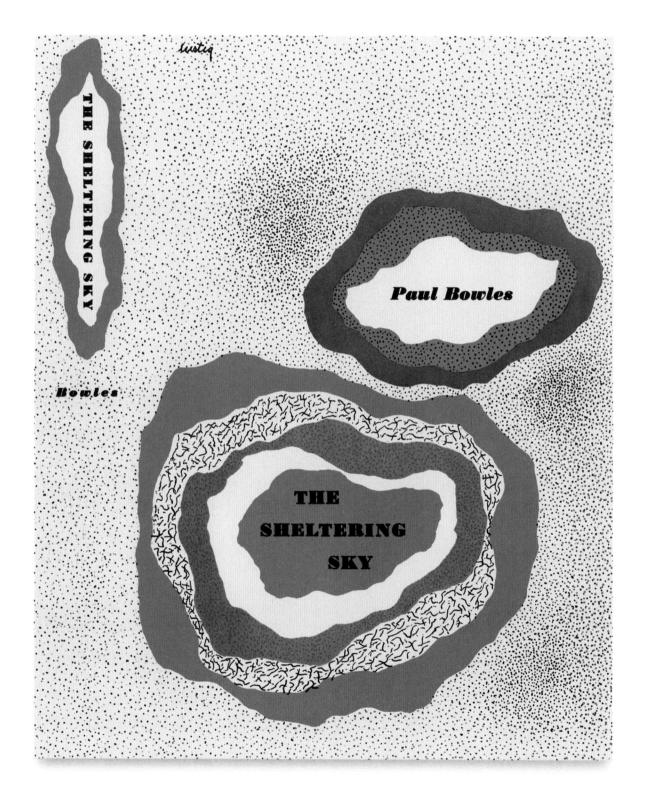

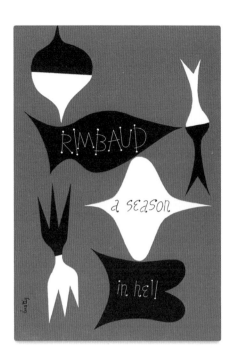

ALVIN LUSTIG

USA · 1915–1955

Whether or not the more pictorial of Alvin Lustig's brilliant dust-jacket designs could be described as *illustration* is debatable. What is clear is that whether suggesting recognizable forms or working entirely with geometric shape and pattern, Lustig's primary concern was for *design*, with control of all aspects of his dust-jackets' identity and, where relevant, that of the series in which it was situated. It might also be argued that his unique visual vocabulary elevated design in this particular context to the status of art.

Lustig was an artist who chose design as the area best suited to express his ideas. As a Modernist, his approach was considered highly innovative and challenging by many people during the 1940s and early 1950s. Initially, some of his work incorporated motifs, shapes, lines and textures that referenced the work of his artistic peers, such as Joan Miró. Alongside (and informing) his commissioned work, Lustig constantly explored his talent through painting, drawing and printing. He used the process of letterpress printing to create abstract, geometric designs and did typographic experiments with wood and metal.

In the context of the design of a dust jacket these innovations were never gratuitous but were always employed in the service of a distillation of the book's content and spirit into simple but powerful visual form (or in the words of another designer of the period, Abram Games: 'maximum meaning, minimum means'). Lustig felt strongly that literal or naturalistic representation of specific events within a text was reductive.

In many ways, Alvin Lustig was ahead of his time in his propagation of the idea of designer as author and artist. As with Barnett Freedman in the UK, he despaired at what he saw as the false barriers placed between art and design. Besides doing dust jackets, Lustig moved freely between architectural design and that of furniture, interior spaces, textiles, signage systems and more. To him, design was almost a religion – a means of making the world a better place – and he disseminated his strong views on the importance and role of design through lectures and art school teaching. His impact is all the more astonishing given his tragically short life. Having contracted an incurable form of diabetes in his teens, Lustig lost his eyesight in 1954 at the age of 39. Even then, he continued to design, with the assistance of his wife, Elaine, who was able to help him realize the concepts that still formed in his mind's eye. But he soon succumbed to the disease and died the following year, leaving a prodigious body of highly influential work that has been rediscovered in recent years and received the recognition it deserves.

The Growth of the Book Jacket
Charles Rosner
Harvard University Press · 1954
239 × 170 mm · 9⅜ × 6⅝ in.

Rosner's important survey of dust
jackets, ranging from the earliest-
known 19th-century examples through
to the 1950s was published five years
after the exhibition 'The Art of the
Book Jacket' that he organized at
the Victoria and Albert Museum in
London. Lustig's highly conceptual
jacket design was one of his last.

A Street Car Named Desire
Tennessee Williams
New Directions
(New York) · 1947
235 × 159 mm · 9¼ × 6¼ in.

The human figure, gender and
narrative themes are rendered down
to primitive representations of shape
and colour for the jacket of the first
edition of Tennessee Williams's
Pulitzer Prize-winning play.

Anatomy for Interior Designers
Francis de N. Schroeder
Whitney Publications
(New York) · 1948
260 × 235 mm · 10¼ × 9¼ in.

Lustig's distinctive hand-rendered
lettering was a key pictorial feature
of the early editions of this striking
jacket design. Sadly, in later editions
this was removed and replaced by
a font – a rather ill-fitting Akzidenz-
Grotesk Bold.

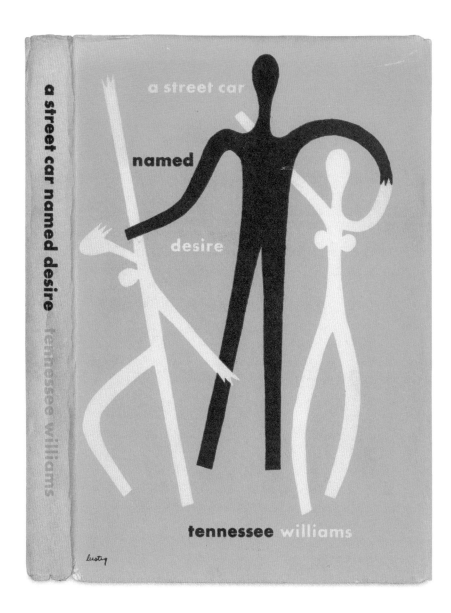

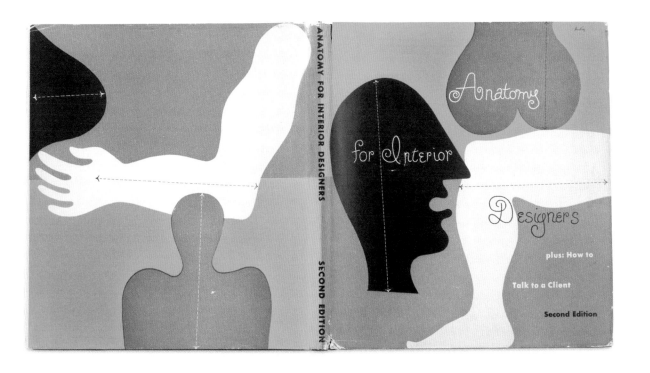

ROBERT MICKLEWRIGHT
UK · 1923–2013

A stalwart of illustration in Britain in the 1950s and 1960s, Robert Micklewright was often described as 'the illustrator's illustrator'.[58] This was perhaps attributable to his professionalism and reliability as much as to his exacting formal draughtsmanship. He was a regular contributor of black-and-white line drawings to *Radio Times* for many years and his book illustrations spanned from the 1950s to the 1980s.

Micklewright was born in West Bromwich but grew up in South London, enrolled at Croydon School of Art in 1939 and then moved to Wimbledon School of Art. His studies were interrupted in 1942 when he was called up; his company commander in the Rifle Brigade was the glass engraver Laurence Whistler. After the war, he returned to Wimbledon to continue his studies and was then admitted to the Slade School of Fine Art. The Slade was very much a fine-art painting school and Micklewright later observed that it 'wasn't an awful lot of use to ordinary mortals like myself'.[59] Like many of those whose studies were interrupted by the war, he was also conscious of being much older than the other students, and he married while studying at the Slade. However, this very formal training, which involved drawing and painting from the model on a daily basis for the best part of three years, clearly served him well in terms of underpinning his work with secure draughtsmanship.

All of Micklewright's drawings, illustrations and paintings are painstakingly constructed and immaculately structured. His working process involved cutting up drawings and moving them around, recomposing over and over again until satisfied with the finished result. As with all illustrators working in an essentially realist or representational idiom in pre-Internet days, the working day involved regular trips to the local library to research geographical and historical settings, the building of a substantial collection of visual references, and drawing from direct observation wherever possible. He cited Leonard Rosoman as a key influence on his work, remarking, 'I remember seeing his drawings and, in a sort of blinding flash, I suddenly knew how to do black-and white-drawings.'[60]

Designing dust jackets was one of many important areas of Robert Micklewright's freelance career. Here again, the work is characterized by carefully constructed figure compositions and total command of media. Early jackets mostly involved the creation of separate artwork for each colour for letterpress line-block printing, sometimes using mechanical tints to add texture. Later, as offset lithography took hold, his jackets were painted as full-colour artworks, for example in his designs for children's books by Malcolm Saville in the 1970s.

Homecomings
C. P. Snow
Macmillan · 1956
190 × 121 mm · 7½ × 4¾ in.

Using just two available colours, Micklewright employs a night-day metaphor for this jacket. The contrasting houses no doubt reflect the two marriages of the protagonist Lewis Eliot in C. P. Snow's sixth published novel (but seventh in the sequence) in the *Strangers and Brothers* series. It follows Eliot's life in the Second World War, including the suicide of his first wife.

Excelsior!
Paul Hyde Bonner
André Deutsch · 1955
204 × 140 mm · 8 × 5½ in.

The American diplomat and novelist Bonner wrote a number of books of international intrigue. With this jacket Micklewright ably conveys the fashionable glamour of the story of the machinations of a Swiss banker's family. He gains maximum impact with only three available colours by using a mechanical tint and sparingly revealing the unprinted white of the paper to pick out details such as the glove and pearls of the foreground figure. It would have been printed letterpress.

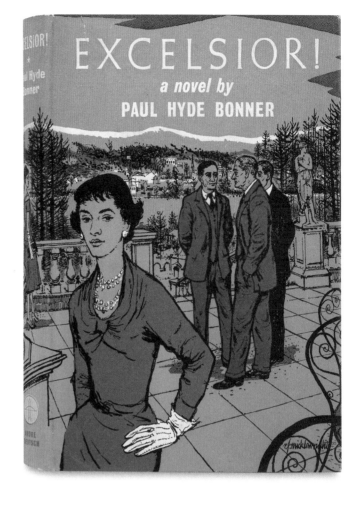

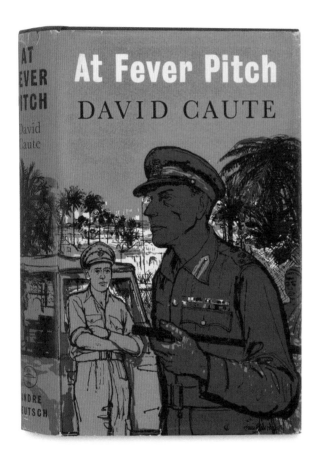

At Fever Pitch
David Caute
André Deutsch · 1959
190 × 130 mm · 7½ × 5⅛ in.

Caute's first novel is set in an unnamed African country that is about to achieve independence from the British. Micklewright's jacket design is one of his best known, evoking the heat and tension of the novel's theme. The book won the John Llewellyn Rhys prize in 1960.

Country Practice
Hubert Bagster
André Deutsch · 1957
216 × 140 mm · 8½ × 5½ in.

The limited use of a mechanical tint to describe the shadow cast by the portico gives extra depth and texture to this design. The window cleverly curves around the spine.

The Derelict Day:
Poems in Germany
Alan Ross
John Lehmann · 1947
195 × 130 mm · 7¾ × 5⅛ in.

One of Minton's earliest jacket designs for John Lehmann, this is now one of the most collectable. The classic Minton overhead view and sombre tones capture the mood of Ross's poems.

French Country Cooking
Elizabeth David
Macdonald · 1958
204 × 135 mm · 8 × 5⅜ in.

The success of David's revolutionary books must owe at least a little to the brilliance of Minton's jacket designs. They provide a perfect visual counterpart to the books' sensuous exploration of Gallic culinary culture. This 1958 Macdonald reprint reproduces the original 1951 design for John Lehmann.

Time Was Away:
A Notebook in Corsica
Alan Ross
John Lehmann · 1948
240 × 170 mm · 9½ × 6¼ in.

Arguably one of the most spectacular dust-jacket designs of the twentieth century, this must have seemed particularly exotic and alluring in the postwar austerity of 1948. Lehmann funded Ross and Minton's trip to Corsica.

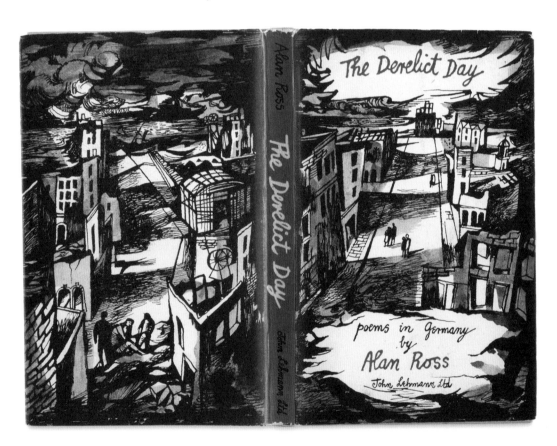

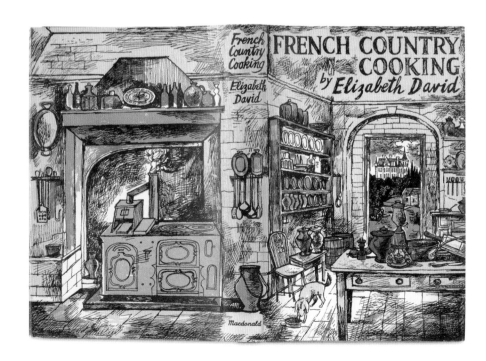

JOHN MINTON
UK · 1917–1957

In the heady decade between the end of the Second World War and the mid-1950s the illustrations of John Minton achieved a standard and status that has rarely been matched since. At its best, Minton's graphic work was sublime, but at its worst, in the years of decline with a troubled personal life, running up to his premature death at the age of thirty-nine, it was almost unrecognizable. As a painter, Minton never achieved the recognition that he craved. To some extent this may have been attributable to establishment prejudices that have often been a disincentive for artists to engage with both the fine and commercial arts. Minton's popularity and wide exposure as a virtuoso illustrator may have counted against him.

The publisher John Lehmann commissioned much of Minton's finest work, including books that were fully illustrated by him such as *Time Was Away: A Notebook in Corsica* (1948), a key twentieth-century illustrated book that was produced in collaboration with the writer Alan Ross after the two spent some weeks on the island. Minton's designs for Elizabeth David's highly influential cookery books for Lehmann were also among the highlights – *A Book of Mediterranean Food* (1950; p. 25) followed by *French Country Cooking* (1951). As well as producing sublimely evocative dust-jacket designs by means of letterpress line-block

separations, Minton illustrated the books throughout with elegant black-and-white line drawings. The Elizabeth David books opened up a new world of cuisine to the British public and Minton's illustrations described Mediterranean culture in its broadest sense, complementing and enhancing the writing.

Over a period of ten to twelve years, John Minton produced a prodigious amount of commissioned graphic work, in book and magazine illustration, advertising, mural, poster and wallpaper design and more. In all, he designed sixty-one dust jackets, many for Lehmann but also for the plethora of small, independent publishers of the day including Rupert Hart-Davis, Secker & Warburg, André Deutsch and Chatto & Windus. Where he was able to use his distinctive free flowing, hand-rendered typography the overall design of the jackets was fully integrated, image and text working seamlessly together. Minton relished the challenge posed by the limitations of the line-block letterpress printing process, cleverly producing separations for each of two, three or four colours, while only able to see the final image in his mind's eye.

Minton was, by all accounts, a generous teacher in his role as tutor in the painting school at the Royal College of Art. His manic personality and chaotic life are strongly hinted at in contemporary paintings of him. Lucian Freud's tiny, intense portrait of Minton (1952) hangs in the Senior Common Room of the Royal College of Art and is almost painful in its depiction of internal agony. Rodrigo Moynihan's *Portrait Group, 1951* (Tate) is a posed study of the staff of the RCA painting school, with Minton seated to the left of the group, looking detached and haunted.

Rain on the Pavements
Roland Camberton
John Lehmann · 1951
204 × 134 mm · 8 × 5¼ in.

Camberton's two novels of London life have been rediscovered and republished in the last few years, largely thanks to the keen interest of writer Iain Sinclair. He memorably described the 1950s jacket designs of Lehmann's books as 'having the louche swagger to complement an edgily cosmopolitan list'.[61] Camberton's other novel, *Scamp* (1950), also featured a jacket design by Minton.

Let it Come Down
Paul Bowles
John Lehmann · 1952
200 × 140 mm · 7⅞ × 5½ in.

Minton was the perfect artist to represent Bowles's writings of the seedy underbelly of North African expatriate life. Compare Minton's treatment of the book to Edward McKnight Kauffer's design for the American edition (p. 29).

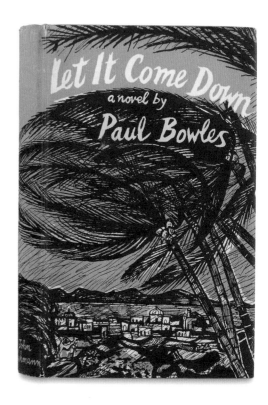

Heirs of the Wind
Michele Prisco
Derek Verschoyle · 1953
225 × 140 mm · 8⅞ × 5½ in.

Although uncredited, this wraparound design for short-lived publisher Derek Verschoyle shows Minton at his best. First published in Italy in 1950 as *Gli eredi del vento*, this was the second novel by the upcoming Italian writer Michele Prisco.

The Pocket Guide to the West Indies
Sir Algernon Aspinall
Methuen · 1954
170 × 110 mm · 6¾ × 4⅜ in.

A visit to Jamaica informed Minton's
treatment of the jacket for this small-
scale (though rather substantial for
'pocket' sized) guide. The lush greens
are created by overlaying the yellow
and blue line-block separations.

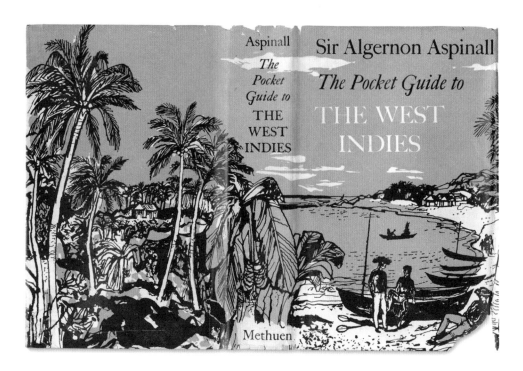

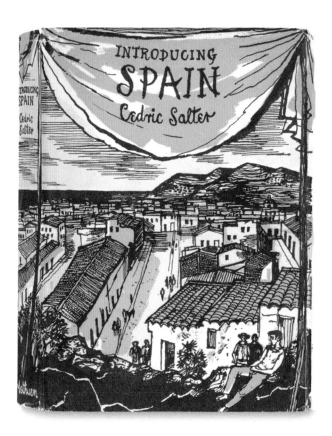

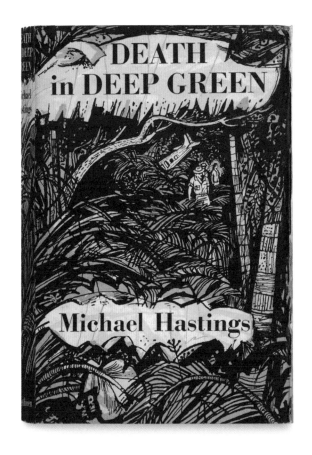

Introducing Spain
Cedric Salter
Methuen · 1953
200 × 140 mm · 7⅞ × 5½ in.

By the time he undertook this
commission, Minton had visited and
painted in Spain. This jacket features
many of his favourite motifs, including
the languid male foreground figure,
the elevated street view, and hand
lettering over draped cloth.

Death in Deep Green
Michael Hastings
Methuen · 1952
190 × 125 mm · 7½ × 5 in.

Minton was particularly known for
his flair in rendering lush tropical
vegetation. In Michael Hastings's
adventure a plane crashes in the
Malaysian jungle and the passengers
are left to fend for themselves. Once
again, the artist overlays colour
separations to great effect.

Touch the Harvest Moon
Madeleine Myers
Henry Holt (New York) · 1955
210 × 140 mm · 8¼ × 5½ in.

One of the few jackets designed by
Mitchell other than *Catcher in the
Rye*, this exhibits the same linear
panache as his more famous work.
The novel follows the fortunes of
20-year-old Lydia Wayne and her
brother, Rod, when they inherit
a farm in New England.

E. MICHAEL
MITCHELL
USA · 1920–2009

Whatever the qualities of his wider body of work, and they were
considerable, E. Michael Mitchell will be largely remembered
for one particular, instantly recognizable piece of graphic art:
his design for the jacket of J. D. Salinger's seminal novel *The
Catcher in the Rye*. Published in 1951, it has sold over sixty-five
million copies in most of the world's major languages. Mitchell's
dramatic jacket design has become a 'logo' for the book. It draws
loosely on the final scene at a carousel in Central Park, New
York, but is primarily a highly charged, eye-catcher. With the
merest glimpse of the yellow type over cascading red we know
which book this is.

Mitchell was born in Toronto, Canada, and served in the
Royal Air Force in the Second World War, seeing active service
in Britain and mainland Europe. After the war, he studied
at Ontario College of Art and then moved to the US, where
he contributed illustrations to a number of the more stylish
magazines, including *Cosmopolitan* and *Collier's*, from 1948 to
1953. These illustrations, often printed in two or three colours,
are characterized by supremely assured draughtsmanship and
dynamic composition.

Salinger and Mitchell were neighbours and friends in
Westport, Connecticut, when Salinger was writing *The Catcher
in the Rye*. The two would visit each other's houses regularly.
Mitchell was working on a variety of commercial commissions
and exhibiting, as well as being one of the instructors at the
Famous Artists School, a highly successful art correspondence
course based in Westport. As Salinger's fame grew and he
became increasingly reclusive, he moved to New Hampshire.
Thereafter, the friendship between him and Mitchell continued
mostly through a regular correspondence that ranged over
more than forty years; some of their letters are now held
in the Morgan Library in New York.

From the late 1970s Mitchell worked mainly as a concept
artist for animation and film, based in Southern California. He
was employed on many well-known TV series and contributed
substantially to a number of successful films, the latter including
Flash Gordon (1980) and *FernGully: The Last Rainforest* (1982).
In his later years he taught drawing to animation students at
CalArts (California Institute of the Arts), near Los Angeles.
As a teacher, he was highly regarded for his innovative approach
and artistic integrity, and is fondly remembered by generations
of former students.

Like that of his friend Salinger, E. Michael Mitchell's life
is somewhat shrouded in mystery and myth but there are
glimpses of him quietly discussing his approaches to life
drawing in short videos made by his students at CalArts. His
striking appearance, with piratical eye patch, contrasts with
his unassuming modesty as he explains that 'I try to keep one
foot in the Renaissance and one in the contemporary world…
[I'm] healthily schizophrenic.' When asked about his dust-
jacket design for *Catcher*, he mumbles, 'that was a minor project.
Salinger was a friend. I did that as a favour for him.'[62]

Catcher in the Rye
J. D. Salinger
Little, Brown (Boston) · 1951
220 × 146 mm · 8⅜ × 5¼ in.

Instantly recognizable and universal,
E. Michael Mitchell's jacket design
for one of the most successful novels
of all time is inseparable from it in
the consciousness of most American
readers. The first edition and initial
Book Club edition featured a
photograph of Salinger on the back
of the jacket. The famously reclusive
author insisted on its removal from
subsequent editions.

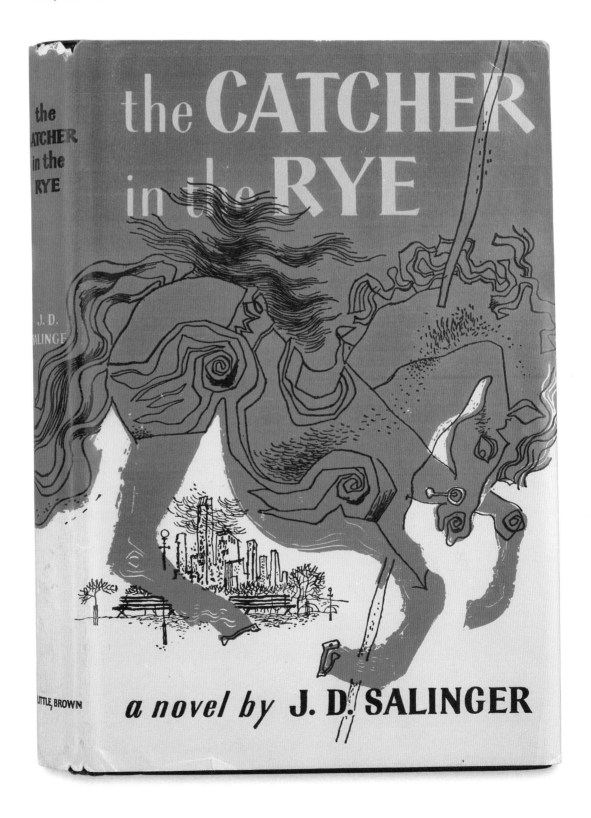

JOHN NASH

UK · 1893–1977

John Nash is often described as a 'countryman' and 'plantsman', and he lived for much of his life in the country, first in Buckinghamshire and then from 1943 until his death at Bottengoms farm in Wormingford, Essex. He was a painter of landscapes, cornfields, rolling hills and brooding woodlands. In the First World War he joined the Artists' Rifles and was later appointed an official war artist. His most famous painting, *Over the Top* (1918), now hangs in the Imperial War Museum. He was also a prolific and highly regarded illustrator and the subject matter of his commissions tended to reflect his interest in the natural world.

Nash's older brother, Paul, is generally regarded as the 'senior' painter of the two but Paul himself was extremely protective of his younger sibling's talents and his sensitive 'untrained eye'. John initially planned a career as a journalist but was further encouraged to pursue painting by the artist Claughton Pellew-Harvey, who had studied with Paul at the Slade School of Art.

He and John shared walking and painting trips to the North Norfolk coast, but John did not undertake any formal art training.

An early influence on the young Nash brothers was the work of the painter and humorist Edward Lear. The brothers' Aunt Gussie had been a close friend of Lear and she owned many of his paintings and drawings. She introduced her nephews to Lear's nonsense verse and drawings and John's humorous drawings display a similarly anarchic tendency, especially in early work such as the illustrations for *Dressing Gowns and Glue* by Lance Sieveking (Cecil Palmer & Hayward, 1919). Nash's irrepressible visual humour was evidenced by a tendency to cover his correspondence with comic drawings.[63] But the majority of his work as a painter and illustrator is characterized by an almost naïve directness, unhindered by any fluency or facility in draughtsmanship. This extends to his excursions into the exacting craft of wood engraving, where his use of the graver is awkward and almost clumsy.

John Nash's dust-jacket designs for Batsford's *British Nature Library* editions of 1938 were produced through the process of autolithography, where each colour to be printed was drawn separately by the artist straight onto the lithographic plate or stone. The results have a directness and rustic charm. Nash modestly said of his lithography: 'I strove nobly and long, but I never mastered the craft.'[64]

Men and the Fields
Adrian Bell
B. T. Batsford · 1939
220 × 140 mm · 8⅝ × 5½ in.

This exquisite collaboration of words
and pictures by two countrymen
friends is perhaps best described by
the writer Ronald Blythe, who was
a lifelong friend of John Nash: 'The
book evokes in the purest of terms the
last moments of the great agricultural
depression. Both writer and artist
knew farming only in the slump.
A second war would bring subsidies
and, for a while, unprecedented
wealth. But it would also destroy
the apparently timeless universe
of *Men and the Fields*.[65]

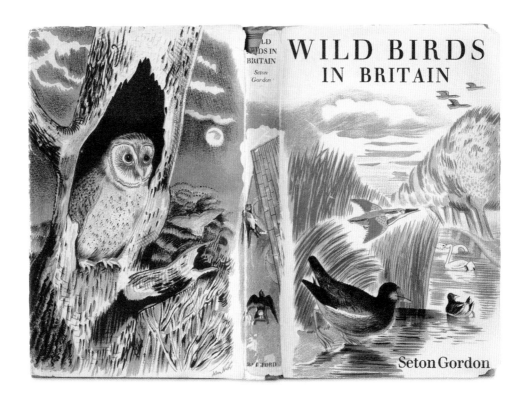

Wild Birds in Britain
Seton Gordon
B. T. Batsford · 1938
220 × 140 mm · 8⅝ × 5½ in.

Wild Animals in Britain
Frances Pitt · B. T. Batsford · 1938
220 × 140 mm · 8⅝ × 5½ in.

Batsford's *British Nature Library* titles,
which also included *Wild Flowers
of Britain*, drew on Nash's extensive
knowledge of the subject matter.

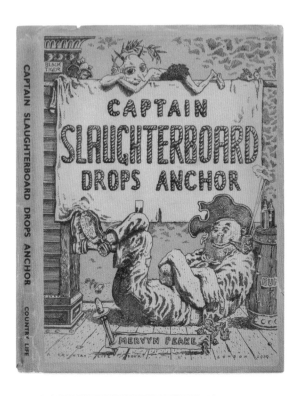

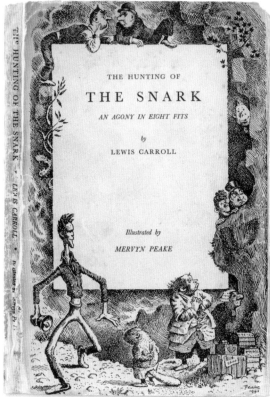

MERVYN PEAKE
UK · 1911–1968

The remarkable pictorial imagination of Mervyn Peake was at the root of all aspects of a creative output that included painting, illustration, novels, poetry and plays. The highly visual nature of his own writing is evident throughout his best-known work, the *Gormenghast* trilogy, published between 1946 and 1959.

Peake did not begin illustrating books until his late twenties, despite having painted and drawn all his life, when his first book, *Captain Slaughterboard Drops Anchor*, was published by Noel Carrington at *Country Life* in 1939. Many copies of the first edition were destroyed during the Blitz (making those that survived extremely collectable) but the book was reprinted in 1945, rather less lavishly due to postwar shortages. *Shapes and Sounds*, a collection of Peake's poetry, was published by Chatto & Windus in 1941, with the artist's intricately rendered dust-jacket design. He went on to illustrate many important works of literature including *Alice in Wonderland* and *Treasure Island*. Despite having such a powerful and instantly recognizable visual vocabulary, Peake recognized that a key aspect of the art of illustration is the ability to find a way into the inner world of the writer: 'there must be above all things the power to slide into another man's soul.'[66]

Peake had been born in China, in the hill town of Kuling, in Kiang-Hsi (Jiangxi) Province. His parents were Congregationalist missionaries and the first twelve years of his life were spent mostly in Tientsin (Tianjin), southeast of Beijing. The family returned to England in 1923, and in 1929, after a brief spell at Croydon School of Art, Peake attended the Royal Academy Schools.

In the years running up to the publication of *Slaughterboard*, Peake primarily devoted himself to painting and had his first one-man show at the Calmann Gallery in London in 1938. He would continue to paint, but it is for his writing and illustration that he is best remembered. In 1940, Peake joined the Royal Artillery, his application to become an official war artist having been turned down. Later, he was given special dispensation by his commanding officer to continue writing his novel *Titus Groan* (1946). It was during the war that Peake's interest in illustration grew. He was commissioned by Chatto & Windus to illustrate *The Hunting of the Snark* (1941) and spent time studying the techniques of many of the great narrative artists, such as Francisco de Goya, Albrecht Dürer, Honoré Daumier, William Hogarth and George Cruikshank. He left the Army in 1942. In June 1945, with a commission from the *Leader* magazine, he visited the liberated concentration camp at Bergen-Belsen and did several drawings of the terrible scenes he saw there.

The immediate postwar years were the most productive of Peake's career, in terms of both writing and illustration. By the late 1950s, however, he was showing early symptoms of dementia. He continued to work and to teach at the Central School of Art for some years more. Peake died in 1968 at a nursing home run by his brother-in-law at Burcot, near Oxford.

Captain Slaughterboard
Drops Anchor
Mervyn Peake
Country Life · 1939
255 × 190 mm · 10 × 7½ in.

Copies of this edition of Peake's first book, illustrated throughout, are rare since most of the print run was destroyed by enemy action during the war, the outbreak of which coincided with publication. A second edition was produced in 1945 with plates coloured by Peake.

The Hunting of the Snark
Lewis Carroll
Chatto & Windus · 1941
210 × 135 mm · 8¼ × 5⅜ in.

Peake was the ideal choice to illustrate Lewis Carroll's nonsense verse, some sixty years or so after the original publication. In 1948, Chatto issued a slightly smaller edition under the Zodiac Books imprint with the illustrations printed on a yellow paper dust jacket.

Grimm's Household Tales
Eyre & Spottiswood · 1946
210 × 170 mm · 8¼ × 6¾ in.

Text and image are kept apart on
this early postwar edition of *Grimm's
Household Tales*. Inside, Peake
contributed a striking full-colour,
hand-lettered design for the title page
and further colour and black-and-
white illustrations.

Witchcraft in England
Christina Hole
B. T. Batsford · 1945
225 × 150 mm · 8⅞ × 5⅞ in.

The choice of Peake to illustrate this
survey of English witchcraft lore was
highly appropriate. The jacket blurb
on the second edition, printed the same
year, describes the book as 'luridly
embellished by Mervyn Peake with
many macabre drawings', which are
'in striking contrast to the objectivity
of the writing'. The wraparound jacket
was printed in two-colour half-tone.
The image perhaps shows the influence
of Peake's visit to Bergen-Belsen
concentration camp in June 1945.

Who Goes Home
Maurice Edelman
Alan Wingate · 1952
190 × 130 mm · 7½ × 5⅛ in.

Edelman was a journalist, novelist
and Member of Parliament. The title
of this, his second novel, is taken from
the traditional cry at the end of each
Parliamentary day in the Palace of
Westminster. Peake's design for the
jacket is rather let down by the poor
quality of the half-tone reproduction.

Harlequin Phoenix
Thelma Niklaus
The Bodley Head · 1956
232 × 167 mm · 9⅛ × 6½ in.

The dust-jacket design is repeated
on the title page of Niklaus's history
of the figure of Harlequin from his
origins in Italian *commedia dell'arte*.

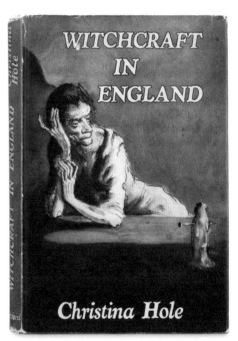

CELESTINO PIATTI

Switzerland · 1922–2007

The Swiss graphic artist Celestino Piatti was best known for his poster designs, of which he designed more than five hundred, winning many national and international awards, but he worked across many areas of design including children's books, book-cover and dust-jacket design. He was born in Wangen-Brüttisellen in the canton of Zurich, the son of a Ticino stonemason, and studied for a year at the Kunstgewerbeschule (School of Applied Arts) in Zurich. Piatti then spent four years as an apprentice at a Swiss printing studio in Basel under the tutelage of Fritz Bühler. (It is interesting to note that Ben Shahn learned his craft in a similar manner.) During this time, Piatti continued his education by taking evening classes at his old school. In 1948, he set up a studio of his own in collaboration with his wife, Marianne Piatti-Stricker.

During his lifetime Piatti's poster designs featured in exhibitions throughout the world. In 1959, he was awarded first prize at the Foire internationale de Lyon in France. By the early 1960s his standing was such that he was entrusted by the newly established Munich publishing house Deutscher Taschenbuch Verlag (DTV) with the typography and graphic design of the firm's paperbacks, along with the advertising and promotional material. He created the company's image, or 'brand' as it would now be known, with his distinctively muscular use of line along with the typeface Akzidenz-Grotesk printed in black against a white background. Over the course of thirty years he designed most of DTV's books. Examples of his work can be found in the collections of museums and galleries in Munich, Zurich and Stockholm.

Animals were a constant presence in Celestino Piatti's work and the motif of the owl in particular makes a regular appearance (in 1964 he even wrote and illustrated a book called *The Happy Owls*). When asked about this for a magazine interview in 1992 he is said to have commented, 'You can draw an owl a thousand times, and never find out its secret.'

The Golden Apple
Celestino Piatti and Max Bolliger
The Bodley Head · 1970
304 × 216 mm · 12 × 8½ in.

In this moral tale by the Swiss children's author Max Bolliger, each animal considers the golden apple in the forest belongs to him but in the end none can obtain it. Piatti's animals tended to be depicted as static designs rather than as animated characters. He delighted in their shapes and here anchors them with heavy outlines.

'n HAUM-kinderboek
vertel deur Kalie Heese
en geïllustreer deur Celestino Piatti

Die Kersnag

Der Kersnag: die verhaal van die geboorte van Christus (Christmas Eve: The Story of Christ's Birth)
Kalie Heese
HAUM (Cape Town) · 1969
206 × 292 mm · 8⅛ × 11½ in.

In this retelling of the Christmas story for children, Piatti combined subtle layering of light tones over dark to create a painterly moonlit scene of Joseph and Mary.

Graphis Annual 58/59
Amstutz & Herdeg, Graphis Press (Zurich) · 1958
305 × 240 mm · 12 × 9½ in.

Piatti's owl motif makes an appearance on the jacket of this who's who of international graphic design. However many times the owl was used, Piatti found new and original ways to employ him.

The Unquiet Grave
Palinurus · Hamish Hamilton · 1945
210 × 140 mm · 8¼ × 5½ in.

One of Piper's best-known jacket designs makes use of the artist's keen interest in collecting rubbings from headstones. Palinurus was a pseudonym (taken from a character in Virgil's *Aeneid*) of the literary critic Cyril Connolly. The book consists of aphorisms and musings on being 40. It was first published in 1944 by *Horizon* magazine, which Connolly edited.

The Castles on the Ground
J. M. Richards
Architectural Press · 1946
216 × 140 mm · 8½ × 5½ in.

J. M. Richards, editor of the *Architectural Review*, and Piper collaborated on this rather patronizing celebration of English suburban style. Piper's three-colour jacket and two-colour interior lithographs revel in the subject matter.

South
William Sansom
Hodder & Stoughton · 1948
210 × 140 mm · 8¼ × 5½ in.

Piper's jacket design for William Sansom's collection of short stories set in Corsica, Italy and the Riviera uses his favoured classical columns as a framing device, as with his designs for Murray's *Architectural Guides*.

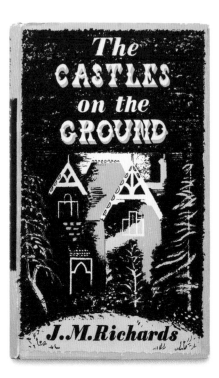

JOHN PIPER

UK · 1903–1992

John Piper's work across so many areas of art and design perhaps places him as one of the best examples of the polymath that it was still possible to be in the mid-twentieth century. As with his English contemporaries, Edward Bawden, Eric Ravilious and Barnett Freedman, he combined a working life as a highly respected fine artist with a keen interest in design for print. His curiosity and activities extended further, notably into architecture, theatre design, ceramics, fabrics, stained glass and even fireworks.

Piper's father was a partner in a firm of solicitors and he was insistent that John should join the firm. It was not until after his father's death that he was able to enrol at art school. Being a few years older than the other students, unusual in the late 1920s, he was impatient to make his way in the world. At the Royal College of Art he found the design school to be of more

interest than the painting school. Ultimately, he left without completing his diploma.

Although the design of dust jackets may have been a relatively minor aspect of Piper's prodigious overall output, the outcomes can be seen to embody many of the passions and preoccupations that drove his work. His visual vocabulary was rooted in direct observation, in particular of the relationship between architecture, natural forms and decay, but he was also fascinated by the geometry of form and by typography. Consequently, his jacket designs feature theatrical framing, architectural motifs and surface textures, along with sometimes ornately decorated letterforms. Often the textures were taken in the form of rubbings from gravestones and other inscribed monuments and surfaces.

Collaboration with his contemporary John Betjeman was inevitable given Piper's interest in all aspects of church architecture and a shared sensibility for what Piper called 'pleasing decay'. Together, the two are perhaps best remembered for their work on architectural guidebooks. The *Shell Guides* were sponsored by Jack Beddington at Shell-Mex BP, who was responsible for commissioning many of the great artists of the mid-twentieth century in the service of advertising.

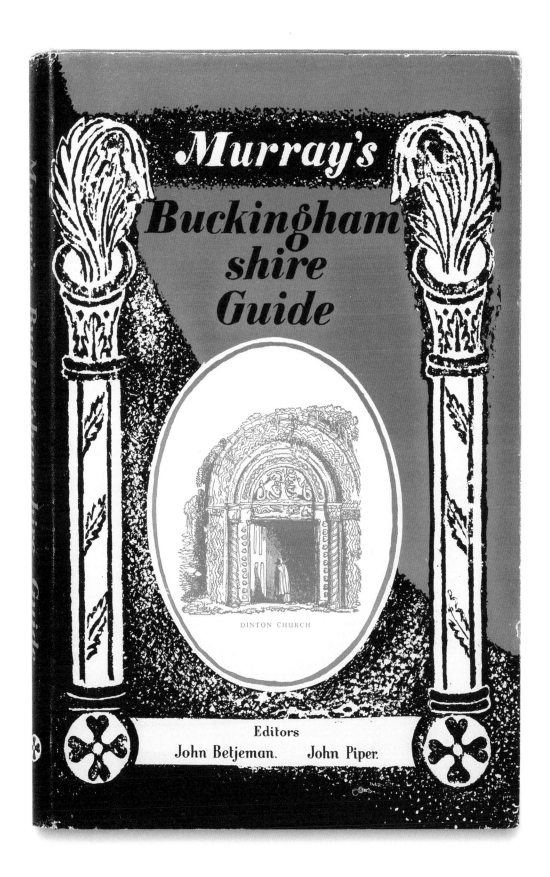

Murray's Buckinghamshire Guide
Edited by John Betjeman
and John Piper
John Murray · 1948
240 × 170 mm · 9½ × 6¾ in.

In a letter to a reviewer, found in
this copy of the first of the Murray's
guides, publisher John Murray writes,
'It is something of an experiment and
we hope very much that the public
will approve of it and that it may be

possible to carry the series through
to all the counties.' Only Berkshire
and Lancashire ensued in the series
edited by John Betjeman and Piper.
The latter's jacket design was
created to be printed in a different
colour for each county and with an
oval space on the front into which
an architectural detail from the
relevant county could be inserted.
The numerous photographs inside
the book were taken by Piper.

Buildings and Prospects
John Piper
Architectural Press · 1948
249 × 190 mm · 9¼ × 7½ in.

The dust jacket of Piper's *Buildings and Prospects* describes a walk around the English market town of Devizes. It is repeated inside the book as a title page. The artist had a gift for capturing how buildings relate to one another, even if every detail was not delineated. This collection of Piper's writings about English architecture also included reproductions of prints, engravings, drawings and photographs by the author.

The Language of Pictures
David Bell
B. T. Batsford · 1953
230 × 152 mm · 9 × 6 in.

The author's quest is to enlighten the layman on the meaning of paintings. As the dust jacket text explains, this is 'not a question of erudition, but a simple matter of enjoyment, a form of pleasure, alike in the artist and layman'. Piper's jacket echoes these aims through joyful mark-making.

First and Last Loves
John Betjeman
John Murray · 1952
216 × 152 mm · 8½ × 6 in.

A shared love of architecture is the premise for this collaboration between Betjeman and Piper. As well as the jacket, Piper contributed interior drawings, including a fold-out panorama of the spa town of Cheltenham.

The Spire
William Golding
Faber and Faber · 1964
190 × 125 mm · 7½ × 5 in.

The lettering and cleaner lines
of this jacket show the influence
of the 1960s. Golding's story of the
construction of a spire at a medieval
cathedral obviously appealed to
Piper's interest in architecture.

Forlorn Sunset
Michael Sadleir
Constable · 1947
190 × 125 mm · 7½ × 5 in.

Piper's brooding textures suit this
jacket for Sadleir's novel set in
Victorian London's underworld.

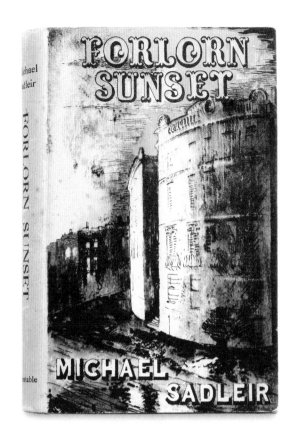

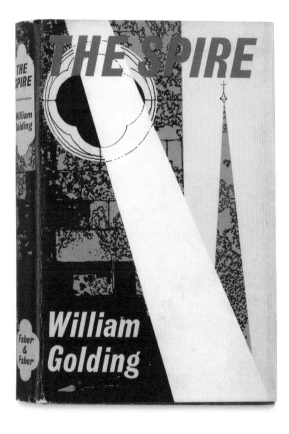

An Innocent Grows Up
Norman Hancock
J. M. Dent · 1947
190 × 125 mm · 7½ × 5 in.

One of Piper's most dramatic and
atmospheric jackets was for this
title, featuring textural pyrotechnics
including collaged marbling, which
is repeated inside as the title page.
This is perhaps more exciting than the
autobiographical story of what the
blurb calls a 'plain man', which begins
and ends in the family drapery shop,
picked out in red on Piper's design.

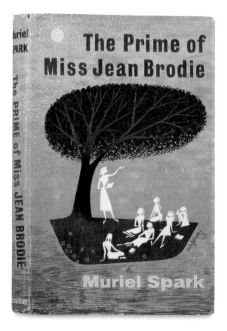

VICTOR REINGANUM

UK · 1907–1995

....

In the early stages of his career as an illustrator, 'Reinganum' (as he always signed his designs) tended to be employed to illustrate subject matter relating to what would later become known as 'the Jazz Age'. His mastery of stencilling and airbrush brought him plenty of work but as he recalled in a later interview with Peter Harle, 'I was rather typecast to begin with as a "bright young thing", and I was asked to draw subjects like cocktail bars, dancing girls, the sort of swinging-20s kind of thing. Eventually I graduated to the sort of drawing I preferred to do.'[67]

Reinganum had been educated at Haberdashers' Aske's School in north London, before going on to study at the Heatherley School of Art, London's oldest art school, from 1925. He then progressed to the Académie Julian in Paris and also studied privately under the distinguished artist Fernand Léger at his studio in Montmartre. On returning to England, Reinganum took a job as art director at Elstree Studios but stayed only for a year before leaving to pursue work as an artist and freelance illustrator. This was in the late 1920s and it was at this time that he exhibited works with a loose group of fellow artists, including Nicolas Bentley, who called themselves the Pandemonium Group, showing regularly at the Beaux-Arts Gallery. The artists broadly shared an interest in abstraction but Reinganum was wary of such labels. In later life, he would regularly be invited to exhibit under the banner of Surrealism. He himself preferred to describe some of his more formal compositions as 'diagrams', which is perhaps a better term for the imaginative fusion of the pictorial and schematic that characterized much of Reinganum's output. This work was in increasing demand before the Second World War as the more adventurous commissioners of advertising art in England such as Jack Beddington at Shell-Mex BP and Frank Pick at London Transport began to seek him out.

Like most illustrators of his time, it was as a black-and-white line artist that Reinganum was most frequently commissioned and best known, in particular for his weekly contributions to *Radio Times* over a period of several decades. In the interview with Harle he spoke of his perennial dismay at the standards of colour reproduction during his working life, 'I was delighted to have the commissions and I enjoyed doing them but, unfortunately, I was always very disappointed by the final result, which in my opinion bore very little resemblance to my original artwork as far as colour was concerned.'[68]

As with his output as a whole, Reinganum's dust-jacket designs spanned the decades from the 1920s to the late 1960s and covered a wide range of subject matter, fiction and non-fiction. However, it his designs for the jackets of the novels of Muriel Spark that he is most widely remembered. His jacket designs, as with all his work, are instantly identifiable, while gradually evolving stylistically through the trends and movements of the twentieth century, a fact that may not be unrelated to his final comment in the Harle interview: 'I was, of course, trained as a painter, there was no such thing as a commercial art course then, and I'm very glad there wasn't. I was just taught to be an artist.'[69]

Captain Conan
Roger Vercel
Constable · 1935
190 × 125 mm · 7½ × 5 in.

This early jacket shows Reinganum's already well-formed stylistic approach. His highly skilled use of airbrush and stencil was later abandoned in favour gouache painting.

Anywhere Else
H. J. Kaplan
Secker & Warburg · 1951
190 × 125 mm · 7½ × 5 in.

In Kaplan's novel, set in Paris, John Phillip Clifford is a 'man of affairs seeking, far from the conference table, for the decisive moment of his manhood', according to the blurb. Reinganum symbolizes Clifford's dilemma in his modernist jacket design that cleverly represents time and space.

The Prime of Miss Jean Brodie
Muriel Spark
Macmillan · 1961
204 × 134 mm · 8 × 5¼ in.

Spark's celebrated novel features Reinganum's best-known jacket design. The image sketches the eponymous teacher and her six pupils, called the 'Brodie set', whose lives are played out against the background of a girls school in 1930s Edinburgh.

The Ballad of Peckham Rye
Muriel Spark
Macmillan · 1960
197 × 140 mm · 7¾ × 5½ in.

Spark's 'novel of constant movement', as the dust-jacket blurb declares, is encapsulated in this dynamic evocation of South London life at the start of the 1960s.

Rosoman had a long and highly productive life as an illustrator, painter, muralist, printmaker and teacher. An important feature of his work, or rather his approach to it, was a total absence of snobbery or sense of hierarchy in relation to the fine and applied arts. Like Edward Bawden and John Piper, he was as engaged with illustration and design as he was with painting, and was equally respected for his work in both fields. In an article in *Image* in 1950, Michael Middleton remarked how Rosoman

> assumed that he could not be an illustrator. In fact, of course, what now gives value to his drawings for reproduction is just the absence of that barrier. Illustration has come out of the pigeonhole and is merely an extension of his work in other fields – indeed, of his whole outlook on life. Rosoman is an example of the integrated artist – a distinguished member of a generation that aims to bring the fine and applied together in harness again.[70]

Rosoman stated later that he had been encouraged to believe that book illustration was something inferior: 'It is not so… illustration and easel painting are closely related and equally important…I find the extremes of scale stimulating.'[71] Furthermore, in an interview with Peter Harle, he commented, 'You see, involvement in other fields has always been very important for me.'[72] Other areas of activity included his work as an official war artist towards the end of the Second World War on HMS *Formidable* in the Pacific, and running the new department of mural painting at Edinburgh College of Art in the late 1940s. He was elected a Royal Academician in 1969 and in 1986 painted the mural in the restaurant at the Royal Academy's home, Burlington House. Two years later, he was commissioned to paint the ceiling of the chapel in Lambeth Palace, the London residence of the Archbishop of Canterbury.

Rosoman was born in Hampstead, London, and his artistic education was at King Edward VII School of Art in Newcastle, the Royal Academy Schools and the Central School of Arts and Crafts (under Bernard Meninsky). His first real break as a book illustrator came in 1937 when he was commissioned by the Cresset Press to illustrate a children's book, *My Friend Mr Leakey*, by the scientist J. B. S. Haldane. He was also commissioned by the legendary Jack Beddington at Shell-Mex BP to design a poster based on a folly. At the outbreak of war he joined the Auxiliary Fire Service and his experiences during the Blitz inspired one of his most famous paintings, *A House Collapsing on Two Firemen, Shoe Lane, London EC4* (1940), now in the Imperial War Museum. Returning to London after his wartime service in the Far East, Rosoman became friends with fellow artist-illustrator John Minton, who invited him to join the teaching staff at Camberwell School of Arts and Crafts. He taught at art schools for much of his working life; stints at Chelsea and the Royal College of Art followed after Edinburgh.

The Pyramid
William Golding
Faber and Faber · 1966
190 × 125 mm · 7½ × 5 in.

Rosoman's slightly offbeat visual language perfectly introduces Golding's light-hearted novel of teenage frustrations in English suburbia.

The Endless Colonnade
Robert Harling
Chatto & Windus · 1958
204 × 135 mm · 8 × 5⅜ in.

There is a slightly eerie detachment
to Rosoman's style of drawing.
Figures go about their business in
a strange and uneasy atmosphere.
Harling, a typographer and writer
on the graphic arts, also wrote
fiction, including this novel set
against the background of ancient
and modern Rome.

The Gold-Rimmed Spectacles
Giorgio Bassani
Faber and Faber · 1960
190 × 125 mm · 7½ × 5 in.

A Prospect of Ferrara
Giorgio Bassani
Faber and Faber · 1962
190 × 125 mm · 7½ × 5 in.

Two jackets for Faber and Faber in
the early 1960s feature the artist at
his most formal and objective. The
ink drawing is carefully composed
and constructed, and laid over
two-colour separations. Both titles
were part of a cycle of books set in
Ferrara, where Bassani was brought
up. *The Gold-Rimmed Spectacles*,
a novella about Athos Fadigati,
a gay doctor in the 1930s who is
marginalized and eventually commits
suicide, was the first of the cycle.

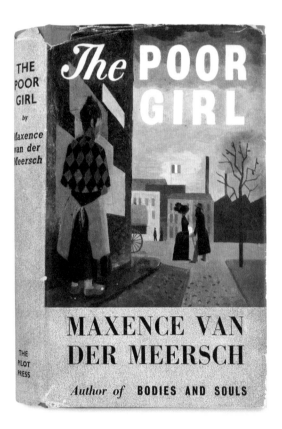

KENNETH ROWNTREE
UK · 1915–1997

The years after the Second World War in England were rich in artist-illustrators who were as comfortable responding to a brief as they were with creating for the gallery wall. Kenneth Rowntree, who was among that group, was a decade or so younger than Bawden, Ravilious and Piper and so was able to learn a great deal from them. He knew them well, teaching with them and in the case of Ravilious and Bawden, living in the same Essex village for several years.[73]

Rowntree was born in the Yorkshire town of Scarborough, where his father was the owner of a family department store. He left in 1932 to study at the Ruskin School of Drawing in Oxford, where he received the encouragement of the principal of the school, Albert Rutherston. Here he was also taught by Barnett Freedman and Ravilious. In 1935, he progressed to the Slade School of Art in London but dropped out without completing his studies. As a Quaker and pacifist, he did not fight when war broke out but was instead commissioned by Kenneth Clark to contribute to the Recording Britain project, making drawings and paintings in Yorkshire, Derbyshire, Essex and Wales. His interest in the landscape and life of Wales was developed after the war into a book in the *King Penguin* series, *A Prospect of Wales*, with the addition of an essay by Gwyn Jones. Rowntree's flair for design is evident in the carefully conceived cover, showing a portfolio within a portfolio.

Kenneth Rowntree's work as both a painter and illustrator is instantly recognizable. It is playfully odd and intriguing, never self-conscious or mannered even though he was an artist who moved with the times and happily embraced changing trends and influences. He liked to paint landscapes and interiors, often using strangely 'flat-on' compositions. Rowntree was also fascinated by letterforms and many paintings and illustrations feature gravestones, notice boards or signage, with every detail of the wording carefully inscribed. From 1949 he taught mural painting at the Royal College of Art and in 1951 contributed his own example of the medium, *Freedom*, to the Lion and the Unicorn pavilion at the Festival of Britain, celebrating various decisive moments in British history.

Rowntree and his wife, Diana, an architect and architectural writer, moved north in 1959 when Kenneth accepted the position of Professor of Fine Art at Newcastle University, succeeding his former teacher, Lawrence Gowing. With such an interest in pure shape and construction, it was inevitable that his painting would explore abstraction in later years. Nonetheless, many of these works from the 1960s and later retain a playful element of the pictorial, such as *Putney Bridge Night Scene* and *Landscape Catalogue III* (1972).

In his dust-jacket designs of the late 1940s and early 1950s, Kenneth Rowntree was often able to play with his favoured motifs and preoccupations – landscape, letterforms and pattern.

The Poor Girl
Maxence van der Meersch
Pilot Press · 1949
220 × 140 mm · 8⅝ × 5½ in.

A simple, squared painting introduces the author's story of poverty and exploitation in French factory life.

Master Mariner
Leo Walmsley
Collins · 1948
204 × 140 mm · 8 × 5½ in.

Rowntree's distinctive jacket design for Walmsley's tale of drink, religion and U-Boats afforded him the opportunity to play with letterforms, pattern and texture.

Do I Wake or Sleep
Isabel Bolton · Chapman & Hall · 1947
190 × 125 mm · 7½ × 5 in.

The artwork (below) is far more subtly
toned and textured than the solid black
of the rather crudely printed jacket.
This was the first book of the three
New York Mosaic novels written under
a pen name by Mary Britton Miller.

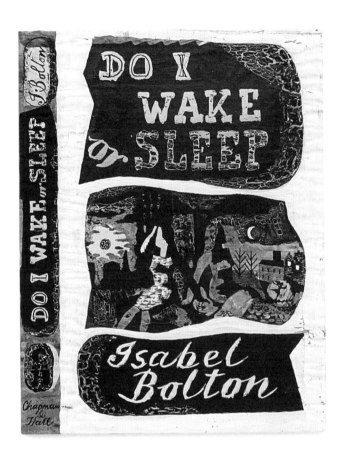

The Village
Marghanita Laski
Cresset Press · 1952
190 × 125 mm · 7½ × 5 in.

Rowntree uses the white of the
paper cleverly and sparingly to give
the effect of a third colour on this
hand-lettered, full-width design.
Laski's novel about lovers divided
by class conveyed the tensions of
British society as people adjusted
to the social consequences of the
Second World War, a transformation
perhaps subtly indicated by
Rowntree's use of the broken line.

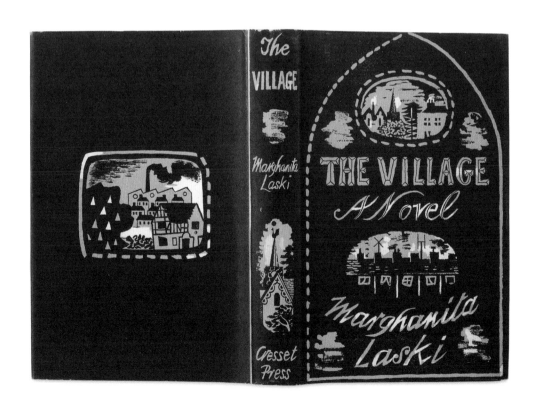

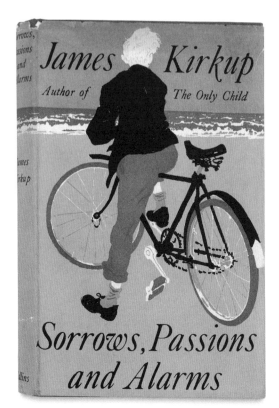

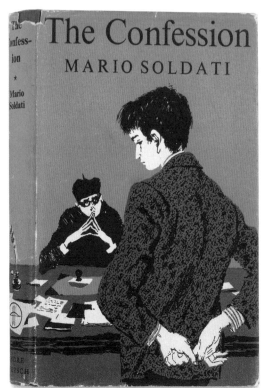

Sorrows, Passions and Alarms
James Kirkup · Collins · 1959
204 × 142 mm · 8 × 5⅝ in.

In this jacket, Russ uses solid blocks of colour only, without recourse to line. Image and text are considered in partnership. James Kirkup was visiting poet at Bath Academy of Art for three years from 1952 and would have been one of Russ's colleagues. The book is an autobiography of his childhood in South Shields.

The Confession
Mario Soldati
André Deutsch · 1958
190 × 125 mm · 7½ × 5 in.

A 14-year-old pupil at a Jesuit school in Turin is sure that his future lies in the priesthood. But, according to the blurb, 'instincts had begun to stir and he knew that he had sinned'. Russ describes the confession visually with expert use of body language.

Beggars on Horseback
James Mossman
The Bodley Head · 1966
204 × 134 mm · 8 × 5¼ in.

The white of the paper is used prominently as a 'colour' in this vibrant design. The fleeing white man (in every sense), who is seen from on high as a native population looks on, captures the topical story of the manoeuvring and intrigue in an unnamed Middle East country at the end of the colonial era.

May We Borrow Your Husband?
Graham Greene
The Bodley Head · 1967
204 × 134 mm · 8 × 5¼ in.

The good life of the 1960s is vividly evoked in luminous pink on Russ's jacket for Graham Greene's collection of short 'comedies of the sexual life'.

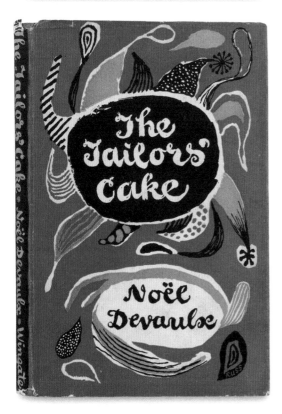

STEPHEN RUSS

UK · 1919–1983

Stephen Russ was one of the finest designer-illustrators of dust jackets of his generation. He is perhaps best known among the wider public for the design of the phoenix rising from the flames motif on the front of the famous Penguin edition of D. H. Lawrence's *Lady Chatterley's Lover* from 1960. Russ is also closely identified wth the covers for the paperback *Penguin Poets* series in the 1960s, which were produced in the form of individual patterns and textures to represent or evoke the broad theme of the collection in each edition. Nonetheless, from the mid-1940s until well into the 1970s Russ was creating numerous pictorial dust-jacket designs for a range of hardback fiction titles for publishers such as André Deutsch, Collins and the Bodley Head.

Before the outbreak of the Second World War, Russ studied under Edward Bawden and Eric Ravilious at the Royal College of Art. From 1950 until his retirement in 1982, he taught printmaking and design at Bath Academy of Art (now part of Bath Spa University). Alongside his work as an illustrator he was heavily involved in fabric design and was an advisor on this subject to the United Nations Technical Assistance Board, which provided guidance for local industries and craftsmen and women throughout the world.

Print processes and design were key to Stephen Russ's commercial work, the two coming together in his dust-jacket designs. The majority of these were printed by letterpress and originated by the artist in the form of colour separations. As a printmaker-designer, Russ was fully equipped to make maximum use of the processes at his disposal. He shared his knowledge, not only with his students at Bath but also with the wider public through his authored books on various aspects of printmaking. *Fabric Printing by Hand* was published by Studio Vista (and Watson-Guptill in the US) in 1965. This was followed by *Practical Screen Printing* (Studio Vista/Watson-Guptill, 1969) and finally *A Complete Guide to Printmaking* (Thomas Nelson/ Viking Press) in 1975. All three books combine technical information and guidance with clearly conveyed insight into issues of design in relation to pattern and rhythm.

It is a mark of the excellence of Stephen Russ's dust-jacket designs that, notwithstanding the comings and goings of 'retro' trends, his work looks as fresh and contemporary today as it did in its original context.

Miguel Street
V. S. Naipaul
André Deutsch · 1959
190 × 125 mm · 7½ × 5 in.

The early editions of Naipaul's novels for André Deutsch are highly collectable. The jackets were designed by Robert Micklewright or Stephen Russ, the latter designing the jacket for this third novel. Maximum graphic effect is achieved through the use of textures and tints.

The Tailor's Cake
Noël Devaulx
Allan Wingate · 1946
190 × 125 mm · 7½ × 5 in.

One of Russ's earliest jackets was this wraparound design for the publishing house Allan Wingate, founded by André Deutsch. The design is redolent with the shapes and motifs of early postwar neo-romanticism, including the free-flowing hand lettering that was so popular at the time.

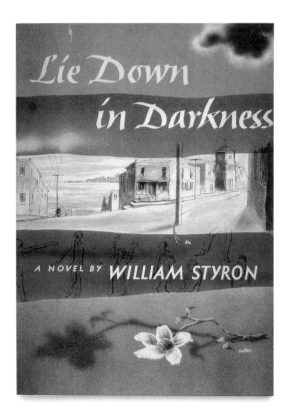

Lie Down in Darkness
William Styron
Bobbs-Merrill
(Indianapolis) · 1951
204 × 140 mm · 8 × 5½ in.

Horizontal bands of colour feature
regularly in Salter's designs. Here
they are used to represent the various
layers of meaning in the author's
tale of a dysfunctional and tragic
Virginia family against a backdrop
of religious fundamentalism, racism
and increasing industrialization.

East of Midnight
Forrest Rosaire
Alfred A. Knopf
(New York) · 1945
185 × 125 mm · 7¼ × 5 in.

Salter draws on the aesthetic of
consumer advertising for this sultry
and slightly menacing image. The
languid gaze is immediately arresting,
leading us into the author's first
novel, which explores the impact of
childhood experiences on adult life.

GEORGE SALTER

Germany & USA · 1897–1967

Georg (later George) Salter was born into a musical family in Bremen, Northern Germany, although he was brought up in Berlin. The family was Jewish, but in the year of Georg's birth converted to Christianity, as was common at the time. After serving in the German army in the First World War, Slater enrolled at the Kunstgewerbe- und Handwerkerschule (School of Applied Arts and Crafts) in Berlin in 1919 and studied design for the stage. He would go on to design productions for, among other clients, the Berliner Volksoper while also building a freelance career in book design. By 1927 the strains of juggling both areas of creative endeavour were becoming too great and he decided to devote himself primarily to book design and illustration. The experience of working in the theatre, however, clearly influenced his dust-jacket and book-cover work. Dramatic lighting and composition remained an instantly recognizable feature of his work on a two-dimensional surface. During the 1920s and early 1930s Salter built a considerable reputation in German publishing circles as a designer of decorative bindings and dust jackets, particularly as many of his designs appeared on bestsellers by major writers. He worked closely with the graphic artist and type designer Georg Trump who invited him to lead the commercial art department at the Höhere Graphische Fachschule (Institute of Graphic Arts) in Berlin in 1931.

All of this came to an end when Trump was required to enforce new Nazi race laws and to dismiss Salter due to his Jewish ethnicity. In 1934, in part thanks to his youngest brother Stefan, who had gone to the States in 1928, Salter obtained an American visa and arrived in New York in November that year. His reputation had gone before him and within a very short time he was earning a living as a freelance designer and dust-jacket artist in the USA. And in 1937 he began to teach at Cooper Union, an association that would continue for thirty years. Many of his design and calligraphy students went on to illustrious careers in the field, among them Milton Glaser.

After gaining American citizenship in 1940, Salter changed his first name to George. His reputation continued to grow throughout the decade and his election to the Grolier Club in New York in 1951 indicates the esteem in which he was held by bibliophiles and others in the book world. He was one of the most prolific and highly respected artists in the graphic arts in the postwar era, bringing a new and highly distinctive fusion of literary and visual intellect to the field. His jackets adorned books by a variety of authors, including Thomas Mann, Ayn Rand, Patrick White, Ngaio Marsh and Arthur C. Clarke. A collection of jackets designed by Salter together with artwork are among his papers held at Smith College, Northampton, Massachusetts.

Der Tunnel
Bernhard Kellermann
S. Fischer Verlag (Berlin) · 1931
190 × 125 mm · 7½ × 5 in.

A striking example of Salter's early
work in Berlin. The design speeds us
into the novel, which explores the idea
of a transatlantic underwater train,
in the classically streamlined, highly
stylized manner of the machine age.

The Wall
John Hersey · Alfred A. Knopf
(New York) · 1950
210 × 140 mm · 8¼ × 5½ in.

It is interesting to compare Salter's
design with that of Barnett Freedman
for the English edition (see p. 85).
They take a similar approach, placing
elements of the human experience
against the wall of the Warsaw ghetto.

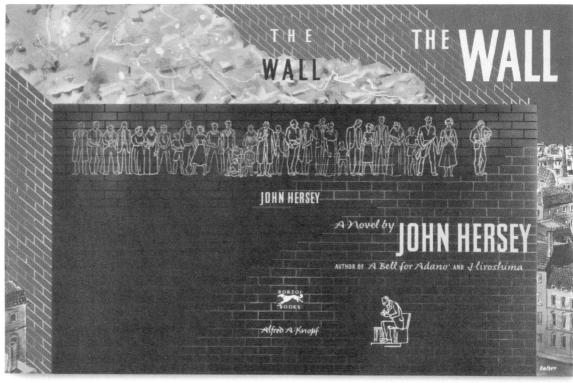

RONALD SEARLE

UK · 1920–2011

The illustration of dust jackets could be said to form a relatively minor portion of Ronald Searle's prodigious and instantly recognizable output of graphic work. Yet even within this particular field of creative endeavour, the number of examples constitutes sufficient to reflect the evolution of his work over the span of his long career, which saw him work professionally as an artist for around seventy-five years, from the age of 15 to 90.

Searle was born in the university city of Cambridge, to a working-class couple. His father was employed on the railways and the family took in lodgers to make ends meet, something the young Ronald disliked intensely.[74] He drew from an early age, inspired by regular visits to the city's museums, especially the Fitzwilliam. As a teenager he precociously approached the *Cambridge Daily News* on hearing that the resident cartoonist had moved on to better things in London. He left a portfolio of drawings with the editor, who subsequently commissioned Searle to produce regular Saturday cartoon strips, dealing with topical local issues. At this time, in the mid-1930s, he was attending evening classes at Cambridge School of Art, but the award of a scholarship in 1938 allowed him to study full time. He was taught drawing by former Henry Tonks student John Hookham and was a member of the sketch club run by the great illustrator and wood engraver Gwen Raverat, who took her pupils out on cycling trips to the countryside to draw the rural scene. Another early influence was the work of George Grosz.

Ronald's joy at becoming a full-time art student was cut short by the outbreak of war, in which he enlisted in the Royal Engineers. His experiences as a prisoner of the Japanese at the notorious Changi gaol in Singapore and on the Burma-Siam 'Death' Railway were graphically documented through an extraordinary body of drawings.[75]

Searle returned to England with his draughtsmanship honed through hours of furtive observational drawing and a burning ambition to make up for lost time. After exhibiting the war drawings at Cambridge School of Art and publishing a selection of them with Cambridge University Press,[76] he headed for London with his portfolio. He had already had humorous drawings published in the popular magazine *Lilliput*, after sending them for consideration before his period of captivity. In the headily optimistic years of postwar renewal, Ronald's brand of anarchic graphic wit was very soon in great demand. Before long he became one of those rare things, an illustrator who is a 'household name'. His drawings for the Lemon Hart Rum advertisements could be seen reproduced on the country's billboards and at an even bigger scale around Piccadilly Circus in London. The *St Trinians* series of books had begun life in the pages of *Lilliput* and would go on to become an international publishing phenomenon along with Searle's illustrations to Geoffrey Willans's *Molesworth* books.

However, Searle's work was about much more than humour for children. His reportage and documentary drawings for newspapers and magazines around the world could be powerfully hard hitting and his biting graphic satire addressed political and environmental issues throughout his career. His book illustration was wide ranging, some of it produced under his own publishing imprint, Perpetua Books, which he established in the 1950s.

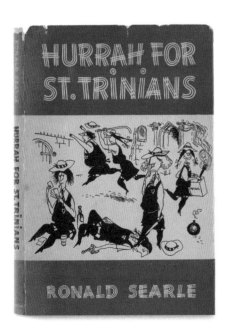

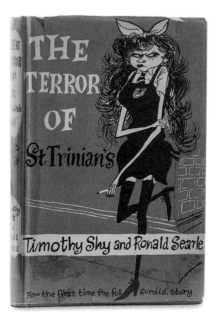

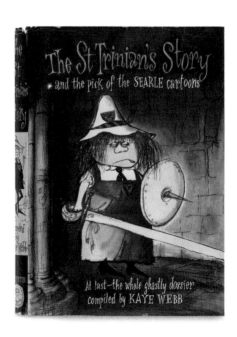

The Rake's Progress
Ronald Searle
Perpetua Books · 1955
255 × 190 mm · 10 × 7½ in.

In this volume, William Hogarth's
original concept of *The Rake's
Progress* was reworked by Searle in
the context of the mid-1950s, showing
contemporary 'modern day' characters
and their various follies and foibles
as they fall from grace. Searle said
that the caricatural drawings of the
German artist George Grosz had made
an impact on him and echoes of that
work can be seen here.

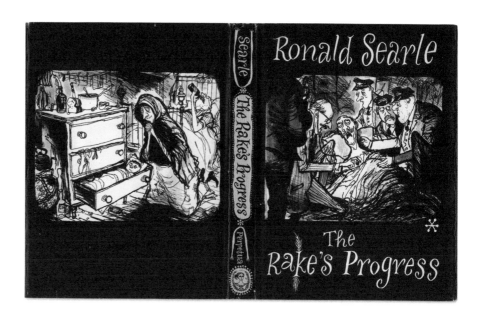

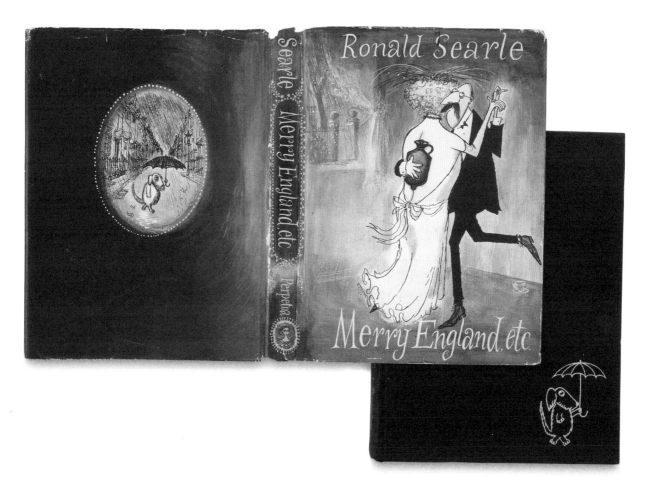

Hurrah for St Trinians
Ronald Searle · Macdonald · 1948
200 × 134 mm · 7⅞ × 5¼ in.

The St Trinians phenomenon was
launched in book form with this
collection of the cartoons that had
appeared in *Lilliput* magazine. The
book became a huge seller, running
into numerous editions.

The Terror of St Trinians
Timothy Shy and Ronald Searle
Max Parrish · 1952
200 × 134 mm · 7⅞ × 5¼ in.

For this publication Searle contributed
a more bespoke jacket: a three-colour
design with his own distinctive
lettering. The main text of the 'full
sordid story' was written by the
journalist D. B. Wyndham Lewis
under the pseudonym Timothy Shy.

The St Trinians Story
Compiled by Kaye Webb
Perpetua Books · 1959
255 × 198 · 10 × 7¾ in.

By 1959, Searle had had enough of
St Trinians, despite its continuing
popularity and the public appetite
for more. Under his own Perpetua
publishing imprint, and with his wife
Kaye Webb's text, the 'whole ghastly
dossier' was put to bed by burning the
school to the ground.

Merry England, etc.
Ronald Searle · Perpetua Books · 1956
255 × 190 mm · 10 × 7½ in.

Merry England, etc. was published at
the height of Searle's fame by his own
Perpetua imprint, which took its name
from Eric Gill's typeface. Searle's
distinctive colophon design can be
seen on the spine. The book featured
a compilation of the artist's satirical
drawings that had been published in
newspapers and magazines.

The Sure Thing
Merle Miller
John Lehmann · 1950
204 × 134 mm · 8 × 5¼ in.

Set in Washington, DC, at the height
of the witch-hunt for Communists,
the novel charts the story of Brad
Douglas, who is eventually dismissed
from his job after an FBI investigation,
hinted at by the dark figure in the
background of Searle's design.

With My Little Eye
Roy Fuller
John Lehmann · 1948
204 × 134 mm · 8 × 5¼ in.

In the late 1940s Searle took a studio
in London's Bedford Gardens, in the
same building as John Minton. The
two exchanged notes and publishers'
contact details. This early jacket design
(and the one for *The Sure Thing*) for
John Lehmann shows that Searle was
influenced by Minton's flamboyant
hand-rendered titling.

Whizz for Atomms
Geoffrey Willans and Ronald Searle
Max Parrish · 1956
200 × 134 mm · 8 × 5¼ in.

Molesworth's Guide to the Atommic Age
Geoffrey Willans and Ronald Searle
Max Parrish · 1956
216 × 146 mm · 8½ × 5¾ in.

How to be Topp
Geoffrey Willans and Ronald Searle
Max Parrish · 1954
210 × 134 mm · 8¼ × 5¼ in.

Down with Skool!
Geoffrey Willans and Ronald Searle
Max Parrish · 1953
210 × 134 mm · 8¼ × 5¼ in.

These highly popular, anarchic
collaborations between Searle and writer
Geoffrey Willans were published by Max
Parrish in a handily pocket-sized format.

BEN SHAHN
USA · 1898–1969

In a talk that he gave to a group of students at the Franklin School in New York in 1950, Ben Shahn discussed his thoughts on the thorny subject of the relationship between 'commercial' and 'fine' art.[77] Shahn himself saw no problem in accommodating both, or in applying the same high standards of engagement and commitment to each. He spoke about the sad case of the stereotypical commercial artist who 'longs to paint'– 'a second drink will usually wring a confession from him'. Then, he observed, there is 'that sort of artist who saves part of himself for his "important work"'. He lamented the attitude that he had noticed among some art students in his early days as a teacher, when, much to his annoyance, his criticisms would be met with comments such as 'But Mr Shahn, I'm only going in for commercial art anyway', revealing a perception that there was less to learn in this field beyond a bag of stylistic tricks. He would point out to them that 'Commercial art, contrary to the general conception, is an unyielding taskmaster, a hard school. It is also an excellent school for any artist, *provided it is not abused.*'[78] The kind of abuse to which Shahn was referring was the practice of visual plagiarism, freely lifting stylistic techniques from other artists.

Ben Shahn was born in Kovno (Kaunas), Lithuania, then part of the Russian empire, to a family of craftsmen. When he was still an infant, his father was exiled to Siberia, although the family was later reunited in the US after Shahn, his mother and two siblings emigrated there in 1906. In all likelihood these early hardships underpinned Shahn's work across the fine and applied arts, which was driven by a deep concern for social issues and a hatred of injustice of any kind.

Having drawn from a young age, Shahn was apprenticed as a craftsman lithographer at a printing firm in downtown Manhattan from the age of 14. The experience perhaps nurtured his strong sense of graphic design and keen affinity with lettering. He undertook more formal art training at City College and the National Academy of Design in the early 1920s. Having initially worked in lithography, Shahn came to prominence in the early 1930s with the series of paintings he made about the case of Sacco and Vanzetti, the victims of a miscarriage of justice who had been executed in 1927 amid worldwide protest. In the mid-1930s he was employed by the Farm Security Administration as a photographer and toured the South with Walker Evans and Dorothea Lange, recording the effects of the Depression on people's lives. He was also hired as a muralist by other New Deal agencies. During the war he was engaged for a time by the Office of War Information.

Thereafter, his work extended to stained glass, magazines, including covers for *Time*, CBS television and dust jackets. However, such was his reputation as a fine artist that he was selected to represent the USA at the 1954 Venice Biennale along with Willem de Kooning. In 1956–57, Shahn gave the Charles Eliot Norton lectures at Harvard University, published as *The Shape of Content* in 1960, in which he set forth his views on both the practice and the purposes of art.

A Boy of Old Prague
Sulamith Ish-Kishor
Chatto & Windus · 1966
235 × 155 mm · 9¼ × 6⅛ in.

Text and image are in perfect harmony in Shahn's jacket design for a children's book set in the ghetto of sixteenth-century Prague. The book also features twenty illustrations by Shahn and was first published in the US by Pantheon in 1963 with the same jacket design. Shahn could be as inspired by a text as by any direct life experience.

Kuboyama and the Saga of the Lucky Dragon
Richard Hudson and Ben Shahn
Thomas Yoseloff (New York) · 1965
285 × 216 mm · 11¼ × 8½ in.

The book tells the story of the Japanese fisherman Aikichi Kuboyama who died of radiation poisoning following the H-Bomb test on Bikini Atoll in 1954. Shahn's powerful drawings are first encountered through a transparent glassine dust jacket printed with solid red text hand-rendered in Shahn's classic style.

The Rising Gorge
S. J. Perelman
Simon and Schuster
(New York) · 1961
204 × 134 mm · 8 × 5¼ in.

In this design, Shahn opts for a simple graphic expression of the outpourings of the great American humorist S. J. Perelman. This collection consists of thirty-six pieces that mostly first appeared in the *New Yorker* magazine in the 1940s and 1950s.

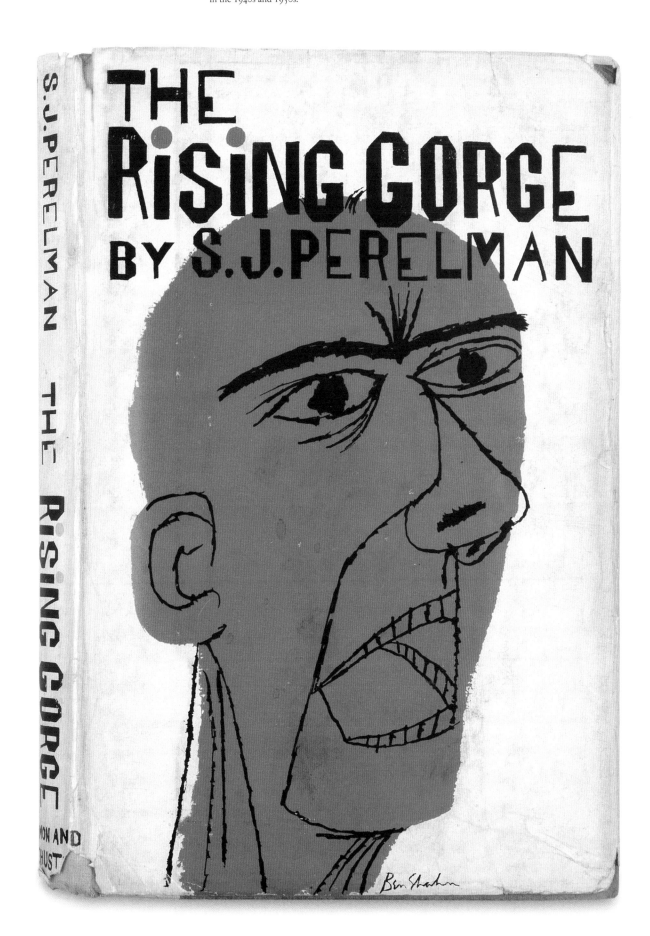

The distinctively stylized signature 'SKRENDA' appeared on the jacket of many romantic novels from the 1920s to the 1940s. His vividly coloured flat, graphic shapes were especially familiar in the context of the works by the prolific novelist Grace Livingstone Hill, who also wrote under the pseudonym Marcia Macdonald. Although set against contemporary events such as the First World War and the Great Depression, the books usually had a Gospel message, but it would be hard to discern this from Skrenda's jackets.

Little is known about Skrenda himself. He seems to have been a prolific artist in the field of dust-jacket design, in demand for new editions of classic novels by authors such as Alexandre Dumas and Charlotte Brontë. He also illustrated *Lefty Leighton* (Grosset & Dunlap, 1930), a children's book by Percy Keese Fitzhugh, and *Minute Wonders of the World* (Grosset & Dunlap, 1934) by Isabel Juergens. More often, however, his skills were called on to project the drama of popular romantic fiction with titles such as *Love's Ecstasy* by May Christie (Grosset & Dunlap, 1928). These designs, despite, or perhaps because of, their melodrama and theatrically overwrought posing, have a richly appealing period charm. Skrenda was particularly adept at billowing skirts and heroic gazes, never more so than in his design for the jacket of Rupert Hughes's collection of short stories entitled *She Goes to War* (Grosset & Dunlap, 1929), published to capitalize on the production of the film taken from the title story.

Skrenda was something of a specialist in designing jackets for books after the original publication had become famous via the movies. In the case of Harry Hamilton's *Banjo on my Knee*, however, Skrenda's design for the novel came first but was quickly reissued with the words 'A 20th Century Fox Photoplay with an All Star Cast' added to Skrenda's design. The film aimed to compete with Universal Studios' *Show Boat* of earlier that same year as a popular river-boat musical but, despite its cast, including Barbara Stanwyck and Joel McCrea, was poorly received.

She Goes to War: and other stories
Rupert Hughes
Grosset & Dunlap
(New York) · 1929
197 × 130 mm · 7¾ × 5⅛ in.

The title story of this collection features a young woman who disguises herself as a man in the First World War and follows her fiancé into the trenches to share the experience. This photoplay edition includes images from the United Artists film released the same year. Skrenda's jacket is suitably heroic. The prolific short-story writer, novelist and screenwriter Rupert Hughes was the uncle of the business mogul Howard Hughes.

The Man in the Iron Mask
Alexandre Dumas
Grosset & Dunlap
(New York) · 1939
210 × 136 mm · 8¼ × 5⅜ in.

Another popular photoplay edition, this time published to capitalize on the success of the film staring Louis Hayward and Joan Bennett released in July 1939. The artist's delight in rendering windswept billowing capes is once again evident.

The Red Signal
Grace Livingston Hill
Grosset & Dunlap
(New York) · *c.* 1929
197 × 140 mm · 7¾ × 5½ in.

The American author Grace
Livingstone Hill wrote over a hundred
novels, many with a Christian theme.
This romance is set against the
backdrop of the First World War and
was first published in 1919 by J. B.
Lippincott. The dust-jacket design for
this later edition is signed 'SKRENDA
28'. Other Hill titles for which Skrenda
designed jackets include *A Voice in the
Wilderness* and *The Girl from Montana*.

Banjo on my Knee
Harry Hamilton
Grosset & Dunlap
(New York) · 1936
190 × 125 mm · 7½ × 5 in.

Banjo on my Knee was first published
by Bobbs-Merrill in 1936 with the
same jacket design but this edition
was quickly rushed out by the reprint
publisher Grosset & Dunlap to
coincide with the release of the film
made by 20th Century Fox in the same
year. The novel concerns the lives of
a group of people living in flatboats
on the Mississippi. Skrenda's use of
strident colour in simplified flat shapes
made him a sought-after artist for
popular fiction.

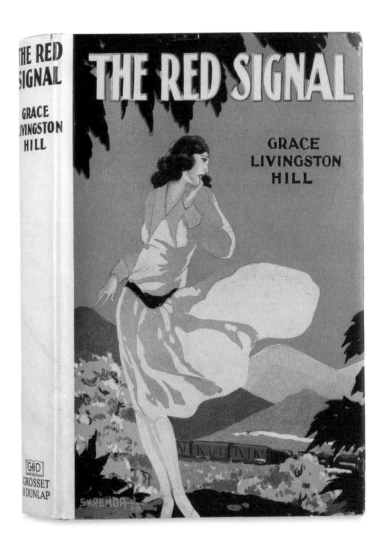

HEATHER STANDRING
UK · b. 1928

There were many freelance illustrators through the mid-twentieth century who might be described as 'jobbing' artists – those whose work was familiar across a range of everyday outlets that included magazines, fashion drawing, general advertising and book illustration. Little is known about a fair number of these people. However, one whose work stands out for its integrity, draughtsmanship and individuality is Heather Standring. Relatively little biographical information is available though she was particularly active in the design of dust jackets for publishers in the UK and USA. Her designs adorned the works of several important and influential writers of the 1950s and 1960s.

Standring's illustration work is rooted in the quality of her line and a flair for compositional tension in carefully posed figure groups that have a slightly unsettling effect at times. She was also highly skilled at introducing colour and texture to her designs, depending on the print processes of the day. She maximized the potential of limited available colours through clever use of separations and was also an early employer of mechanical tints (mass-produced sheets of adhesive transparent plastic printed with varying densities of half-tone dots and other forms of texture and pattern). A good example of this can be seen on one of Standring's earliest jacket designs, for the now scarce first edition of Brian Moore's highly regarded novel *Judith Hearne*, which she designed for André Deutsch in 1955. The design is also notable for the artist's unusually prominent signature, audaciously highlighted in the second colour, almost as clearly as the titles.

Heather Standring was born in the small village of Olveston in Gloucestershire and studied life drawing under Bernard Meninsky at the Central School of Arts and Crafts in London. But her specialism then was in drawing for fashion illustration. On graduating, she worked for two years freelancing in this field and in more general illustration while also taking a number of other jobs to make ends meet. She then travelled abroad for a further two years and took a job in Madrid. On returning to England in 1954, she devoted herself fully to illustration. In John Ryder's *Artists of a Certain Line* from 1960, Standring succinctly expresses an approach with which many illustrators will empathize:

> The merit of my illustration very much depends on the quality of the writing and the time I am given to realise my ideas. For a period I build up a store of impressions and then feel stimulated to expend them during long working hours. The two states do not seem to run concurrently. I try to keep my drawing as simple as possible (eliminating effects for their own sake) and consider the drawing of much less importance than what is expressed through it.[79]

Standring taught illustration part-time for a number of years at Maidstone College of Art. In 1974, she wrote the text for *How to Live in Style* (Laurie Larson Publications), a magnificently opinionated and bombastic guide to filling your home with all that was worst about the 1970s.

Judith Hearne
Brian Moore
André Deutsch · 1955
220 × 170 mm · 8⅝ × 6⅝ in.

Moore's well-regarded novel about a middle-aged Irish alcoholic spinster was later republished as *The Lonely Passion of Judith Hearne*. Standring's keen interest in pattern is particularly evident here, as the eponymous character seems oppressively enveloped by the carpet.

Solitaire
Kay Dick
Heinemann · 1958
190 × 125 mm · 7½ × 5 in.

The original colour separations can be seen here alongside the printed version of Standring's design for Dick's novel set in a Parisian winter. The solid black overlay would have been used to create the plate for the red printing. On the line artwork, the artist has indicated in gold and purple the areas to be printed in those colours.

Mushroom Cooking
Garibaldi M. Lapolla
André Deutsch · 1954
190 × 125 mm · 7½ × 5 in.

Despite being limited to two colours
plus black, the artist achieves maximum
texture and impact with this design,
printed on a mushroom coloured paper
stock. Standring also illustrated the
interior with line drawings.

The Warm Country
Donald Windham
Rupert Hart-Davis · 1960
204 × 140 mm · 8 × 5½ in.

Standring uses single colour to
emphasize the title of this book of
short stories and gains maximum
textural impact through the
pattern of the bricks and the
half-tone shadows.

Laugh Till You Cry
Wolf Mankowitz
Dutton · 1955
190 × 125 mm · 7½ × 5 in.

Following *A Kid for Two Farthings*
(1953), Mankowitz's successful
autobiographical novel about growing
up in the East End of London, this
book was written in a different vein:
the stylized story of the adventures
of a shipwrecked salesman of the Rantz
Joke Company. As well as this striking
three-colour jacket design, Standring
illustrated this title throughout.

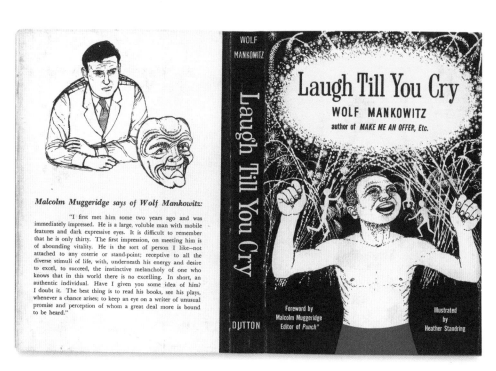

The Visitants
Ernest Frost
André Deutsch · 1955
200 × 135 mm · 7⅞ × 5⅜ in.

Standring was responsible for several dust jackets for André Deutsch during the 1950s, including this design featuring complex use of line, colour separation and multiple textures. She deftly conveys the essence of Frost's fourth novel, concerning the marriage of a 64-year-old man to the 29-year-old niece of his best friend.

Songs to Grow On
Beatrice Landeck
Marks and Sloane
(New York) · 1950
286 × 222 mm · 11¼ × 8¾ in.

Music was a constant presence in Martin's working life. In this design he emphasizes the various stages of childhood through judicious use of the second colour.

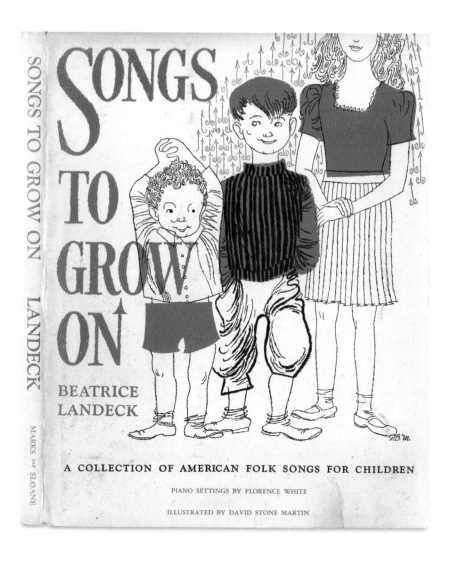

DAVID STONE MARTIN
USA · 1913–1992

It is for his work within the field of music that David Stone Martin (often known as 'DSM') is best known and most celebrated. His album covers for the great jazz artists are keenly collected. These highly influential drawings seem in themselves to be musical notation, a stylish mixing of filigree detailed line work with carefully balanced areas of solid colour. The packaging of LP records provided an important source of work for many artists at a substantial 12 × 12-inch scale before technology brought about its decline. Martin's favoured tool was a crow quill steel pen that was the key to his delicate, at times scratchy, line. A major stylistic influence was Ben Shahn, whose work was becoming increasingly well known during Martin's creatively formative years. During the 1950s he designed more than two hundred album covers for the labels of his long-time friend Norman Granz: Clef, Norgran and Verve. In all, he created over four hundred covers for a variety of labels. Alongside this primary area of specialism, Martin illustrated a number of books and designed several dust jackets.

He was born David Livingstone Martin in Chicago, the son of a Presbyterian minister, and he attended the School of the Art Institute of Chicago in the evenings. In the 1930s, he worked as supervisor of mural projects for the Federal Artists Project, and during the Second World War he was employed as graphic arts director by the Office of Strategic Services and as art director for the Office of War Information. There he worked with Shahn, whom he had first met when he was Shahn's assistant designing murals for the Chicago World's Fair in 1933. An undated painting of a logger by Martin from around this time (*Untitled* (*Logger*), now in the Art Institute of Chicago) is heavily influenced by Shahn, stylistically and in terms of its idealizing of physical toil.

After the war Martin built a strong freelance career; his profile grew as he began to receive awards for his work. As well as dust jackets and book illustrations, he obtained commissions from magazines such as the *Saturday Evening Post*, *Time* and *Life*, and produced posters and advertisements for theatre, film and television, including CBS. In the mid-1960s, his flair for portraiture led to covers for *Time* magazine featuring, among others, the politicians Robert F. Kennedy, Eugene McCarthy and George C. Wallace. His work is held in the collections of the Museum of Modern Art and the Metropolitan Museum of Art in New York, the Art Institute of Chicago and the Smithsonian Institution.

A Back-Fence Story
Augusta Walker
Alfred A. Knopf
(New York) · 1967
208 × 140 mm · 8¼ × 5½ in.
....

This excursion into children's
literature sees Martin in more
traditionally representational mode.
The numerous cats scattered across
the drawing underline the book's
subject: the story of three generations
of cats and the woman who becomes
a cat lover in the process of looking
after them.

Mister Jelly Roll
Alan Lomax
Duell, Sloan and Pearce
(New York) · 1950
216 × 146 mm · 8½ × 5¾ in.
....

Lomax's biography of Ferdinand
'Jelly Roll' Morton was the ideal
commission for Martin, whose stylish
jacket and interior illustrations are
informed by his depth of knowledge
of the subject. The book was based
on recordings and interviews that
Lomax conducted in the late 1930s for
the Library of Congress, and rapidly
became a classic of jazz literature.

"... So in the year of 1902 when I was about seventeen years old I happened to invade one of the sections where the birth of jazz originated from. Some friends took me to The Frenchman's on the corner of Villery and Bienville, which was at that time the most famous nightspot after everything was closed. It was only a back room, but it was where all the greatest pianists frequented after they got off from work in the sporting houses. About four A. M., unless plenty of money was involved on their jobs, they would go to The Frenchman's and there would be everything in the line of hilarity there.

"All the Girls that could get out of their houses was there. The millionaires would come to listen to their favorite pianists. There weren't any discrimination of any kind. They all sat at different tables or anywhere they felt like sitting. They all mingled together just as they wished to and everyone was just like one big happy family. People came from all over the country and most times you couldn't get in. So this place would go on at a tremendous rate of speed—plenty money, drinks of all kinds — from four o'clock in the morning until maybe twelve, one, two, or three o'clock in the daytime. Then, when the great pianists used to leave, the crowds would leave ..."

Strange Fruit
Lillian Smith
Cresset Press · 1945
204 × 125 mm · 8 × 5 in.

For the UK edition of Lillian Smith's examination of interracial romance, Tisdall took a restrained approach, using a powerful visual metaphor to deal with what was at the time a controversial topic.

Before My Time
Niccolò Tucci
Jonathan Cape · 1963
200 × 140 mm · 7⅞ × 5½ in.

Tisdall seemed to regard image and type as equally pictorial and of equal status. Some of his designs would be purely calligraphic, some predominantly image-led, others a fusion of the two, such as this jacket for Tucci's family chronicle, set in a world of infinite wealth at the beginning of the twentieth century.

The Leopard
Giuseppe di Lampedusa
Collins and Harvill Press · 1960
216 × 146 mm · 8½ × 5¼ in.

Tisdall kept scrapbooks and notebooks full of heraldic reference material. The powerful jacket he designed for Lampedusa's best-selling novel about a Sicilian nobleman at the time of the Risorgimento is one of his most immediately identifiable.

HANS TISDALL
Germany & UK · 1910–1997

The instantly recognizable, unique graphic vocabulary of Hans Tisdall featured strongly in bookshops from the 1940s through to the 1960s. His was a world of calligraphic swirls, heraldic motifs and patterns, and a melding of word and image into a single visual language. Many of these jacket designs were commissioned by the publishers Jonathan Cape, but his work also adorned books published by other firms, including Chatto & Windus, Collins/Harvill and the Cresset Press.

Tisdall was born Hans John Knox Aufseeser into an artistic Jewish family in Munich. In 1928, he studied at the Akademie der Bildenden Künste München (Munich Academy of Fine Arts) and took classes in sign-writing before being apprenticed to the Russian sculptor Moisey Keegan in Paris. He moved to London in 1930 and began a career as a painter, with a studio in Fitzroy Street, next door to Vanessa Bell and Duncan Grant. To make ends meet, he gravitated to textile design, working for Edinburgh Weavers, which led to his marriage in 1941 to Isabel Gallegos, a stylist with the firm.

The strong element of pattern and shape in Tisdall's work fed into an ongoing involvement with fabric design, tapestries and mosaics throughout his career. He was also engaged as a muralist, an art form that saw a resurgence of interest in the 1930s, and along with Edward Bawden and John Armstrong was commissioned by the architect Michael Rachlis, a fellow German émigré, to create murals for the International Building Club in Park Lane the year before the war.

Owing to anti-German sentiment, Aufseeser changed his name to Tisdall in 1940 and during the war worked for the Ministry of Information while also continuing freelance work, designing advertisements for the United Steel Companies. He held his first one-man show of paintings at the Leger Galleries in London in 1945 and exhibited in England, France and Germany into the 1990s. His reputation was sufficiently established by this point for him to be invited to contribute to the School Prints scheme in 1946; his lithograph, *Fisherman's Hut*, was inspired by his love of boats and the Sussex coast, and he seized the opportunity to create a playfully surreal composition. Around the same time, two non-fiction children's books were produced in partnership with Oliver Hill for Pleiades Books. The first was about architecture (*Balbus*, 1944) and the second on transport (*Wheels*, 1946). His involvement with the Festival of Britain in 1951 included designing the entrance to the Festival Pleasure Gardens in Battersea. From the 1947 until 1975 Tisdall was a lecturer at the Central School of Arts and Crafts, teaching in both the textile design and painting schools.

Although his working life was spent almost entirely in Britain, Tisdall retained a distinct if hard to define European sensibility that he brought to his designs in a rich variety of media.

The Defeat of the
Spanish Armada
Garrett Mattingly
Jonathan Cape · 1959
235 × 165 mm · 9¼ × 6½ in.

Given a full wraparound jacket
to design, Tisdall makes the
most of the opportunity with
this stunning tour de force of
calligraphic swirls in yellow,
green, red and black. The battle
takes place between the front and
back cover, opposing forces firing
at each other across the spine.

GARRETT MATTINGLY

THE DEFEAT OF THE SPANISH ARMADA

Harvest
Castle Press · 1948
250 × 190 mm · 9¾ × 7½ in.

This uncharacteristically tonal full-
colour illustration was produced for
the dust jacket of the first volume of the
short-lived *Harvest*, a hardback journal
of art and literature. This issue dealt
with the theme of travel. The second
and final issue followed in 1950, on the
subject of 'the household', with a jacket
design by Leslie Hurry.

The Old Man and the Sea
Ernest Hemingway
Jonathan Cape · 1952
190 × 125 mm · 7½ × 5 in.

Tisdall's dust jacket for
Hemingway's classic about an
aging fisherman struggling with a
giant marlin is a dramatic fusion of
painting, design and typography.
The novel was awarded the Pulitzer
Prize for Fiction in 1953.

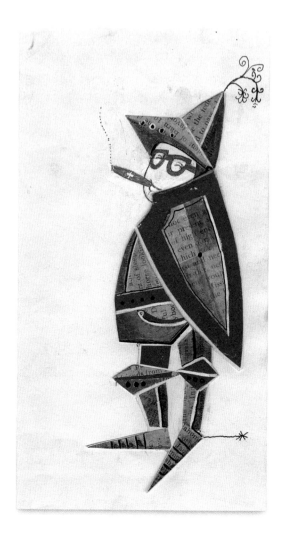

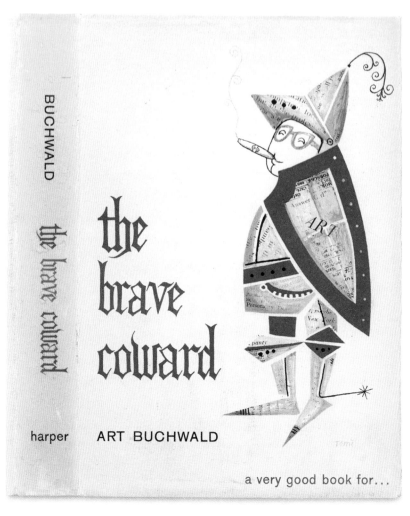

TOMI UNGERER

France · b. 1931

The extraordinary life of Jean-Thomas (Tomi) Ungerer began in Strasbourg, France. He grew up in poverty and hardship. His father, Theodore, died when he was just 3 years old and his mother was forced to move the family back to her own mother's home at Logelbach, near Colmar. Following the fall of France in 1940, Ungerer experienced life in Nazi-occupied Alsace, which, as he later recalled, 'was a schooling in relativity, in figuring out for myself who were the good guys and who were the bad'. Towards the end of the war, when the Allied forces arrived, the family was living in a cellar as their house had been destroyed by bombing: 'my taste for the macabre certainly finds its roots there', he observed.[80]

Education and Ungerer do not seem to have been happy bedfellows. He failed his baccalauréat exam and was described in his school report as a 'wilfully perverse and subversive individualist'.[81] He did not fare much better in the traditionally liberal environment of art school. In October 1953, he enrolled at the Municipal School for Decorative Arts in Strasbourg. He was asked to leave at the end of his first year.

During the early 1950s, Ungerer travelled widely in Europe, walking, hitchhiking and working his passage on cargo ships. In 1956, he arrived in New York with very little money but a trunk full of drawings. His first professional commission was for *Sports Illustrated* magazine, and he was soon doing illustration work for *Esquire*, *Life*, *Holiday*, *Harper's* and the *New York Times*. Early influences were Saul Steinberg and George Grosz. His first book contract was with the renowned children's book editor Ursula Nordstrom at Harper & Row for *The Mellops Go Flying* (1957), a story about a family of daring French pigs. This was the beginning of a long and successful career in the publishing field, in which Ungerer has followed his own creative path wherever it has taken him, often in the direction of controversy, but always innovative and usually surprising. He has illustrated more than 150 books dealing with all aspects of the human condition, including a number for adults that have explored sexuality and eroticism.

Ungerer has created political posters against war and racial injustice and has consistently fought for tolerance and diversity in Europe, especially in his home region of Alsace, where Franco-German relations have been historically delicate. In 1976, he and his family moved to Ireland, also spending time in Strasbourg.

In the field of dust-jacket design, as in all aspects of his work, Ungerer has searched for the most direct and simple means through which to express a concept in graphic form.

The Brave Coward
Art Buchwald
Harper & Bros (New York) · 1957
210 × 135 mm · 8¼ × 5⅜ in.

Humorist and *New York Herald Tribune*
columnist Buchwald offers memoirs
in the form of sketches, including how
he scaled the Empire State Building
and how to get through the Louvre
in six minutes. Ungerer conveys
the nonchalant author of the title by
a cigar-smoking knight in armour.
The original artwork is also shown.

Looking for a Bandit
Anthony Carson
Methuen · 1961
190 × 130 mm · 7½ × 5⅛ in.

Ungerer's design exhibits the
graphic and conceptual fearlessness
and panache that is a hallmark of
all of his work. Peter Brooke, an
habitué of Fitzrovia along with
Dylan Thomas, George Barker and
others after the war, wrote a number
of humorous travel books under the
pseudonym Anthony Carson.

Poor Man's Mimosa
Anthony Carson
Methuen · 1962
190 × 125 mm · 7½ × 5 in.

A second Anthony Carson humorous
travel title for Methuen carries a jacket
with the design printed on utilitarian
brown wrapping paper.

The Clambake Mutiny
Jerome Beatty, Jr.
Young Scott Books
(New York) · 1964
230 × 152 mm · 9 × 6 in.

This design is repeated on boards
and jacket. The book is illustrated
by Ungerer throughout in the same
two colours.

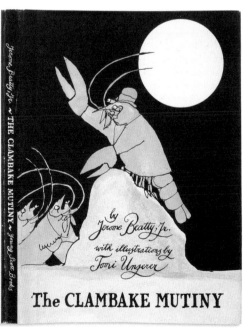

The Spirit of Jem
P. H. Newby
John Lehmann · 1947
200 × 135 mm · 7⅞ × 5⅜ in.

This publication constituted a rare
excursion into children's literature for
writer, illustrator and publisher, none
of whom could be said to have had
a natural affinity with childhood. But
Vaughan's angular compositions and
disinclination to patronize the reader
bring something fresh to the genre.
The richly textured, dramatic jacket
design is something of a classic of the
neo-romantic period. Howard Newby
later became Managing Director of
BBC Radio and his novel *Something
to Answer For* was the first winner
of the Booker Prize in 1969.

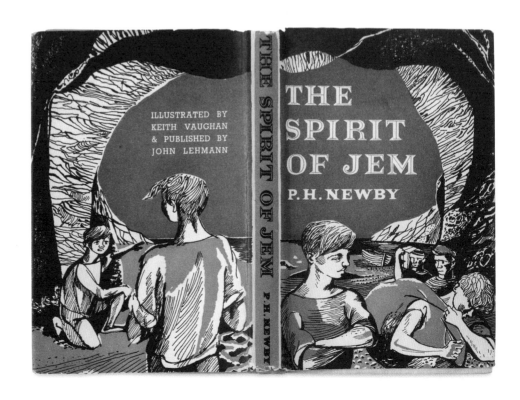

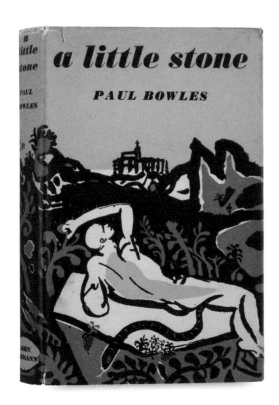

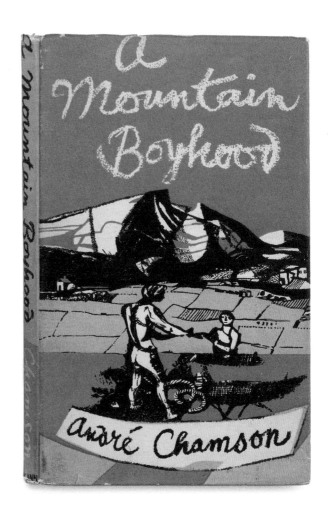

A Little Stone
Paul Bowles
John Lehmann · 1950
200 × 135 mm · 7⅞ × 5⅜ in.

Vaughan's striking jacket for Paul
Bowles's collection of short stories is
a classic of the neo-romantic era with
its rather overwrought theatricality.
Vaughan was the graphic designer
for Lehmann's short-lived publishing
house and contributed a number of
illustrated jackets himself.

A Mountain Boyhood
André Chamson
John Lehmann · 1947
190 × 125 mm · 7½ × 5 in.

This early Vaughan jacket design for
a book of stories of peasant life in
France was produced in the first year
of John Lehmann's publishing house.
Vaughan's muscular stylistic approach
is clearly comparable to the designs
for *The Spirit of Jem* and *A Season
in Hell*.

KEITH VAUGHAN
UK · 1912–1977

A Season in Hell
Arthur Rimbaud
John Lehmann · 1949
220 × 140 mm · 8⅝ × 5½ in.

As well as this, perhaps his finest
dust-jacket design for John Lehmann,
Vaughan produced eight full-page
three-colour lithographs for the
interior of the book, making it one
of the most valuable and sought-
after examples of the mid-century
illustrated book. The images helped
to establish Vaughan's reputation.
Compare his dust-jacket design to
the one by Alvin Lustig for the same
title four years earlier (p. 129).

Vaughan was a complex man, troubled by his sexuality at a time
when homosexual acts were illegal. He was shy, melancholy
and seemingly unhappy. Much of his inner turmoil was revealed
in the journals that he began to keep in 1939 and in which he
continued to document his life until the very moment of his
suicide in 1977 when suffering from cancer.

Although born in Sussex, Vaughan grew up in London, to
which the family moved soon after his birth. His father, a civil
engineer, left the family when Keith was 10 years old. After
an unhappy time at Christ's Hospital school, Vaughan became
a trainee with Lintas, the advertising department of Unilever,
where he worked in the art studio. It is something of a paradox
that, despite this early introduction to commercial art and
absence of formal art training, among the group of postwar
artists and illustrators who were subsequently to be labelled
neo-romantics, it was Vaughan who ultimately went on to
commit most exclusively to painting.

During the Second World War he registered as a
conscientious objector and ended up in the Pioneer Corps.
Throughout his service, he drew whenever he could, mainly
capturing men at work, and his first exhibition of drawings
was held at the Lefevre Gallery in 1944, followed by shows
of his paintings at the same gallery in the postwar years. An
early influence was Graham Sutherland, whom he met in the
war. Vaughan studied painting in depth, writing on the subject
for John Lehmann's anthology *New Writing and Daylight* in
this period, and later for Lehmann's *Penguin New Writing*
paperbacks. After a short period in premises in London with
the volatile Scottish painters Robert Colquhoun and Robert
MacBryde, generally referred to as 'the two Roberts', in 1946
Vaughan shared a house in Hamilton Terrace, St John's Wood,
with John Minton. Minton was able to assist him with contacts
in publishing and also helped Vaughan secure part-time
teaching work at Camberwell School of Arts and Crafts and
the Central. In 1951, he was invited to paint the central mural
in the Dome of Discovery at the Festival of Britain.

It is difficult to imagine two more contrasting personalities
than Vaughan and Minton, one deeply introspective and the
other socially outgoing and charming. However, they both
clearly had their demons. In his journals, Vaughan wrote of his
insecurities and concerns that he was too influenced by Minton
and trying too hard to be like him. Although there are many
confluences in their early work, with Samuel Palmer looming
large as an influence for both, Vaughan never had any of the
fluency or facility of Minton's draughtsmanship. Ultimately
this was part of Minton's problem and a key to Vaughan's
greater adaptability and longevity as an artist.

It was during the late 1940s and early 1950s that Vaughan
designed a number of dust jackets, mostly for John Lehmann
but also for other publishers, including Paul Elek (for whom
he illustrated *The Adventures of Tom Sawyer* in the *Camden
Classics* series, which employed the services of a number of
leading artist-illustrators of the day) and Gerald Duckworth.

The Catcher in the Rye
J. D. Salinger
Hamish Hamilton · 1951
190 × 125 mm · 7½ × 5 in.

Wegner's best-known jacket design
takes us into the book via the semi-
profile of the teenage protagonist
Holden Caulfield. As with E. Michael
Mitchell's jacket for the original US
edition (p. 139), the artist homes in
on the final scene of the narrative.

FRITZ WEGNER
Austria & UK · 1924–2015

Fritz Wegner was born in Vienna into a family of assimilated Jews but a happy early life came to an end with the Anschluss and arrival of the Nazis in 1938. Fortunately, his father was in London and at the age of 14 Fritz escaped to the UK. He was admitted to St Martin's School of Art, which took school-age students at that time, and was taken under the wing of one of his teachers, George Mansell, a distinguished exponent of architectural lettering. He lived with Mansell and his wife for several years, an experience that had a profound influence on the young Fritz and helped instil in him a passion for the arts in the broadest sense.

During the Second World War, Wegner worked as a farm labourer in Buckinghamshire, which led to publication of some early drawings in farming magazines and the beginning of his long career as a freelance illustrator. His excellent draughtsmanship was honed through a wide range of jobbing commissions, turning his hand to anything that would help support the family, having married when he was 21. The popular pocket-sized magazine *Lilliput* was an important source of employment for many artists at this time, especially those who could turn their hand to visual humour such as Wegner, alongside the likes of Ronald Searle, John Minton and André François.

The design of dust jackets became an important aspect of Wegner's work and one of his more regular clients in the 1950s and 1960s was the publisher Hamish Hamilton. Among the many commissions that he executed for them was the jacket design for the first UK edition of J. D. Salinger's *The Catcher in the Rye* in 1951, which is inevitably one of the most familiar examples of Wegner's work. Although choosing the same fairground carousel imagery that E. Michael Mitchell employed for the jacket of the US edition (see p. 139), Wegner chose a much more literal approach, depicting the narrator, Holden Caulfield, in the foreground. He was also in regular demand to design for popular crime fiction, including jackets in the 1950s for UK editions of the novels of Raymond Chandler and George Simenon.

Wegner found his true home in children's literature, where he could fully indulge his comic talents working with authors such as Alan Ahlberg and Michael Rosen as well as creating his own concepts. His technique became increasingly based on a wonderfully fluent and expressive line as a medium better suited to his graphic wit than the more static painting that was employed for many of the earlier dust jackets. Wegner taught at St Martin's School of Art one day a week for twenty-five years and was remembered affectionately by generations of graduates who recalled his always constructive and helpful manner.

Hullabaloo
Edited by Barbara Willard
Hamish Hamilton · 1969
250 × 165 mm · 9⅞ × 6½ in.

The placing of the title text in the gaping mouth of the child perfectly echoes the anarchic tone of Barbara Willard's anthology of mischievous verse.

After the Flesh
Leslie Hedge
Hamish Hamilton · 1963
200 × 135 mm · 7⅞ × 5⅜ in.

Hedge's novel explores the issue of celibacy in the Catholic clergy through the experiences of a young priest. Wegner's dramatic jacket design uses strongly textured black plus two flat colours and the negative space of the white paper.

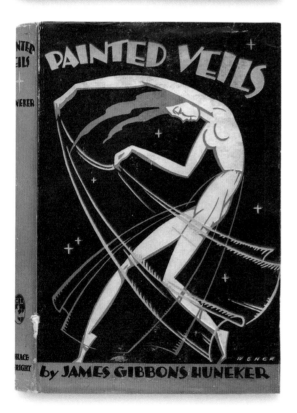

PAUL WENCK
Germany & USA · 1892–1964

The finely sculpted heads and dramatically stylized motifs of Paul Wenck's artwork were a familiar presence on American dust jackets through the 1920s and 1930s. Skilful with a range of media and processes, Wenck designed jackets across a range of literary genres, from highbrow to lowbrow. He could perhaps be described as something of a stylistic chameleon, his techniques being deployed in widely varying ways, depending on the nature of the text. His designs could be playfully comic, heraldic or realistic. However, most of the work was tinged with a strong flavour of Germanic Art Deco.

Wenck's best-known designs are those that were executed for the jackets of the German-born writer Erich Maria Remarque, in particular his most famous novel, *All Quiet on the Western Front* (1929), about the lives of German soldiers in the First World War. Wenck's stark portrait of a young soldier, staring into space, framed by barbed wire against the sickly yellow glow of warfare is a classic of its time (see p. 29). The loose pencil texture adds to the impression of direct documentary drawing. *The Road Back* was published two years later, in 1931 (Little, Brown). Wenck's design is similarly emotive, this time showing a fuller figure composition of the soldier trudging through the wreckage of war. In many other jacket designs, such as that for *Class of 1902* by Ernst Glaeser (Viking, 1929) and *Artemis Weds* by Cicely Farmer (Morrow, 1932), there are stylistic nods to the German Expressionists.

Considering the wide exposure of his work in the field of dust-jacket design, there is scant information on the life of Paul Wenck. He worked in the New York area and his etchings and other prints, always in the Art Deco manner, occasionally come up for sale.

Class of 1902
Ernst Glaeser
Viking (New York) · 1929
197 × 134 mm · 7¾ × 5¼ in.

This striking three-colour design draws on Cubism and German Expressionism in cleverly mixing geometry and representation. The style hints at the origins of this autobiographical novel about a group of adolescent boys growing up in the First World War. It was published in Germany in 1928.

Painted Veils
James Gibbons Huneker
Horace Liveright
(New York) · 1928
216 × 146 mm · 8½ × 5¾ in.

Wenck's composition for *Painted Veils* is generally regarded as a high point in Art Deco dust-jacket design. First published in 1920, Huneker's novel about a young drama critic who falls in love with an opera singer was reissued in this edition of 2,300 numbered copies in 1928.

Three Comrades
Erich Maria Remarque
Little, Brown (Boston) · 1937
216 × 146 mm · 8½ × 5¾ in.

Set in 1920s Germany, Remarque's
third novel follows the lives of three
former soldiers. Wenck's Social
Realist-style dust jacket portrays the
three protagonists in heroic fashion.

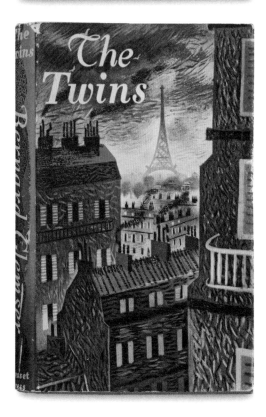

Leslie Wood is best known for his illustrations to Diana Ross's long-running series of *Little Red Engine* books for Faber and Faber. The first title in the series, *The Little Red Engine Gets a Name* (1942), was illustrated by the design duo Lewitt Him (Jan Lewitt and George Him). Their illustrations set the style for the characters and backgrounds and when Wood was asked to take over with the second book, he seamlessly built on the existing visual approach. Such adaptability and professionalism was typical of Leslie Wood. His illustrations were always stylish and stylized, but he was at the same time extremely versatile and not always recognizable in his various guises. This would perhaps explain why relatively little is known about him, like many highly accomplished illustrators who employed a variety of stylistic idioms.

Wood was born in Stockport near Manchester and studied at Manchester College of Art. He won a scholarship to travel abroad but with the outbreak of war was unable to take it up. He went to London instead and in search of commissions showed his portfolio at the offices of Faber and Faber in 1943. The timing was serendipitous as he was immediately offered the chance to take over illustrating *The Little Red Engine* series. Lewitt and Him were keen to continue but were busy on other children's books and in demand for war-related poster and general advertising work, as well as for designing murals for factory canteens. The books that Wood was commissioned to illustrate for Faber could not be published until after the end of the war because of a shortage of paper and printing inks. These included another title by Diana Ross, *Whoo, Whoo, the Wind Blew* (1945), which was issued with a dust jacket also designed by Wood and printed on poor quality postwar paper. It is now extremely rare. *The Little Red Engine* titles and other stories by Diana Ross continued to provide illustration work for Wood until 1972.

There seem to have been several strands to Wood's work. He produced many dust-jacket designs for a number of publishers, but for writing of variable quality. He designed the jackets for Hugh Walters's science-fiction novels, which again are now highly collectable. Although he may have seemed something of a stylistic chameleon, there is an underlying integrity to the work, which exudes panache and sheer pleasure in texture and surface – 'jobbing' illustration at its very best.

Pro
Bruce Hamilton
Cresset Press · 1946
190 × 125 mm · 7½ × 5 in.

The Twins
Bernard Glemser
Cresset Press · 1946
191 × 127 mm · 7½ × 5 in.

The small, independent publishers Cresset Press had a history of publishing finely illustrated books. These two Wood jacket designs show clear indications of the influence of Barnett Freedman and Eric Ravilious but Wood's love of muted browns and greens rendered with pattern and texture is already clear.

Storm of Time
Eleanor Dark · Collins · 1948
210 × 140 mm · 8¼ × 5½ in.

Wood mixes pictorial space and
exuberant pattern in this design for
the second volume of Dark's *Timeless
Land* trilogy, set in colonial Sydney in
the early nineteenth century.

The Blindness of Richard Blake
Peter Sutcliffe · Cresset Press · 1951
190 × 125 mm · 7½ × 5 in.

This jacket features a three-colour
engraved illustration set against
a subtle pattern and using Wood's
favoured italic type. The design
depicts the novel's eponymous
protagonist whose struggles to rebuild
confidence and hope after being
blinded in the war form the basis
of the narrative.

The Foolish Gentlewoman
Margery Sharp · Collins · 1948
190 × 125 mm · 7½ × 5 in.

A moral tale and elegy to prewar days,
a stage version of Sharp's thirteenth
novel opened in London in 1949,
starring Sybil Thorndike. Wood's
elegant design combines pattern with
traditional pictorial space and itself
has the air of a theatre set.

Good Angel Slept
Robert Greenwood
Hodder & Stoughton · 1953
210 × 140 mm · 8¼ × 5½ in.

Wood always enjoyed playing
with the patterns and rhythms in the
coming together of landscape and
industrial buildings. The design for
this jacket is reminiscent of many
of his *Little Red Engine* illustrations.

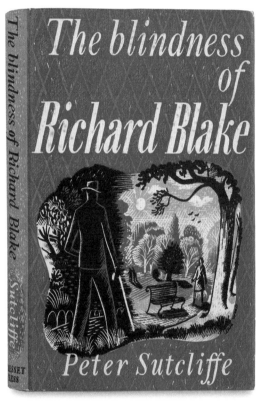

HILDEGARD WOODWARD

USA · 1898–1977

As well as a prolific illustrator and painter, Hildegard Woodward was the author of many children's books herself. She was a recipient of a prestigious Caldecott Honor on two occasions, first in 1948 for her illustrations to *Roger and the Fox* by Lavina Riker Davis and then again in 1950 for *The Wild Birthday Cake* by the same author (both published by Doubleday). Woodward was an all-round professional, 'jobbing' illustrator and as well as the children's books that she was particularly known for, she turned her hand to illustrating books and dust jackets for adult fiction and humour. She was also a highly regarded watercolourist and portrait painter, particularly of children, though she was unmarried and did not have children herself.

Woodward was born in Worcester, Massachusetts, and educated at the School of the Museum of Fine Arts, Boston, and later in Paris. Her first illustrated children's book was Alice Dagliesh's *The Blue Teapot: Sandy Cove Stories*, published by Macmillan, New York, in 1931, and soon established her reputation. In addition to her book work, she taught design and illustration at many private schools in New York, and also at her alma mater in Boston. In 1953, she was commissioned to paint a mural on the wall of the cafeteria at the Center School in Brookfield, Connecticut, the community in which she lived from 1942 until her death. A diabetic, from the early 1960s Woodward began to lose her sight but continued to work. As her vision deteriorated, she developed a way of painting that she called 'painting by touch', using twigs, branches of trees and wads of waxed paper, among other things, to assist her. Her papers are held at the University of Southern Mississippi and there is an archive of her work at the Children's Literature Research Collection at the University of Minnesota.

Woodward's work covered a variety of of subject matter but was particularly good in the areas of historical fiction and non-fiction. The imagery sometimes borders on sentimentality but invariably radiates human warmth.

The Mott Family in France
Donald Moffat
Little, Brown (Boston) · 1937
185 × 130 mm · 7¼ × 5⅛ in.

Woodward's jacket design appropriately evokes for an American audience the romance of European travel. The four solid, flat colours are used to harmonious effect, echoing the great Belle Epoch posters of Henri de Toulouse-Lautrec. Her playfully integrated typography adds to the rumbustious atmosphere. Woodward's illustrations also accompany the story of an American couple, the thinly disguised Moffats, who decide to live for a year in France with their three young daughters.

Little Miss Cappo
Frances Gaither · Macmillan
(New York) · 1937
216 × 142 mm · 8½ × 5⅝ in.

Gaither's third children's novel tells
the story of a girl from Alabama,
brought up on a plantation,
experiencing the strictures of a
Moravian boarding school in Winston-
Salem, North Carolina, in 1820.
Woodward produced illustrations and
decorative endpapers for the book as
well as this delicately coloured jacket.
Gaither, who grew up in the South,
is best known for her trilogy of novels
for adults about slavery, published
in the 1940s.

Philippe's Hill
Lee Kingman
Doubleday (New York) · 1950
210 × 150 mm · 8¼ × 5⅞ in.

Kingman's story of a young French
Canadian boy who learns to ski by
making his own skis from barrel-staves
and uses them to rescue a friend,
brought out the printmaker and poster
designer in Woodward. By using
loosely registered areas of colour and
no outlines she created drama and
movement in the classic ski-poster style.
Kingman herself, as well as being a
writer of many children's books, was
a trained designer and illustrator.

Country Neighborhood
Elizabeth Coatsworth
Macmillan (New York) · 1944
250 × 195 mm · 9¾ × 7⅞ in.

Woodward contributed black-and-white
drawings as well as the jacket design
for this book of anecdotes, impressions
and descriptions of country life in
Maine, where Coatsworth, who won
the Newbery Medal in 1931, had a farm.

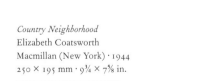

N. C. WYETH

USA · 1882–1945

The lot of the painter-illustrator has never been an easy one. To a greater or lesser degree at different periods in history, depending on the vagaries of public and critical perceptions, artists who choose to combine working for themselves with working for publication have often found responses to their gallery work coloured by awareness of their endeavours in the sphere of publishing. Much of this can be put down to intellectual laziness on the part of critics within the art establishment, sometimes unable to assess the quality of the work on its own terms. Usually, of course, this problem only prevails during the lifetime of the artist, the passage of time allowing for new perspectives on an artist's *oeuvre*.

Wyeth was a passionate appreciator of the beauty of landscape and the natural world. This is abundantly clear in both his paintings and illustrations. But he was troubled by perceptions that he was an 'illustrator first and a painter second'. He longed to be accepted by the art establishment at a time when photography was beginning to compete with realist painting.

Newell Convers Wyeth was born in Needham, Massachusetts. His ancestors on his father's side had arrived from England in 1645 whereas his mother's family were from Switzerland. His emerging talent as an artist, underpinned by a first-hand knowledge of the great outdoors from his upbringing on the family farm, led to Wyeth being accepted in 1902 at Howard Pyle's School of Art in Wilmington, Delaware, and its summer school in Chadds Ford, Pennsylvania. It was here that he learned from the great master of American illustration,

through formal classes in drawing, including historical costume, dramatic movement and gesture.

His precocious talent led to early success in the form of commissions to illustrate covers and stories for the *Saturday Evening Post*. Initially, he tended to specialize in Western subjects and he made several trips to states such as Colorado and Arizona to inform his depictions of the Old West. However, it was as a brilliant illustrator of classic fiction that he would make his name, especially those volumes published by Charles Scribner's Sons. His illustrations to Robert Louis Stevenson's *Treasure Island* (1911) have become universally acknowledged as examples of book illustration at its best. Wyeth's image of Blind Pew tapping his way manically towards the viewer is a masterpiece of composition, light and drama.

Wyeth's turmoil grew the more he achieved success in commercial illustration, working for companies such as Coca-Cola, and leading magazines, including the *Ladies' Home Journal*, *Harper's Monthly* and *McClure's*. His talents were put to use on mural painting in the 1930s and by the government for patriotic images in both world wars. His apparent self-loathing was vividly expressed in many of his letters to friends, in which he wrote despairingly of having 'bitched myself with the accursed success in skin-deep pictures and illustrations'.[82] Whether such statements genuinely expressed his feelings towards the activity of illustration or were projected onto it as a result of the attitudes of critics, it is impossible to know. Nonetheless, his work brought him celebrity and his artist son Andrew Wyeth remembered a host of famous visitors to the house in Chadds Ford, including F. Scott Fitzgerald and Mary Pickford.

The dust jackets of early editions of N. C. Wyeth's illustrated books have rarely survived, partly because of the flimsy nature of the paper stock on which many were printed and partly because of the common practice of discarding them to reveal the lavish pictorial bindings beneath.

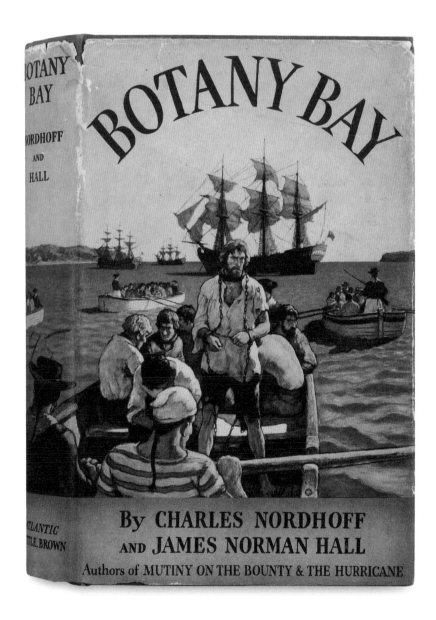

Westward Ho! (endpapers)
Charles Kingsley
Charles Scribner's Sons
(New York) · 1928
235 × 180 mm · 9¼ × 7 in.

Wyeth's two-colour halftone endpaper
design for this edition of Kingsley's
Elizabethan adventure gives a foretaste
of the nine full-colour plates in the book
itself. Much of Wyeth's best work was
executed for Charles Scribner's Sons.

The Yearling
Marjorie Kinnan Rawlings
Charles Scribner's Sons
(New York) · 1939
225 × 159 mm · 8⅞ × 6¼ in.

Rawlings's classic tale of a boy and his
deer, set in the swamps of Florida, won
the Pulitzer Prize for Fiction for 1939.
As well as designing the jacket, Wyeth
contributed fourteen full-colour plates
to the book.

Botany Bay
Charles Nordhoff
and James Norman
Atlantic Little, Brown
(Boston) · 1941
210 × 146 mm · 8¼ × 5¾ in.

Wyeth specialized in historical
dramatic realism. His work was always
painstakingly researched, as for the
jacket of this story about the penal
colony established in Australia in the
late eighteenth century.

Notes

Further Reading

1. Charles Rosner, *The Growth of the Book Jacket* (Cambridge, MA, Harvard University Press, 1954), p. 54.

2. Ibid., p. v.

3. *Observer*, 1949.

4. Alan Horne, *The Dictionary of 20th Century British Book Illustrators* (Woodbridge, Antique Collectors' Club, 1994), p. 35.

5. Peter Curl, *Designing a Book Jacket* (London and New York, Studio Publications, 1956), p. 10.

6. *Second Annual Exhibition, Book Jacket Designers Guild*, exh. cat. (New York, Book Jacket Designers Guild, 1949), n.p.

7. See Jürgen Holstein, *The Book Cover in the Weimar Republic* (Cologne, Taschen, 2015).

8. Steven Heller and Seymour Chwast, *Jackets Required: An Illustrated History of American Book Jacket Design, 1920–1950* (San Francisco, Chronicle Books, 1995), p. 16.

9. As long ago as 1986, a 1902 first-edition copy of Rudyard Kipling's *Just So Stories*, worth at the time around £100 on its own, sold for £2,600 at Sotheby's due to the presence of its rare dust jacket.

10. See Richard Minsky, *The Art of American Book Covers: 1875–1930* (New York, George Braziller, 2010).

11. Steven Heller, *Edward Gorey: His Book Cover Art and Design* (Portland, OR, Pomegranate, 2015), p. 6.

12. *Third Annual Exhibition, Book Jacket Designers Guild*, exh. cat. (New York, Book Jacket Designers Guild, 1950).

13. Leo Manser, Meyer Miller, Jeanyee Wong and Miriam Woods.

14. Dust jackets can be consulted by registered readers in the British Library's reading rooms. Among the dust jackets retained by the Library, those from *c.* 1925 to *c.* 1955 and those from hardback fiction published in the United Kingdom from 1993 onwards are the most readily accessible.

15. Jhumpa Lahiri, *The Clothing of Books* (London, Bloomsbury, 2017), p. 62.

16. Adam Sonstegard, *Artistic Liberties: American Literary Realism and Graphic Illustration, 1880–1905* (Tuscaloosa, University of Alabama Press, 2014).

17. http://mikedempsey.typepad.com/graphic_journey_blog/2014/08/the-grant-gone-but-not-forgotten.html

18. Gabriel White, *Edward Ardizzone* (London, Bodley Head, 1979), p. 25.

19. Brian Alderson, *Edward Ardizzone: A Bibliographic Commentary* (London, British Library, 2003).

20. John Cooper and B. A. Pike, *Artists in Crime* (Aldershot, Scolar Press, 1995), p. xii.

21. J. M. Richards, *Edward Bawden* (Harmondsworth, Penguin Books, 1946), p. 7.

22. Tony Bradshaw, *The Bloomsbury Artists: Prints and Book Design* (Aldershot, Scolar Press, 1999), p. 7.

23. David Ackermann et al., *Buchumschläge und künstlerische Buchgestaltung in der DDR* (University of Leipzig, 2015).

24. Brian Cook, *The Britain of Brian Cook* (repr. London, B. T. Batsford, 2012), p. 6.

25. A. E. Richardson, *The Old Inns of England* (London, Batsford, 1934).

26. Charles C. Knights, 'Colour is catching', *The Print User's Year Book* (London, Print-User's Year Book Ltd, 1935), p. 107.

27. Steven Heller and Seymour Chwast, *Jackets Required: An Illustrated History of American Book Jacket Design, 1920–1950* (San Francisco, Chronicle Books, 1995), p. 26.

28. Leonard J. Leff, *Hemingway and His Conspirators: Hollywood, Scribners, and the Making of the American Dream* (Lanham, MD, Rowman and Littlefield, 1999), p. 51.

29. Ibid., p. 115.

30. In conversation with the author, 2001. The OUP editor referred to would have been Mabel George, who took over the children's books department at OUP in 1956.

31. David Driver, *The Art of Radio Times: The First Sixty Years* (London, BBC Books, 1981), p. 132.

32. Peter Marren and Robert Gillmor, *Art of the New Naturalists* (London, Collins, 2009), p. 5.

33. Wendy Coates-Smith, 'The children's books of André François', *Line: Children's Books*, 2 (Cambridge, Ruskin Press, 2001), p. 19.

34. Quoted in Pierre Peronne, 'André François: artist, illustrator, designer and sculptor', *Independent*, 19 May 2005.

35. Claude Roy, 'Andre François', *Graphis*, 76 (1958), pp. 98–111.

36. Wendy Coates-Smith, 'The children's books of André François', *Line: Children's Books*, 2 (Cambridge, Ruskin Press, 2001), p. 22.

37. Ronald Searle, *The Biting Eye* (London, Perpetua Books, 1960), p. 11.

38. Wendy Coates-Smith, 'The children's books of André François', *Line: Children's Books No. 2* (Cambridge, Ruskin Press, 2001), p. 20.

39. *Eric Fraser: An Illustrator of Our Time, A Travelling Exhibition Sponsored by British Gas*, text by Pat Hodgson, exh. cat. (London, British Gas, 1991), p. 7.

40. Robin Jacques, *Illustrators at Work* (London, Studio Books, 1963), p. 34.

41. Edward Ardizzone, *Baggage to the Enemy* (London, John Murray, 1942), p. 7.

42. Clifford Ross and Karen Wilkin, *The World of Edward Gorey* (New York, Harry N. Abrams, 1996), p. 18.

43. Steven Heller, *Edward Gorey: His Book Cover Art & Design* (Portland, OR, Pomegranate, 2015).

44. Ibid., p. 23

45. Tony Bradshaw, *The Bloomsbury Artists: Prints and Book Design* (Aldershot, Scolar Press, 1991), p. 7.

46. Steven Heller, 'When book jackets were bad, Hawkins's were good', *Print*, 16 November 2012.

47. E-mail from Gil Hawkins to Martin Salisbury, January 2017.

48. BBC News Magazine, 13 March 2014: www.bbc.co.uk/news/magazine-26529309

49. Susan Varley, *Books for Keeps*, 38, May 1986, p. 24: http://booksforkeeps.co.uk/issue/38/childrens-books/articles/other-articles/susan-varley-meets-harold-jones

50. Ibid.

51. Mark Haworth-Booth, *E. McKnight Kauffer: A Designer and His Public* (London, Gordon Fraser, 1979), p. 13.

52. *Portfolio*, 1:1, Winter 1950.

53. *E. McKnight Kauffer*, by Steven Heller, AIGA (American Institute of Graphic Arts), 1992: www.aiga.org/medalist-emcknightkauffer/

54. F. J. Harvey Darton, *Modern Book Illustration in Great Britain and America* (London and New York, The Studio, 1931), p. 57.

55. Letter from Joe Krush to Thames & Hudson, 7 March 2017.

56. Sara Solovitch, 'Marriage of talents for children's books', *Philadelphia Inquirer*, 7 July 1988, p. C01.

57. Ibid.

58. Robin Jacques, *Illustrators at Work* (London, Studio Books, 1981), p. 43.

59. David Driver, *The Art of Radio Times: The First Sixty Years* (London, BBC Books, 1981), p. 122.

60. Ibid.

61. Iain Sinclair, 'Man in a MacIntosh', *Guardian*, 30 August 2008: www.theguardian.com/books/2008/aug/30/fiction

62. www.youtube.com/watch?v=tsLCAUFToIM

63. Ronald Blythe, *First Friends: Paul and Bunty, John and Christine – and Carrington* (London, Viking, 1999).

64. John Lewis, *John Nash: The Painter as Illustrator* (Godalming, Pendomer Press, 1978), p. 94.

65. Ronald Blythe, 'Soil on their boots', *Guardian*, 8 August 2009.

66. BBC Radio broadcast, 1947, in Hilary Spurling, *The Drawings of Mervyn Peake* (London, Davis-Poynter, 1974), n.p.

67. David Driver, *The Art of Radio Times: The First Sixty Years* (London, BBC Books, 1981), p. 38.

68. Ibid.

69. Ibid.

70. Michael Middleton, 'The drawings of Leonard Rosoman', *Image*, 3 (1950), pp. 3–22 at p. 13.

71. John Ryder, *Artists of a Certain Line* (London, Bodley Head, 1960), p. 113.

72. David Driver, *The Art of Radio Times: The First Sixty Years* (London, BBC Books, 1981), p. 106.

73. The village of Great Bardfield in Essex became home to a loosely based 'artists' colony' after Edward Bawden and Eric Ravilious moved there in the mid-1920s.

74. Conversations with the author over a period of time.

75. Ronald Searle, *To the Kwai – and Back: War Drawings 1939–1945* (London, Collins, 1986).

76. Ronald Searle, *Forty Drawings* (Cambridge University Press, 1946).

77. Ben Shahn, 'Some revaluations of commercial and fine art', in John D. Morse (ed.), *Ben Shahn* (London, Secker & Warburg, 1972), p. 122.

78. Ibid., p. 123.

79. John Ryder, *Artists of a Certain Line* (London, Bodley Head, 1960), p. 119.

80. Anita Silvey (ed.), *Children's Books and Their Creators* (Boston, Houghton Mifflin, 1995), p. 659.

81. Ibid.

82. James H. Duff et al., *An American Vision: Three Generations of Wyeth Art* (Boston, Little, Brown, 1987), p. 18.

Bradshaw, Tony, *The Bloomsbury Artists: Prints and Book Design*, Aldershot, Scolar Press, 1999

Brown, Gregory, 'Book jacket design', in R. B. Fishenden (ed.), *The Penrose Annual*, 38, London, Lund Humphries, 1936

Bryant, Julius, Elizabeth James and Rowan Watson (eds), *Word & Image: Art, Books and Design from the National Art Library*, London, V&A Publishing, 2015

Catalogues of the Annual Exhibition, New York, Book Jacket Designers Guild, 1949, 1950, 1951

Connolly, Joseph, *Eighty Years of Book Cover Design*, London, Faber and Faber, 2009

—, *Modern First Editions: Their Value to Collectors*, London, Orbis, 1984

Cook, Brian, *The Britain of Brian Cook*, London, B. T. Batsford, 1987 and 2012

Cooper, John, and B. A. Pike, *Artists in Crime*, Aldershot, Scolar Press, 1995

Curl, Peter, *Designing a Book Jacket*, London and New York, Studio Publications, 1956

Drew, Ned, and Paul Sternberger, *By its Cover: Modern American Book Cover Design*, New York, Princeton Architectural Press, 2005

—, *Purity of Aim: The Book Jacket Designs of Alvin Lustig*, Rochester, NY, RIT Cary Graphic Arts Press, 2010

Hansen, Thomas S., *Classic Book Jackets: The Design Legacy of George Salter*, New York, Princeton Architectural Press, 2005

Heller, Steven, *Edward Gorey: His Book Cover Art & Design*, Portland, OR, Pomegranate, 2015

— and Seymour Chwast, *Jackets Required: An Illustrated History of American Book Jacket Design, 1920–1950*, San Francisco, Chronicle Books, 1995

Holstein, Jurgen, *The Book Cover in the Weimar Republic*, Cologne, Taschen, 2015

Horne, Alan, *The Dictionary of 20th Century British Book Illustrators*, Woodbridge, Antique Collectors' Club, 1994

Jacques, Robin, *Illustrators at Work*, London, Studio Books, 1963

Lewis, John, *John Nash: The Painter as Illustrator*, Godalming, Pendomer Press, 1978

—, *The 20th Century Book*, London, Studio Vista, 1967

McLean, Ruari, *Modern Book Design*, London, Longmans, Green & Co., 1951

Marren, Peter, and Robert Gillmor, *Art of the New Naturalists*, London, Collins, 2009

Minsky, Richard, *The Art of American Book Covers, 1875–1930*, New York, George Braziller, 2010

Powers, Alan, *Front Cover: Great Book Jacket and Cover Design*, London, Mitchell Beazley, 2001

Rosner, Charles, *The Art of The Book Jacket*, London, H. M. Stationery Office, 1949

—, *The Growth of the Book Jacket*, Cambridge, MA, Harvard University Press, 1954

Tanselle, G. Thomas, *Book-Jackets: Their History, Forms, and Use*, New Castle, DE, Oak Knoll Books, 2011

Tedesco, A. P., *The Relationship Between Type and Illustration in Books and Book Jackets*, New York, George McKibbin & Son, 1948

Wilson, Adrian, *The Design of Books*, London, Studio Vista; New York, Reinhold Publishing, 1967

Credits

a: above; b: below; c: centre; l: left; r: right.

2 Kathleen Hale; 7a Eric Ravilious; 7c Paul Nash; 7b Hans Tisdall; 8 Peter Curl. Reproduction courtesy Studio International; 9a, 9b Catalogue of the Second Annual Exhibition of the Book Jacket, Designers Guild, 1949; 11a Willy Herzig. Photo courtesy private collection; 11c George G. Kobbe. Photo courtesy private collection; 11b © The Estate of George Grosz, Princeton, NJ/DACS 2017. Photo courtesy private collection; 12 Illustration from *A Simple Guide to Pictures*, 1914; 13l Illustration from *Hazel Glen*, undated; 13r © The Estate of Edmund Dulac. All rights reserved. DACS 2017; 14a The Estate of Edward Bawden; 14c Boris Artzybasheff; 14b The Estate of Edward Bawden; 15 Victor Reinganum; 16 © The Estate of Vanessa Bell, courtesy Henrietta Garnett; 17al 'Baird'; 17ar 'Acona (Edward D'Ancona'; 17bl 'Patk'; 17br 'Baird'; 18 Alfred Maurer; 19al Illustration from *The Black Eye*, 1946; 19ar Illustration from *The Penthouse Mystery*, 1941; 19bl Illustration from *The Spinster's Secret*, 1946; 19br Robin Macartney; 20 Illustration from *The White Hour*, 1950; 21a Clifford Barry. Penguin Books; 21bl Bateson Mason; 21br © The Estate of John Craxton. All Rights Reserved, DACS 2017; 22, 23a The Estate of Graham Sutherland; 23b James Holland; 24 Illustration from *The Book of Woman's Hour*, 1953; 25al Illustration from *Captain Caution*, 1949; 25ar Ferelith Eccles Williams; 25bl The Estate of John Minton. Courtesy Special Collections, Royal College of Art, London; 25br Thomas Henry; 26a Manfred Reiss; 26bl, 26br Illustrations from *The Daily Mail Boys Annual*, c. 1956; 27al, 27ar; Jenny Dalenoord © DACS 2017; 27b W. J. Rozendaal; 28l N. C. Wyeth; 28r Illustration from *Tender is the Night*, 1934. Collection of Mark Terry/Facsimile Dust Jackets L.L.C. www.dustjackets.com; 29al Paul Wenck. Collection of Mark Terry/Facsimile Dust Jackets L.L.C. www.dustjackets.com; 29ar The Estate of Rockwell Kent (1882–1971). Courtesy the Plattsburgh State Art Museum, Plattsburgh College Foundation, Rockwell Kent Gallery and Collection, Bequest of Sally Kent Gorton, Plattsburgh, NY. Collection of Mark Terry/Facsimile Dust Jackets L.L.C. www.dustjackets.com; 29bl © Simon Rendall; 29br © The Estate of Arthur Hawkins, Jr.; 31al Adrian Bailey; 31ar Illustration from *A Man of Power*, 1960; 31bl Adrian Bailey; 31br Illustration from *Flight into Camden*, 1960; 32al Illustration from *Lest We Lose Our Edens*, 1958. Collection of Maria Ranauro; 32ar Illustration from *Kiss and Part*, 1957; 32bl Illustration from *This Lovely Thing*, 1959. Collection of Maria Ranauro; 32br Illustration from *Love is a Reckless Thing*, 1958. Collection of Maria Ranauro; 33a Alan Ball; 33bl 'Stevens'; 33br 'Grimley'

(Harry Grimley); 36–39 Permission granted by the Ardizzone Estate; 40–41 Boris Artzybasheff; 40l Photo courtesy Bearly Read Books, Sudbury, MA; 40r, 41 Collection of Mark Terry/Facsimile Dust Jackets L.L.C. www.dustjackets.com; 42–45 C. W. Bacon; 43 Photo courtesy Anthony Smith Books, London; 44 Photo courtesy John Hinchliffe; 45br Collection of Mark Terry/Facsimile Dust Jackets L.L.C. www.dustjackets.com; 46–47 Stanley Badmin. Courtesy Chris Beetles Gallery, St James's, London; 48–53 The Estate of Edward Bawden; 48l The Fry Art Gallery, Saffron Walden, UK; 49r Collection of Roger Thorp; 54–55 © The Estate of Vanessa Bell, courtesy Henrietta Garnett; 54bl, 54br, 55b Victoria University Library, Toronto; 56–57 The Estate of Eberhard Binder; 58–61 Brian Cook. Batsford Pavilion Books: 60–61 Collection of Hannah Webb; 62–65 Cleon (Cleonike Damianakes): 62, 63a, 63bl, 63br Collection of Mark Terry/Facsimile Dust Jackets L.L.C. www.dustjackets.com; 64 Photo courtesy Michael Pyron, Bookseller, Ann Arbor, MI; 65 Photo courtesy Books of Choice, Bookseller; 66–69 © 1944, 1946, 1948, 1949, 1950, 1952 by Roger Duvoisin. Used by permission of the Literary Estate of Roger Duvoisin in care of the Jean V. Naggar Literary Agency, Inc. (permissions@jvnla.com); 66b Photo courtesy www.RareBookCellar.com; 67l Mabel Watts Papers, de Grummond Children's Literature Collection, University of Southern Mississippi Libraries (DG1032, box.30 cu.ft.); 70–73 © The Estate of Susan Einzig. Courtesy Hetty Einzig; 74–75 Clifford and Rosemary Ellis; 76–77 André François (André Farkas) © ADAGP, Paris and DACS, London 2017; 78–83 Courtesy the Fraser Family; 84–89 The Estate of Barnett Freedman: 84 Photo courtesy Maggs Bros. Ltd, London; 86a, 86bl Collection of Roger Thorp; 90–93 Reproduction courtesy Milton Glaser Studio: 91 Collection of Mark Terry/Facsimile Dust Jackets L.L.C. www.dustjackets.com; 94–97 By permission of the Edward Gorey Charitable Trust: 96a, 96b, 97a, 97c, 97b Private collections; 98–99 © The Estate of Duncan Grant. All rights reserved, DACS 2017: 99a Photo courtesy Ashton Rare Books, Leicester; 100–103 Aubrey Hammond: 100a Photo courtesy Andy Collins & Brenda Greysmith/Pedlar's Pack Books, Torquay; 100b Photo courtesy Babylon Revisited Rare Books; 102–103 Collection of Mark Terry/Facsimile Dust Jackets L.L.C. www.dustjackets.com; 104–105 © The Estate of Arthur Hawkins, Jr.: 104al, 104ar Photo courtesy Yesterday's Gallery, ABAA of Woodstock, CT; 104b Photo courtesy Hyde Brothers Booksellers, Fort Wayne, IN; 105a Collection of Mark Terry/Facsimile Dust Jackets L.L.C. www.dustjackets.com; 106–107 The Estate of Adolf Hoffmeister: 106b, 107a, 107b Collection of Roger Thorp; 108–111 © Tove Jansson, 1950, 1952, 1957, 1958, 1963, 1975 Moomin Characters™: 108a, 108b, 109a, 109b, 111 Collection of Roger Thorp;

112–115 The Estate of Barbara Jones: 113b, 114b Collection of Susanna Ingram; 115a Collection of Brian Webb; 116–117 © Harold Jones, 1937, 1938, 1940, 1957, 1958. Permission granted by the Harold Jones Estate; 118–121 © Simon Rendall: 118al Collection of Brian Webb; 118r Photo courtesy Peter Ellis, Bookseller; 118bl, 119 Private collections; 120a Collection of Roger Thorp; 121b Photo courtesy Novel Ending Books; 122–123 The Estate of Rockwell Kent (1882–1971). Courtesy the Plattsburgh State Art Museum, Plattsburgh College Foundation, Rockwell Kent Gallery and Collection, Bequest of Sally Kent Gorton, Plattsburgh, NY; 122a Collection of Mark Terry/Facsimile Dust Jackets L.L.C. www.dustjackets.com; 122b Photo courtesy Scott Emerson Books; 123b Photo courtesy Between the Covers Rare Books, Inc.; 124–127 By permission of Joe Krush; 124l Photo courtesy Peter Harrington Books; 124c Photo courtesy Marie Bottini, Bookseller, Cotati, CA; 126r Photo courtesy Bill Wickham/Wickham Books South, Naples, FL; 128–131 Reproduced by permission of the Alvin Lustig Archive: 128 Collection of Mark Terry/Facsimile Dust Jackets L.L.C. www.dustjackets.com; 129l, 129c, 129r Photo courtesy the Alvin Lustig Archive; 131a Collection of Mark Terry/Facsimile Dust Jackets L.L.C. www.dustjackets.com; 132–133 Robert Micklewright; 134–137 The Estate of John Minton. Courtesy Special Collections, Royal College of Art, London; 138–139 E. Michael Mitchell; 140–141 John Northcote Nash (1893–1977)/© The Estate of John Nash/Bridgeman Images; 142–143 Illustrations by Mervyn Peake reprinted by permission of Peters Fraser & Dunlop (www.petersfraserdunlop.com) on behalf of the Estate of Mervyn Peake: 142a Photo courtesy Les Sklaroff (Cameron House Books); 144–145 Reproduced by permission of Ursula Piatti: 145b Photo The History of Advertising Trust www.hatads.org.uk; 146–149 © The Piper Estate/DACS 2017: 148br Photo courtesy Clearwater Books, London; 150–151 Victor Reinganum; 152–153 The Estate of Leonard Rosoman; 154–155 Kenneth Rowntree; 155al Collection of Alan Powers; 156–157 Stephen Russ; 158–159 The Estate of George Salter; 160–163 The Estate of Ronald Searle: 160l Photo courtesy Michael Johnson; 160c Photo courtesy Maggs Bros. Ltd, London; 163bl Photo courtesy Time Tested Books; 163bc, 163br Photo courtesy Dave Shoots, Bookseller, Saint John, New Brunswick, Canada; 164–165 © The Estate of Ben Shahn/DACS, London/VAGA, NY 2017; 166–167 Alfred Skrenda: 166a Photo courtesy Dale Steffey Books, Bloomington, IN; 167b Photo courtesy The Odd Book, Canada; 168–171 Heather Standring: 168 Photo courtesy Adrian Harrington Rare Books www.harringtonbooks.co.uk; 169al, 169ac, 169ar Collection of Terry Sole; 172–173 David Stone Martin: 172 Photo courtesy Arthur Frank, Round Table Books, L.L.C. Glenview, IL; 174–179 Hans Tisdall; 180–181 Illustrations by Tomi

Ungerer © Tomi Ungerer/Diogenes Verlag AG Zurich, Switzerland. All rights reserved: 180l Museum Tomi Ungerer, Centre international de l'Illustration, Strasbourg; 181al Collection of Roger Thorp; 182–183 © The Estate of Keith Vaughan. All rights reserved, DACS: 183 Photo courtesy Dominic Winter (Auctioneers); 184–185 The Estate of Fritz Wegner; 184 Photo courtesy Chapter 1, Johannesburg, South Africa; 186–187 Paul Wenck: 186a Photo courtesy Daniel Wechsler/Sanctuary Rare Books, New York; 186b Photo courtesy Yesterday's Gallery, ABAA of Woodstock, CT; 188–189 By permission of the Estate of Leslie Wood; 190–191 The Estate of Hildegard Woodward: 191bl Photo courtesy Gretchen Goldberg from Books For You, Colorado Springs, CO; 191br Photo courtesy Morley's Books, Carson City, NV; 192–193 N. C. Wyeth: 193a Collection of Mark Terry/Facsimile Dust Jackets L.L.C. www.dustjackets.com

Page 30, untitled poem © 2017 Raymond Briggs. Reproduced by kind permission of Raymond Briggs

Index

Considerable thanks are due to the many antiquarian and second-hand booksellers and other individuals who have kindly allowed us to reproduce images of books and artworks to fill the gaps in my own collection, especially the following: Roger Thorp, Terry Sole, Alan Powers, Brian Webb and Ashton Rare Books. I am also grateful to Gil Hawkins, Ursula Piatti and Thomas S. Hansen for their helpful assistance. Most of all, thanks to everyone at Thames & Hudson, especially Julia MacKenzie, Maria Ranauro and Alex Wright, who have all played such a big part in making this book.